INVENTING A HERO

Inventing a Hero

The Posthumous Re-Creation of Andres Bonifacio

GLENN ANTHONY MAY

published in cooperation with
New Day Publishers

University of Wisconsin
Center for Southeast Asian Studies
1996

Library of Congress
Catalogue Card No. 96–085119

ISBN Cloth 1-881261-18-2
ISBN Paper 1-881261-19-0

Published by the
Center for Southeast Asian Studies
University of Wisconsin-Madison
Madison, Wisconsin 53706 USA

Telephone: (608) 263-1755
FAX: (608) 263-3735

Designed by Ingrid Slamer

Copyright © 1996

The Board of Regents of the
University of Wisconsin System

All rights reserved

Printed in the
United States of America

Distributed in the Philippines
exclusively by New Day Publishers;
and in the rest of the world
exclusively by the University of
Wisconsin-Madison, Center for
Southeast Asian Studies

FOR HELEN

Contents

Acknowledgments *ix*

A Note about Spelling *xi*

Introduction:
History, Invention, and Nationalism *1*

1. Bonifacio before the Revolution *19*
2. The Mysterious Letters of Andres Bonifacio *53*
3. Ricarte's Bonifacio *83*
4. Agoncillo's Bonifacio *113*
5. Ileto's Bonifacio *137*

Afterthoughts:
Nationalism and Myth *163*

Notes *167*

Index *195*

Acknowledgments

Many people and institutions have assisted me in the making of this book. I am grateful to the Social Science Research Council and the Oregon Committee for the Humanities for research grants to support my fieldwork in the Philippines. I would also like to thank the University of Oregon for awarding me two summer research grants and a research fellowship in the Oregon Humanities Center.

I owe my greatest debts to nine individuals. Ben Anderson, Al McCoy, Jim Mohr, Ambeth Ocampo, and John Schumacher all gave close readings to earlier drafts of this book and offered sage counsel about how to improve the text. (Anderson and Ocampo also provided important research materials.) Jan Opdyke, a terrific editor, tightened my prose. My wife Helen Liu cheerfully endured the many ups and downs of this research project, helped me to refine my arguments, and sustained me throughout. My daughters Elizabeth and Rachel reminded me that there is more to life than scholarship.

In addition, I am indebted to a host of other people for all manner of assistance. Librarians have located hard-to-find books, colleagues and students at the University of Oregon have given me feedback about my ideas, Southeast Asian specialists around the world have answered my queries, and research assistants have helped me to understand and translate difficult Tagalog texts. Let me express my gratitude to the following individuals: Ellen Alfonso, Jiffin Arboleda, Celia Bautista, Cynthia Brokaw, Holly Campbell, Nayan Chanda, Malcolm Churchill, Nita Churchill, Dan Doeppers, Emmanuel Encarnacion, Laura Fair, Carol Foster, Bill Frederick, Lewis Gleeck, Andrew Goble, Bryna Goodman, Mila Guerrero, Michael Haddigan, Joanne Halgren, Julie Hessler, Kimloan Hill, Bong Ibay, Jr., Biff Keyes, Jack Maddex, Ruth Ann Maguire, Pepot Marpa, May Kyi Win, Helen Mendoza, Rose Marie Mendoza, Kay Mohlman, Teresita Pangan, Robin Paynter, Tina Ranche, Tony Reid, John Roosa, Jim Rush, Rosanne Rutten, Boni Salamanca, Steve

Shankman, David Shehigian, John Shurts, Peter Stanley, Edwin Tuble, Ramon Villegas, John Wiersma, Stephanie Wood, and Aimee Yogi.

Finally, I wish to express my appreciation to the editors and publishers of the journal *Pilipinas* for giving me permission to use material from a previously published article.

A Note about Spelling

In accordance with local usage, I have rendered the names of all Filipino people, places, and organizations without accents—hence, Jose Rizal, Jose P. Santos, Andres Bonifacio, and so forth. The Tagalog passages found in the text are reproduced as they appear in the sources. Some of those passages come from late-nineteenth- and early-twentieth-century documents, and, since the Tagalog of that period differs considerably from late-twentieth-century Tagalog, they contain more than a few orthographic peculiarities. For example, the contemporary word *ginhawa* ("prosperity") is spelled *guinhawa* in the documents, and *katwiran* ("reason" or "straightness") is spelled *katuiran*.

As a general rule, I have spelled the names of all Spanish people, places, and organizations according to accepted Iberian usage, including the use of accents: thus, Manuel Sastrón, Instituto de Cooperación Iberoamericana, and so forth.

Andres Bonifacio

(Credit: Reproduced from Manuel Artigas, *Andres Bonifacio y el "Katipunan"* [Manila, 1911])

INTRODUCTION

History, Invention, and Nationalism

This book tells a bizarre story about a famous man. The man in question is the Philippine national hero Andres Bonifacio, the leader of the Philippine Revolution of 1896, who died almost a century ago. The story concerns the successful efforts of a number of historians and one memoirist to transform Bonifacio in the years since his death.

In effect, Bonifacio has been posthumously re-created. He has been given a new personality and a childhood that may bear little resemblance to his real one. Literary compositions have been attributed to him that he almost certainly did not write, and, as a consequence, he has been credited with ideas he did not have. Key events in his life have been altered beyond recognition. The national hero who has emerged from this process of re-creation—the Bonifacio celebrated in history textbooks and memorialized in statues around the Philippines—is, in reality, something closer to a national myth.

In the pages that follow, I demonstrate that almost every line of poetry heretofore thought to have been written by Bonifacio cannot be shown to be his literary product. Indeed, most of his personal correspondence was probably forged. Perhaps the single most astonishing fact about the Philippine national hero is that most of what we will ever know about him must be refracted through the lenses of his contemporaries. Furthermore, I argue that the historians and the one memoirist who were largely responsible for producing the image of Bonifacio we have today often adopted questionable methods. More than one consciously dissembled. More than one altered evidence.

More than one interpreted the evidence at their disposal in very strange ways. One placed into circulation a small collection of seemingly bogus documents. I have entitled this book *Inventing a Hero* because that is precisely what those people did.

I

I did not originally plan to write such a book. In September 1989, I arrived in Manila, intending to launch a research project on the Philippine Revolution of 1896. The centennial of the revolution was approaching, and I believed that the existing literature about it was deficient. A reconsideration seemed to be in order. But over the next three months, as I worked my way through the holdings of archives and libraries and spent hundreds of dollars on xeroxed copies, my focus slowly shifted from the revolution itself to the leader of the secret society that launched the uprising against Spain, Andres Bonifacio. The more documents I read about Bonifacio, the more I felt that historians' accounts of the man were wholly off the mark. So my projected book about the Philippine Revolution became a book about Bonifacio.

The research project did not progress well. Back in the United States, working my way through accumulated research notes, various books and articles written about Bonifacio over the years, and thousands of xeroxed pages of texts written in difficult, deep, turn-of-the-century Tagalog, I began to realize that something was not quite right. The scholarly literature was even more problematic than I had originally thought; contributions considered reliable turned out to be seriously flawed. Furthermore, the sources I was reading appeared to contradict each other often, sometimes on matters of small detail and sometimes on important issues. Could I ultimately make sense out of the mess of contradictions?

A colleague suggested that I try to write something on Bonifacio based on the research I had done thus far. In the summer of 1991, I produced two article-length pieces: the first a reconsideration of the most influential book ever written about Bonifacio, Teodoro Agoncillo's *The Revolt of the Masses: The Story of Bonifacio and the Katipunan*, and the second a study of the Tejeros assembly, a meeting held by the Filipino revolutionaries in the province of Cavite in March 1897—an event that is often depicted as a crucial turning point in the revolution against Spain. The first, eventually published in the journal *Pilipinas*, laid out some of the concerns I had about Agoncillo, a scholar who dealt with historical evidence in demonstrably peculiar ways.[1] The second pointed out the dubious nature of some of that evidence and made an honest effort to determine whether it was possible, given such flawed sources, to figure out what really happened at Tejeros. In that summer of 1991, I came to the tentative conclusion that it was possible—and I wrote as much at the time—but I was uncertain about some of my findings. I did not attempt to publish the second piece.

For the next three years, I spun my wheels. I continued to do research, spending many hours alone with my refractory Tagalog texts, but I made little headway, and my doubts increased about my ability to write a book about Bonifacio. The sources would not permit it. They were too untrustworthy and too biased. The secondary literature was even more difficult to fathom. How could so many highly regarded scholars make so many obvious mistakes? More than once, I decided to drop the project entirely, only to return to it a month later, hoping my mind had cleared sufficiently to allow me to find a path through the documentary/scholarly forest.

In the end, I did find a path, but the process was more the result of trial and error. Three developments, only one of which I can place firmly in time, set me on that path. The first was my growing realization that, of all the baffling texts I had examined, the most baffling of all were certain letters supposedly written by Andres Bonifacio to his fellow revolutionary Emilio Jacinto. What bothered me most about them, aside from the vagueness of too many passages, was that some of the factual information they contained did not agree with that conveyed in any other source.

The second development occurred on a research trip to the Philippines in November 1993. My principal reason for going there was to examine firsthand the "original" texts of those same Bonifacio letters, which had recently been purchased by a well-known collector of rare Filipiniana. With some difficulty, I managed to see photocopies and determined that, in all likelihood, those presumed "originals" were forgeries.

The third development took place over the following eight months as I puzzled over what to do next. Despite my seemingly confirmed doubts about key sources, I remained committed to the goal of writing a book about Bonifacio. But then, slowly, two simple questions became clear. Why was I persisting in my effort to produce a study of Bonifacio if the sources would not permit me to do so? And, if the sources and the published books and articles about Bonifacio were really as odd as they appeared to be, why not write about them? Such were the origins of this book.

II

At this juncture, let me briefly explain the book's organization and summarize its contents. Each of the next five chapters examines an important component of the Bonifacio myth. My focus throughout is not so much on Bonifacio as on the process by which he was posthumously re-created and the six individuals who did the re-creating: three pre–World War II historians, Manuel Artigas, Epifanio de los Santos, and Jose P. Santos; the memoirist, the famous revolutionary Artemio Ricarte; and two highly regarded post–World War II historians, Teodoro Agoncillo and Reynaldo Ileto.

The first chapter looks at what historians have written about Bonifacio's life before the outbreak of the revolution of 1896, paying particular attention to the contributions of Artigas, de los Santos, and Santos. As I demonstrate, the writings of those three about the young Bonifacio have influenced every subsequent account of the national hero's life: they tell us almost everything we know about Bonifacio's childhood and about the prose and poetry he supposedly composed. But, in fact, the picture of Bonifacio that emerges from their writings cannot necessarily be given credence. Most of the data about his childhood are not supported by reliable evidence, and the aforementioned prose and poetry cannot be shown to be his compositions. Chapter 2 deals with the remaining body of primary source material attributed to Bonifacio—his personal correspondence. De los Santos and Santos again play prominent roles in the story I recount. The first apparently located the Bonifacio correspondence and then published it in translation; the second executed the Tagalog-language transcriptions of the original letters that scholars have relied on for the past four decades.[2] As it turns out, however, the famous Bonifacio correspondence was probably forged.

Chapter 3 turns to a different re-creator, Artemio Ricarte, a historical actor rather than a historian. Ricarte's memoir of the Philippine Revolution, first published in the 1920s, provides one of the fullest (and certainly one of the most frequently cited) accounts of what is arguably the most important event in Bonifacio's life—the Tejeros assembly. But, as I show, Ricarte's influential narrative bears little resemblance to reality.

The final two chapters examine the writings of two of the most influential Philippine historians of the postwar period: Teodoro Agoncillo and Reynaldo Ileto, both of whom have made significant contributions of their own to the Bonifacio myth. In chapter 4, a revised version of my earlier article, I focus on Agoncillo's problematic discussion of Bonifacio's personality in his prize-winning book, *The Revolt of the Masses*. In the next, I call into question Ileto's more recent efforts to add a millenarian tinge to the Philippine national hero.

My investigation of Bonifacio's posthumous invention is admittedly selective. I do not scrutinize every component of the Bonifacio myth, nor do I discuss at length all the historians who have produced significant studies of the national hero or the revolutionary period. I write relatively little, for example, about Gregorio Zaide, Carlos Quirino, Renato Constantino, Nick Joaquin, and Alfredo Saulo. In my view, none of these historians, however widely read their books may be, have made contributions to the Bonifacio myth comparable with those of the five historians and one memoirist on which I focus. This book is not, I should make clear, a historiographical study in the conventional sense; it is rather an analysis of historical re-creation. Furthermore, I have not attempted to examine the representations of Bonifacio in paintings, public statuary, plays, films, and popular fiction, nor have I touched on the well-orchestrated public campaign of the 1960s to make Bonifacio a national hero—the naming of streets and schools, the appearance of postage stamps, and so forth. All of those things are relevant to our understanding of popular conceptions of Bonifacio, and I regret that I have not had the time, resources, or energy to treat them in this book. I hope that other scholars will someday pick up where I have left off.

III

In addition to exposing certain myths about a Philippine historical figure of undisputed importance, this book deals explicitly with four interrelated issues that transcend the particularities of the Philippine case: the political uses of history, nationalism, heroic biography, and historical invention. For all the historians whose writings I scrutinize, a primary reason for posthumously re-creating Bonifacio and casting him in a heroic mold appears to have been political. All were, in their respective days, prominent, outspoken nationalists, deeply committed to the ideal of Philippine nationhood. To such people, a reconstructed Bonifacio—idealized and also sanitized in ways I will discuss—served a vital political function as a symbol of Philippine nationalism and a model for Filipino youth. More than anything else, their common commitment to a nationalist agenda probably explains the liberties they took with historical evidence and other deficiencies of their scholarship.

Of course, the Philippines is hardly the only place in which historians have used their writings to promote political objectives. In Western Europe, the United States, and other parts of the planet, Marxist historians have often been charged with attempting, through their books, to promote the possibility of social transformation, and conservative ones have been accused of providing an intellectual justification for existing political and socioeconomic hierarchies. Liberals and environmentalists have agendas; so, too, do feminists and postmodernists. Indeed, it can be argued, and sometimes is, that all historical writing, including the most esoteric, has a political dimension, even if the writers do not acknowledge (or may not be aware of) it.[3] The Philippines is also not the only place where the dominant political agenda is a decidedly nationalist one. In every nation-state of which I am aware, historical writing usually passes through a nationalist phase in which, as in the Philippines, the goal of nation building appears to determine many of the subjects investigated, the topics ignored, and, more often than not, the interpretations given to the data uncovered.[4]

Nor is the Philippines the only place where heroic biography is written. Long before Thomas Carlyle celebrated the notion of writing biographies of presumably great men, historians produced such studies, invariably hagiographic in nature, and up to the present heroic biography continues to flourish.[5] In no country, perhaps, is the genre as well developed as in the United States, and in none has more attention been given to assessing whether a particular man or woman deserves to be accorded heroic status. The list of American heroes seems endless: Washington, Jefferson, Franklin, Boone, Crockett, Jackson, Lincoln, Lee, Barton, Buffalo Bill, Theodore Roosevelt, Ford, Pershing, Lindbergh, MacArthur, Kennedy, King, and on and on.[6] The new states of Latin America have their own heroes—Bolívar, San Martín, O'Higgins, Father Hidalgo, Juárez, and Zapata. The newly independent African nations have Nkrumah, Kenyatta, Mugabe, Mandela, and others.[7] In all these nation-states, not only are the heroes' exploits recounted (and exaggerated) in massive tomes, but, like Bonifacio, their birthdays are celebrated as national holidays, their faces are found on postage stamps and currency, and bronzed representations of their bodies tower above crowded intersections in capital cities.

Nor, for that matter, is the Philippines the only country in which supposedly priceless historical documents have turned out to be certain or probable forgeries. Readers familiar with Chinese history are no doubt aware of the celebrated career of Sir Edmund Backhouse, once regarded as a leading China specialist, who forged lengthy diaries of court officials, invented elaborate tales about how he had discovered them, translated them into English, and published the translations to universal acclaim. The field of U.S. history has been bedeviled with such inventions: the probable fabrication of many letters attributed to the author Stephen Crane by his once-lauded biographer Thomas Beer; the certain invention of letters and other documents concerning the lives of William Penn, John Paul Jones, and Andrew Jackson by the historian Augustus C. Buell; the possibly nonexistent letters of Margaret Johnson Erwin, a nineteenth-century Mississippian, which formed the basis of a book published in 1981 by a respected university press. In European history, one can point to, among the many notorious fabrications thus far exposed, the fake Hitler diaries and the spurious sources upon which the Marquis de Sade based his account of the life of Isabelle of Bavaria. In Latin American history, there are the apocryphal documents published in 1940 relating to the famous Bolívar–San Martín meeting at Guayaquil.[8]

Hence, the general historiographical matters I touch on in my examination of the Bonifacio myth are hardly unique: history invariably serves a political function; nationalist historians around the world wave the flag; and heroic biography and hagiography are widely produced, as are forged historical documents. Beyond that, such things are much written about. On the other hand, less written about, but still not unique, is the particular *combination* of variables one finds in the Bonifacio case. The historians I discuss in this book—or at least some of them—have not simply placed history in the service of a political agenda, celebrated and exaggerated Filipino accomplishments, and used problematic historical records; they have, on this occasion, done all of them at once. A close connection consequently exists between certain sacred canons of Philippine nationalist historical literature and a body of seemingly bogus sources.

What is more, these are not the only canons that rely heavily on such dubious documents. One can point to other well-known examples of certain or probable fabrications of Philippine historical texts, and virtually all of them involve sources that have figured prominently in nationalist historical writing. Two of the most spectacular inventions— the "Maragtas Code," a compilation of the customs of prehispanic Filipinos putatively derived from very old manuscripts, and the "Code of Kalantiaw," a legal code dating from the fifteenth century—were exposed by the late William Henry Scott in his book *Prehispanic Source Materials for the Study of Philippine History*. The first reference to the Maragtas Code can be found in a volume published in 1907 by a local official from Iloilo by the name of Pedro Alcantara Monteclaro; the Code of Kalantiaw initially came to light in the next decade, when Jose E. Marco, a shadowy figure from Occidental Negros, revealed that he had uncovered a nineteenth-century manuscript written by a certain Father José María Pavón that included translations of the code. Scott's scrutiny of the sources revealed that no reliable evidence existed concerning the first code and that the manuscript by Pavón, which was filled with anachronisms and absurdities, was a crudely executed forgery. In addition, Scott concluded that more than half a dozen other supposedly old documents uncovered by the same Jose E. Marco—all of which, like the Pavón manuscript, were filled with data about the prehispanic Philippines—were likewise "deliberate and definite frauds."[9]

A few years after the appearance of Scott's book, John Schumacher exposed another batch of forgeries, all of them relating to the life of the martyred nineteenth-century priest Father Jose Burgos, a man credited with playing a key role in the emergence of Philippine nationalism. Once again, Jose E. Marco was involved, since every one of the forged texts can be traced in one way or another to him. Among the sources shown by Schumacher to be fabrications were a novel attributed to Burgos and a long narrative by a Spaniard about events in which Burgos participated. The latter included what appeared to be excerpts of the court-martial of Burgos and two other priests. As was the case with the sources examined by Scott, the fake Burgos texts were filled with anachronisms and unbelievable data. Schumacher also determined that Burgos's signature on the text of the fabricated novel did not match that on authentic documents of the period.[10]

As I have suggested, one striking characteristic of all of these problematic texts—the bogus codes, the fabricated texts relating to Burgos, the Bonifacio letters—is that they have been taken seriously by scholars and even cited in footnotes. That has been so, in large measure, because all contained ostensibly vital information on subjects of importance to Filipinos. The codes furnished data on the prehispanic Philippines, a period about which very little was known. The Burgos and Bonifacio manuscripts fleshed out the pictures of two famous historical figures. Perhaps understandably, therefore, Philippine historians were quick to seize on them. Referring to the Pavón manuscript and various other forgeries that can be traced to Jose E. Marco, William Henry Scott commented:

> Whether Jose E. Marco executed these manuscripts in his own hand, otherwise participated in their production, or simply purveyed them in good faith, he seems clearly to have responded, early and late, to a deep Filipino yearning for illuminating institutions like law codes and political confederations in a dark past, and to have supplied customers too eager to examine the merchandise and ask questions.[11]

The men who participated in re-creating Father Burgos and Andres Bonifacio also responded to a deep "yearning," this time about more recent developments. Whereas the old codes enabled Filipinos to feel pride about the prehispanic period, the Burgos inventions and the Bonifacio probable forgeries fed their hunger for modern heroes.

Outside the Philippines, there are comparable examples of the connection between nationalism and historical invention, but the list does not appear to be long. Perhaps the best known comes from the historical literature of the first new nation-state, the United States, and it, too, involves hero creation. The hero in question was George Washington, the subject of a large number of heroic biographies in the early years of the Republic, none more influential than Mason L. Weems's *The Life of Washington*. First published in 1800, Weems's book was filled with fabulous anecdotes about Washington's life and character that illustrated the man's greatness. In later years, the book went through a number of reformulations and reprintings, which added even more fabulous stories, including the one about Washington and the cherry tree. By his own account, Weems had nationalistic motives in producing such a picture of Washington; he intended the former president to serve as a national symbol and a model to be emulated. In describing his projected biography to a friend, he wrote: "I then go on to show that his unparalleled rise & elevation were due to his Great Virtues. . . . Thus I hold up his great Virtues . . . to the imitation of Our Youth." Weems was not the only biographer of Washington to take substantial liberties with the historical record. In the 1830s, Jared Sparks, who later became professor of history at (and still later president of) Harvard University, produced a twelve-volume edition of *The Writings of George Washington* in which he selectively bowdlerized Washington's prose.[12]

A second example comes from a state that no longer exists, the Soviet Union. The invented hero was Joseph Stalin—today no longer accorded heroic status, but such was not always the case—and the people responsible for the invention were Stalin himself and a cadre of official biographers. In fact, it turns out that much of what historians used to write about Stalin's early years—details about his family and education, his precocity and rebellious tendencies, his participation in strikes and revolutionary events, his role in the development of Transcaucasian Bolshevism—was simply fabricated. Stalin was, as one historian has commented, "the most striking example in all history of a man who has succeeded in inventing himself." He even concocted a story about a letter he had received from Lenin in 1903, several years before there was any contact between the two men. While it may be argued that this particular example of hero creation was intended more to promote the cult of personality and Stalin's personal agenda than the cause of nationalism, there can be little doubt that nationalism was also served by the effort, since the invented Stalin, a man with impeccable revolutionary credentials, functioned

INTRODUCTION

as a symbol of national unity in a new, troubled, ethnically diverse state.[13]

What sense can we make of such willful, wholesale distortions of the historical record in the service of nationalism? To be honest, I am uncertain, primarily because it is unclear to me how widespread the phenomenon is. It may be that, in some places, certain circumstances—a paucity of sources relating to issues of presumed significance, for example—have made it easier to introduce and circulate inventions. But it is just as likely that the connection between nationalism and invention is much more widespread than the scholarly community has up to now suspected. That is to say, the relatively limited amount of scholarly discussion about the connection may not indicate that it rarely exists but that historians have largely discounted the possibility of its existence. My own best guess—I must admit it is no more than that—is that, at some point in the future, the invented Andres Bonifacio may very well be viewed as the rule rather than the exception and that, instead of appearing to be an aberration, the kind of invention I describe in this book will be seen as merely one manifestation (albeit an extreme one) of the nearly universal tendency of nationalist historians to reshape the historical record.

IV

Before proceeding to my account of Bonifacio's posthumous re-creation, I need first to provide a modicum of information about the era of the Philippine Revolution, so that nonspecialists will have a sporting chance of understanding references to important people, organizations, places, and events. This overview is intended to be both brief and basic. One important reason for the brevity is that, given what I now know (and plan to share with readers) about the work of the mythmakers, I am uncertain about many key details of the revolutionary period.

The Philippine Revolution of 1896 followed a century of rapid change in the archipelago. Beginning in the last half of the eighteenth century, the Philippines, then a backwater of the Spanish empire, began to undergo a major economic transformation as a consequence of its integration into the world market system. In region after region, increasing numbers of Filipino cultivators shifted from the production of subsistence crops (rice and corn, in particular) for local consumption to the growing of cash crops (sugar, tobacco, abaca, and coconuts) for export. Sugar first became a crop of importance in the provinces of Pampanga and Batangas, both on the island of Luzon, and then later on the island of Negros. Tobacco was widely produced in the Cagayan Valley of northern Luzon, and abaca in the Bikol provinces of southern Luzon. Coconuts were grown in various parts of Luzon and on several other islands.[14]

By the mid–nineteenth century, largely as a result of this economic transformation, a substantial number of Filipinos were able to accumulate modest fortunes from cash cropping and trading activities. They used their newly acquired wealth to buy more land, build splendid houses, import furniture and other items from Europe, and otherwise consume conspicuously. But, in addition, more than a few of them invested some of it in the education of their sons. By the late nineteenth century, tens of thousands of young male Filipinos had attended secondary schools in the Philippines, and every year more than fifteen hundred were enrolled in the University of Santo Tomas, located in Manila. Dozens more went to Spain and other places in Europe to pursue further studies.[15]

Not surprisingly, like educated young men in other colonies, some members of this emerging intellectual elite began to grumble openly about the colonial situation. Especially dissatisfied were a small group of Filipinos, most of them university students, who were residing in Spain—a group that collectively launched the so-called Propaganda Movement in the 1880s. The Propagandists, the best known of whom were Marcelo H. del Pilar and the brilliant novelist Jose Rizal, identified many deficiencies of the Spanish colonial regime: censorship of the press; the abuses of the Guardia Civil, the principal law enforcement agency in the archipelago; unfair taxation; and, above all, the inordinate political and economic power of the regular Catholic religious orders (Augustinians, Dominicans, and so on) in the Philippines. In their newspapers and other writings, the Propagandists lobbied vigorously for change.[16]

They made little headway in Spain, and by 1892 Rizal, frustrated about the lack of progress and increasingly at odds with other members of the movement, decided to return to the Philippines. Often characterized as a "mere reformist," Rizal had increasingly become convinced that separation from Spain was necessary. He arrived in Manila in June 1892 and quickly began to organize the Liga Filipina, an organization that aimed to lay the foundations of a national community in order to prepare the way for eventual self-rule. Rizal's leadership of the Liga was short-lived. He was arrested in early July and soon thereafter deported to a remote town on the island of Mindanao.[17]

As the Liga Filipina fell apart in the aftermath of Rizal's deportation, another organization came into being in Manila—a secret society called the Kataastaasan Kagalang-galang na Katipunan ng mga Anak ng Bayan (Highest and Most Honorable Society of the Sons of the Country), or Katipunan, as it is generally known. One of its founders was Andres Bonifacio. Our knowledge of the aims and activities of the Katipunan is limited, due in part to the fact that it was, after all, a *secret* society and in part to the problematic character of the documentation that has survived. Much of the information found in the literature about its operations turns out to be derived from a source—the so-called minutes of the Katipunan—that a number of authorities believe to be bogus. Other key details are based the account of a nonmember, Isabelo de los Reyes.[18]

Even so, a few things can be said with reasonable confidence about the Katipunan.[19] First, the secret society grew very slowly for several years; by the beginning of 1896, it is unlikely that the organization had more than a few hundred members. Second, as time passed, Bonifacio's influence in the Katipunan appeared to increase. In either 1893 or 1894, he attained the position of *supremo*, although it must be acknowledged that we do not know how much power the holder of that position actually had. Third, beginning in January 1896, the secret society's membership expanded considerably—the causes of the expansion have never, in my view, been convincingly explained—so that, by August 1896, the month in which the Philippine Revolution broke out, it probably numbered in the thousands.[20] Fourth, the Katipunan was an almost exclusively Tagalog organization; up to outbreak of the uprising, its membership and influence did not extend beyond the boundaries of the eight Tagalog-speaking provinces of central Luzon.

Because of the rapid growth that occurred in the first eight months of 1896, it is hardly surprising that information about the existence of the secret society eventually came to the attention of the Spanish authorities. That discovery led to a crackdown by Spanish law enforcement agencies, and the crackdown, in turn, led to a decision by Bonifacio and his fellow *katipuneros* in late August 1896 to raise the flag of rebellion. Almost immediately, thousands of nonmembers rallied in support of the Katipunan, both in Manila and in the surrounding provinces.

Over the next few weeks, commanded by Bonifacio and other leading figures in the Katipunan, an army composed of katipuneros and their supporters fought a series of battles against Spanish forces in the environs of Manila. All of the military encounters had similar results—overwhelming victories for the Spaniards, who were better armed, better supplied, and better trained, and who benefited from the inexperience of the Filipino troops. By the end of September, the units under Bonifacio's command were badly beaten and the supremo himself was in hiding.

Outside Manila, however, the Tagalog forces fared a good deal better. To a certain extent, their success was due to the fact that the Spanish military units they faced in their initial operations were small in size. But, in addition, most of the provincial commanders, unlike Bonifacio, had a limited amount of previous experience with military operations. Among the leading figures in the Katipunan in the provinces were a number of men—Emilio Aguinaldo of the town of Kawit in Cavite Province, for one—who had held the position of *gobernadorcillo* in their native towns. In that capacity, as the ranking officials in their communities, they had been obliged from time to time to lead the local police force in operations against bandits. Because of that, gobernadorcillos were familiar with firearms and knew something about small-scale military actions. Hence, at the same time that Bonifacio was avoiding battle, Tagalog units in nearby areas were seizing control of many municipalities.[21]

Particularly noteworthy successes were achieved by revolutionary troops in Cavite, just south of Manila. After the expulsion of the Spanish forces, the province of Cavite was administered by two organizations known as *sangguniang bayan* ("municipal consultative bodies"). One sangguniang bayan, with its headquarters in the town of Kawit, was named Magdalo—which was also the Katipunan name of one of its leaders, Emilio Aguinaldo. The other, based in the town of Noveleta, was called Magdiwang, and among the prominent Caviteños associated with it were Mariano Alvarez and his son Santiago. The jurisdiction of the Magdalo organization (Sangguniang Magdalo) included several towns in eastern Cavite; the Magdiwang organization (Sangguniang Magdiwang) had jurisdiction over western Cavite. Each

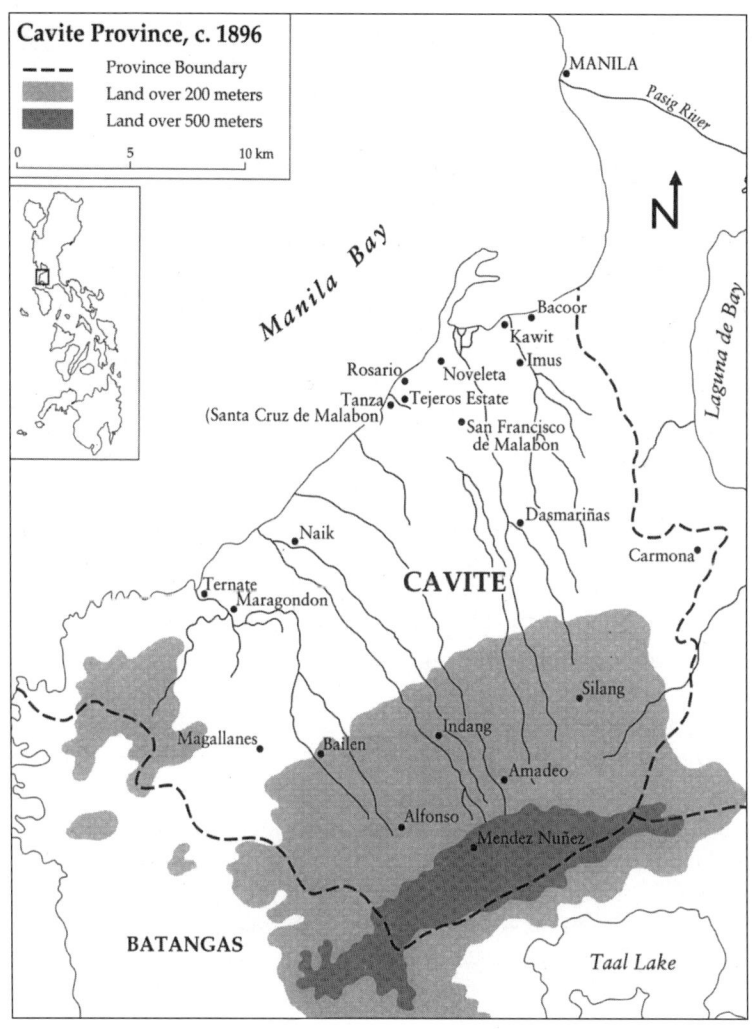

Map of Cavite Province

organization fielded its own military units commanded by its own generals.[22]

Toward the end of 1896 (the sources disagree about the date), Bonifacio was invited to Cavite by Mariano Alvarez, the Magdiwang leader, who was also the uncle of Bonifacio's wife Gregoria de Jesus. Bonifacio accepted the invitation, arriving in the province with a small retinue. From the start, there was tension between Bonifacio and several members of the Magdalo organization—most notably Daniel Tirona. Furthermore, a few months after Bonifacio arrived, the Spanish Army, having been reinforced with fresh troops from the mother country, launched an offensive in Cavite and immediately began winning back the towns earlier occupied by the revolutionaries.

The Spanish offensive exacerbated the existing fissures within the revolutionary ranks, as various commanders found it impossible to cooperate with others. Those developments—together with a perception that the existing revolutionary organization (which was based on the old secret society) was anachronistic and a growing dissatisfaction with Bonifacio—led some of the revolutionaries to favor radical changes in institutions and leadership. In late March 1897, as the Spanish forces were preparing to advance on the town of Imus, an assembly of revolutionaries convened at the friar estate house at Tejeros, close to the municipality of Santa Cruz de Malabon. That meeting produced two significant results—the replacement of the Katipunan by a new governmental structure and the election of Emilio Aguinaldo, the Magdalo field commander, as president of that government. Bonifacio, for his part, refused to accept the verdict of Tejeros.[23]

In the seven weeks following the Tejeros meeting, relations between Bonifacio and the new government headed by Aguinaldo grew steadily worse. No longer in charge, Bonifacio still had some supporters, especially in the province of Batangas just south of Cavite. Meanwhile, rumors of the wildest kind circulated in Cavite. Aguinaldo and his followers claimed that Bonifacio was plotting against them; Bonifacio made the same claims about his rivals. Attempts by intermediaries to arrange a reconciliation failed, and, in the end, superior force prevailed. Aguinaldo ordered Bonifacio's arrest and, after a skirmish, the former supremo was taken into custody. Shortly thereafter, a trial was held. Bonifacio was found guilty of treason and sentenced to death. On May 10, 1897, the sentence was carried out.

The change in leadership did nothing to improve the fortunes of the Filipinos in the military struggle against Spain. By the end of May 1897, the Spaniards had recaptured all of Cavite and Aguinaldo was forced to abandon the province. He eventually went north, establishing his headquarters in Bulacan. Toward the end of 1897, he worked out peace terms with the mother country. In exchange for cash payments and empty promises, he and the other ranking field commanders of the Filipino forces agreed to go into exile in Hong Kong.

Such then, in summary, was the historical context in which Andres Bonifacio, the man who was to become the Philippine national hero, operated. The Philippines was experiencing rapid economic and social change; new elites were emerging; new political organizations were being formed; and Spanish authority was being challenged, first in print and subsequently on the battlefield. In this time of ferment, Bonifacio, the leader of the organization that launched the uprising of 1896 against Spain, was obviously an important player.

But, as the preceding overview has doubtless hinted, he was a very controversial player as well—a revolutionary leader who became embroiled in conflicts with, and ultimately was put to death by, some of the very revolutionaries he had led. However brave he may have been and however much he may have contributed to the revolutionary movement, such a man was, it must be recognized, a somewhat curious choice as a national hero. To raise the dead Bonifacio to heroic status obliged the prospective raisers not merely to tell his story; they also had to contend with the perception that he was a man with serious human flaws.

In addition, as we shall see, they had to contend with a reality that under normal circumstances would have been sufficient to convince many historians to undertake a different research project: a lack of source material relating to Bonifacio's life. Save perhaps for a few printed orders on which his signature appears, virtually nothing written by Bonifacio was passed down to posterity. But this sparse documentary record—something that appeared to pose formidable obstacles to the recovery of the past—actually made it easier for nationalist historians to invent the man. Unhampered by existing documents, they were freer to attribute certain ideas and personal characteristics to Bonifacio, to explain away the apparent human flaws, and, in the process, to create a suitable national symbol. Let us see how they did it.

Bonifacio statue sculpted by Guillermo Tolentino, at Liwasang Bonifacio, Manila

(Credit: Jose Duran)

CHAPTER ONE

Bonifacio before the Revolution

Every significant survey of Philippine history written in the past fifty years—which is to say the books of Gregorio Zaide, Teodoro Agoncillo and Milagros Guerrero, Renato Constantino, Jose Arcilla, and O. D. Corpuz—devotes at least several paragraphs (and, in the case of the longer ones, a dozen pages or more) to the early years of Andres Bonifacio.[1] Although there are slight interpretive differences in the texts, all of them provide more or less the same seemingly hard data. What follows is a composite sketch of the young Bonifacio based on the biographical information found in those books.

Andres Bonifacio was born on November 30, 1863, in the Tondo district of Manila. His parents were Santiago Bonifacio, a tailor, and Catalina de Castro, generally described as a housewife. He had three brothers (Ciriaco, Procopio, and Troadio) and two sisters (Espiridiona and Maxima). For a while, young Andres attended a school run by Guillermo Osmeña, a native of Cebu, but, at the age of fourteen, he lost both his parents and was obliged to enter the world of work in order to support his siblings. Initially, Bonifacio made and sold walking canes and paper fans; he also produced posters for various commercial firms in Manila. Before he had reached the age of twenty, he found employment as a "clerk-messenger" in the Manila-based, foreign-owned business firm of Fleming and Company. In time, he became an "agent" of the company, selling rattan, tar, and other products, and then he switched to another commercial house, Fressell and Company, where he also served as an agent.[2] Bonifacio married twice.

His first wife, a neighbor named Monica, died after a year of wedlock. In 1893, he married Gregoria de Jesus, the daughter of a local official of the town of Caloocan.

Despite his limited formal education, the young Bonifacio evidently had a love of learning. "The little leisure that he had was employed in self-study," wrote Agoncillo and Guerrero in *History of the Filipino People*. "He read books by the lamplight at home."[3] Included in his library were two novels of Jose Rizal, *Les misérables* by Victor Hugo, Eugène Sue's *The Wandering Jew*, and books on the French Revolution, international law, the penal and civil codes, and the presidents of the United States. The historical surveys do not tell us in what languages those books were written.

By 1892, Bonifacio began to manifest a strong interest in political matters. He joined the Liga Filipina, founded by Rizal in early July 1892. Furthermore, at virtually the same time, Bonifacio and a handful of other men inaugurated the Katipunan, which appeared to have somewhat more "radical" objectives. "The Katipunan had two aims," wrote Gregorio Zaide, "namely, (1) to unite the Filipinos into one solid nation and (2) to win Philippine independence by means of revolution."[4] Initially, Deodato Arellano served as supremo of the secret society. He was succeeded by Roman Basa in 1893, and sometime later Bonifacio was elevated to that position. Under his leadership, the organization launched a newspaper called *Kalayaan*, which was intended to sow revolutionary seeds.[5]

Although Bonifacio played a prominent role in organizing the Katipunan, the principal theoretician of the organization and the author of its most important texts was his close associate Emilio Jacinto, a graduate of the prestigious secondary school the Colegio de San Juan de Letran, who, at the time he joined the secret society, was attending the University of Santo Tomas. Even so, Bonifacio produced several literary contributions of consequence before the outbreak of the revolution, all of them written in Tagalog—a number of poems; a translation into Tagalog of one of Jose Rizal's poems; a text entitled "Katungkulang Gagawin ng mga Z. Ll. B." ("The Duties of the Sons of the Country"), a list of rules for the members of the Katipunan, which has often been referred to as Bonifacio's decalogue; and "Ang Dapat Mabatid ng mga Tagalog" ("What the Tagalogs Should Be Aware Of"), a short contribution to *Kalayaan*.

Such, we are told, was the young Bonifacio—a poor lad who by pluck and determination was able to overcome bad fortune and make something of himself. Unlike Rizal, the other national hero to whom Bonifacio is often compared, he did not have wealthy relatives to bail him out when times got tough. Nor did he receive an education at the best secondary schools in the Philippines. Nor did he have an opportunity to pursue university studies in Europe. Bonifacio was, rather, a Filipino version of a Horatio Alger hero or, to invoke an analogy from the realm of historical mythology rather than popular literature, a Filipino Abraham Lincoln.

Where did this picture of the young Andres Bonifacio come from? Is it actually supported by reliable evidence? What was the pre-revolutionary Bonifacio really like? In the remainder of this chapter, I attempt to answer these questions to the extent that they can be answered. My discussion is divided into four parts. The first two subject to scrutiny what has been said about Bonifacio's childhood and early adulthood; the third and fourth deal with his writings.

I

To understand the origins of the traditional picture of Bonifacio's early years, we need first to turn to the references provided in the surveys mentioned above. Arcilla furnished neither footnotes nor endnotes, nor, for that matter, did he include a bibliography or a list of recommended readings. The other authors did indicate, in one way or another, the sources on which they relied—Zaide in footnotes; Agoncillo and Guerrero in a list of "Selected References" found at the end of their book; and Constantino and Corpuz in endnotes.

Gregorio Zaide (1907–86) was undoubtedly the most prolific Philippine historian of the twentieth century. The holder of a Ph.D. from the University of Santo Tomas, Zaide began his academic career as an instructor at the University of the Philippines but subsequently moved on to Far Eastern University, where he rose to the rank of professor. The author of more than fifty books, most of them on Asian history and government, Zaide was best known for his works of historical synthesis, and his textbooks were widely used in Philippine universities. But, early in his career, Zaide also wrote research monographs of some importance, and he was an acknowledged specialist on the revolutionary period, having published a history of the Katipunan in 1939 and a monograph on the Philippine Revolution in 1954.[6]

Zaide's treatment of the prerevolutionary Bonifacio in his popular historical survey text was essentially a summary of material he had published in his earlier monographs. More important for our purposes, his footnotes merely repeated references found in those previously published books. Zaide cited five sources to document his account of Bonifacio: an article published by Epifanio de los Santos in the *Philippine Review* in 1918, two biographies of Bonifacio (the first by Manuel Artigas, the second by Jose P. Santos, the son of Epifanio de los Santos), and newspaper articles by Austin Craig and Zaide himself.[7] Since the newspaper pieces were clearly not works of original scholarship, Zaide's list of five should properly be reduced to three: de los Santos, Artigas, and Santos. In due course, we will return to these featured sources and examine them in detail, but for the moment let us proceed to the other surveys to learn how their authors derived their information about Bonifacio.

Teodoro Agoncillo (1912–85), the principal author of *History of the Filipino People*, was, like Zaide, a respected specialist on the revolutionary period. His best-known publication was the prize-winning monograph *The Revolt of the Masses: The Story of Bonifacio and the Katipunan,* which, together with Agoncillo himself, will be the focus of a later chapter. The lengthy treatment of the young Bonifacio and the Katipunan that appeared in *History of the Filipino People* was, as the coauthors themselves acknowledged at one point, "to a large extent a résumé of several chapters" of *The Revolt of the Masses*. For "important references" on both subjects, they directed interested readers to the earlier book.[8]

A reading of Agoncillo's detailed endnotes in *The Revolt of the Masses* reveals that, in constructing his account of Bonifacio's life up to the time of his involvement in the Katipunan, he relied on a relatively small number of sources: the article by de los Santos, the book by Artigas, a biography of Bonifacio written by Aguedo Cagingin, a book by Jose P. Santos, and several interviews with Bonifacio's contemporaries.[9] Cagingin's biography—brief, unfootnoted, and probably intended for schoolchildren—could not have told Agoncillo anything of consequence and does not merit our serious consideration.[10] The interviews were valuable more for what they told Agoncillo about

Bonifacio's personality than for any details they provided about his daily existence, and they will, in any event, be investigated carefully in a later chapter. That leaves us with three sources to consider, the authors of which were the same authorities mentioned by Zaide: de los Santos, Artigas, and Santos.

Unlike Zaide and Agoncillo, Renato Constantino (1919–) did not make his reputation as a historian of the Philippine Revolution. A journalist by profession, he was one of the most popular newspaper columnists in the Philippines in the days before Ferdinand Marcos's declaration of martial law. During that period, in addition to turning out countless columns of high quality, he wrote a bit of history, producing clever, controversial, and influential interpretive essays on Jose Rizal, U.S. colonialism, and other subjects. But, because of the virtual censorship of the Philippine press that prevailed under martial law, Constantino's journalistic career came to an abrupt halt and he turned increasingly to the writing of history. His major literary productions as a historian were two works of synthesis he wrote in collaboration with his wife Letizia. *The Philippines: A Past Revisited*, which first appeared in 1975, was an overview of Philippine history from the Spanish conquest to the early years of U.S. colonial rule. *The Philippines: The Continuing Past*, published in 1978, was a sequel that brought the story up to the 1960s. The first of these books contained Constantino's lengthy discussion of the Philippine Revolution, an event he viewed as seminal. His account pictured Bonifacio as a patriotic, committed man of humble origins who was ultimately overthrown and eliminated by upper-class usurpers led by Emilio Aguinaldo.[11]

In drawing his portrait of the young Bonifacio, Constantino appeared to rely on sources different from those cited by both Zaide and Agoncillo. He listed four in his endnotes: two journal articles (one by Leopoldo Serrano and the other by Esteban de Ocampo), a study by Teodoro Kalaw, and a book by Epifanio de los Santos entitled *Marcelo H. del Pilar*.[12]

The two articles were brief but not without interest. While both relied heavily on the existing historical literature—Serrano on Artigas, de los Santos, Santos, and Agoncillo; Ocampo on de los Santos and Agoncillo—both also included some heretofore unmentioned details, most of which were learned from the national hero's sister Espiridiona. Serrano, for example, revealed that Bonifacio had a talent for music and also that, once he became head of the household following the death of his parents, he was a strict disciplinarian. Ocampo related that Bonifacio's mother was a Spanish mestiza from Zambales who had worked in a cigarette factory. Serrano did not explain exactly how Espiridiona communicated that information to him. Ocampo, on his part, claimed that he had interviewed the national hero's sister several times.[13]

Kalaw's book *The Philippine Revolution*, published in 1925, was one of the earliest scholarly accounts of the revolutionary period and also one of the most comprehensive. Kalaw, who was a well-known journalist and political figure, covered events from the founding of the Katipunan (1892) to the final official acts of the Philippine-American War (1902). His description of the prerevolutionary Bonifacio included virtually all of the data found in the accounts written several decades later—the humble origins, the limited education, the love of books, the list of favorite titles, and the employment with foreign commercial houses.[14] Since Kalaw did not use footnotes or endnotes, we cannot know for sure where he learned all that, but an examination of his bibliography helps to narrow the possibilities. Among the forty-nine items listed were two publications by Manuel Artigas and two by Epifanio de los Santos.[15] Almost inevitably, the paper trail leads us back to them.

And, of course, even if it didn't, Constantino himself pointed us in their direction, since, as we have already seen, one of the sources he cited was a book by Epifanio de los Santos. His citation was somewhat misleading, however. The book's full title was not *Marcelo H. del Pilar* but *Marcelo H. del Pilar, Andres Bonifacio, Emilio Jacinto*, and it consisted of nothing more than reprints of three biographical sketches de los Santos had published in the *Philippine Review*.[16] The only relevant data on Bonifacio's early life were found in the second sketch. In reality, then, Constantino was citing exactly the same source—de los Santos's brief biography of Bonifacio—that was relied upon by both Zaide and Agoncillo.

O. D. Corpuz (1926–), author of the most recently published Philippine historical survey considered here, has had two quite different careers—one as an academic, the other as a government official. The recipient of a Ph.D. in government from Harvard University, he quickly rose through the faculty ranks at the University of the Philippines, producing important books on

Philippine politics and history and subsequently serving as president of the university (1975–79). But he was also tapped for government service on two occasions, holding Cabinet positions under President Ferdinand Marcos in 1968–71 and 1979–83. After resigning from government service in 1983, Corpuz returned to scholarship, eventually publishing a massive two-volume account of Philippine history from the arrival of the Spaniards to the early years of U.S. rule.[17] Corpuz's description of the prerevolutionary Bonifacio, which appeared in the second volume of his survey, was based on standard sources: Epifanio de los Santos's famous article on Bonifacio and Teodoro Agoncillo's book *The Revolt of the Masses*.

II

One thing that should be obvious by now is that just about everything we are likely to read about the prerevolutionary Bonifacio is based on the scholarly contributions of three long-dead pioneers of the Philippine historical profession: Manuel Artigas, Epifanio de los Santos, and Jose P. Santos. Artigas published his biography of Bonifacio in 1911.[18] De los Santos's seminal article on the national hero first appeared in Spanish in the November 1917 issue of the *Philippine Review*, although the version most often cited by later scholars is an English translation by Gregorio Nieva published in an early 1918 number of that same periodical.[19] Jose P. Santos's principal works on Bonifacio were published in the mid-1930s.[20] Since those three men were the real authorities on Bonifacio's early years, the time has come to direct our attention to them.

Manuel Artigas y Cuerva (1866–1925), the son of a Philippine woman from Bulacan and a Spaniard who came to the Philippines as a ship's navigator and then went into business, was educated at the Ateneo Municipal, the elite Jesuit secondary school in Manila, and the University of Santo Tomas, where he began, but did not complete, the study of medicine.[21] In 1883, at the age of seventeen, he entered government service and over the next fifteen years worked in various agencies of the imperial bureaucracy. At the same time, however, he pursued a journalistic career, working for daily newspapers and periodicals. He also wrote books, initially ones intended for government officials like himself. *El Manual del Empleado* ("The Employee's Manual") was published in 1891, and five other books appeared in 1894. One of the five, a two-volume compilation of documents on municipal government in the Philippines from the beginning of Spanish colonial rule, signaled Artigas's emerging interest in the Philippine past. The Philippine Revolution of 1896 brought his career as a colonial official to an end, and in 1897 he went to Spain, where he continued to work as a journalist and held an assortment of jobs. He also traveled to France.

Artigas returned to the Philippines in 1902. A U.S. colonial administration was now in place, and Artigas initially sought employment in the private sector, finding work as a journalist and as general secretary of a labor union. In 1907, he entered government service once more, this time as a librarian. From 1908 until his death in 1925, he worked for the Philippine Public Library (later to be called the National Library and Museum, and still later the National Library), playing a prominent role in developing the library's collection of Filipiniana. Artigas rose by slow stages through the bureaucratic ranks. In 1911, he was appointed chief of the Filipiniana Division. In January 1916, he became assistant librarian and three months later librarian. On three different occasions, he served as acting chief of the library. In the meantime, he continued to write articles for periodicals and to publish books, one of which was his short biography of Bonifacio. Some of the material included in that book first appeared in an article published in the December 1910 issue of the periodical *Renacimiento Filipino*.[22] Artigas finished writing his biography in the same month, and it was published in June of the following year.[23]

To appreciate Artigas's contributions to our collective understanding of Andres Bonifacio, we must examine briefly what had been written about the supremo before the publication of his biography. In fact, in the fourteen years since Bonifacio's premature death, he had been consigned to a kind of obscurity. Very little had been written about him, and the little that had was highly pejorative. Artigas himself commented on that state of affairs at the beginning of his book, intimating that one of his chief objectives was to provide readers with information about a man, Bonifacio, and an organization, the Katipunan, both of which had been dealt with unfairly in the existing literature. He singled out for criticism several Spanish authors, including Manuel Sastrón and Wenceslao Retana,[24] though two

British writers, William Brecknock Watson and John Foreman, had described Bonifacio in similarly unflattering terms. The former claimed that Bonifacio had "possessed . . . an unfathomable ambition"; according to the latter, he advocated "barbarous persecution and extermination of the Europeans."[25]

Furthermore, the policies of the U.S. colonial administration contributed to Bonifacio's posthumous predicament. Whereas American rulers encouraged the ruled to honor the memory of Jose Rizal—in part, no doubt, because they were encouraged to do so by the prominent Filipinos they courted, and in part, too, perhaps, because he was a reformer and opposed the Katipunan's decision to rebel against Spain—they did not do the same for Bonifacio the revolutionary. One of the early acts of the U.S. Philippine Commission was to change the name of the province of Morong to Rizal. The history curriculum in Philippine elementary schools called for discussion of Rizal but not of Bonifacio. A Philippine history textbook intended for high school students—written by David Prescott Barrows, then director of the Philippine education system—devoted about four pages to Rizal but mentioned Bonifacio only once.[26]

Still another possible reason for Bonifacio's predicament—and one alluded to by de los Santos in his article—was the ambivalence felt by Filipinos about him.[27] On the one hand, he was the leader of a patriotic struggle against alien overlords and hence a hero. But, on the other, he was a revolutionary leader who had been challenged, demoted, and eventually killed by his fellow revolutionaries. Doubtless, too, some Filipinos had heard the stories spread by Bonifacio's enemies, like Aguinaldo, about the supremo's intolerance and unwillingness to compromise.[28] To the extent he was known, therefore, Bonifacio was an ambiguous figure.

Beyond all that—beyond the bad press he had received from Spanish and British writers, the decisions of American colonial officials, and the disturbing known particularities of his life—there was another reason for Bonifacio's predicament: a lack of basic information about the man. Jose Rizal was a better candidate for secular sainthood not only because his politics were more palatable to the rulers but because his literary output (in particular, his correspondence with family, friends, and fellow reformers) was enormous, and as a consequence seemingly every important question relating to his life could be answered. As of 1911, the year in which Artigas's biography was published, Andres Bonifacio was a virtual tabula rasa. No collection of correspondence and writings had surfaced. The details of his early life and even of his contributions to the revolutionary movement were largely unknown.

Manuel Artigas made an effort to provide such details in his biography. He reproduced the entry in the Tondo parish register recording Bonifacio's baptism (on December 2, 1863, a few days after his birth). He conveyed other bits of information about Bonifacio's life before his involvement with the Katipunan—his parents, siblings, schooling, vocational history, and the like. Artigas also included a considerable amount of data on Bonifacio's role in the Katipunan, the course of the revolution, and his conflict with Aguinaldo. Still, Artigas's book was hardly a full-fledged biography of the supremo; indeed, the new data notwithstanding, it was a rather sketchy treatment of Bonifacio's life. The entire text ran to only slightly more than ninety pages, and of that total approximately half were taken up with transcriptions of documents relating to the Katipunan, revolutionary manifestos, and Artigas's lengthy critical comments about other books on the revolution. The book also included rambling, seemingly interminable footnotes, in many of which Artigas launched further acrimonious attacks on other writers (most notably Wenceslao Retana).

As a result, Artigas's entire discussion of Bonifacio's youth and early adulthood was only two pages in length. New data there were, but not great quantities of them. What is more—and what is more directly to the point—despite the fact that Artigas did include footnotes in his book, *not a single one of them* revealed the sources from which he derived the information he imparted about Andres Bonifacio's early years.[29]

Artigas's failure to provide footnote citations to sources is a fact worthy of our attention, not simply for what it tells us about Artigas's approach to history but for what it reveals about Philippine historical scholarship in the era in which he lived. Although "professional" historical methodology—which involved, among other things, the use of footnotes to acknowledge the sources upon which one relied—was fairly well established in scholarly circles in Western Europe and the United States by the early twentieth century, that was definitely not the case in the Philippines until about 1950. As we have seen, Teodoro Kalaw's influential study of the Philippine Revolution, published in 1925, did not contain such citations. In fact, the bulk of the historical literature then produced in the Philippines lacked footnote references. The historians of that era wrote almost exclusively for a popular audience; often the books they produced were longer versions of articles they had published in the popular press. All that changed in time, as more Filipinos received graduate training in history and Euro-American canons of historical scholarship became more widely accepted, but the change was gradual and it certainly had not begun when Manuel Artigas set pen to paper to write his biography of Andres Bonifacio.[30]

None of the above should be interpreted as a criticism of popular history. Around the world, a certain amount of well-researched history has always been written by women and men who provide no footnotes or endnotes, and such was certainly the case in the era in which Artigas wrote.[31] Nor do I wish to imply that footnoted scholarship is necessarily more reliable or better. Lots of dreadful history books—ones riddled with factual errors, misuse of evidence, incorrect quotations, insupportable interpretations, and the like—contain footnotes or endnotes that follow the guidelines laid out by Kate Turabian and the University of Chicago Press. My point is simply that Artigas, popular historian that he was, did not document most of the important things about which he wrote. In that respect, he did differ appreciably from the two other historians who played key roles in creating our image of the prerevolutionary Bonifacio: Epifanio de los Santos, who was a contemporary; and Jose P. Santos, who was not.

What conclusions can be drawn from the fact that almost all of Artigas's statements about the young Bonifacio were uncorroborated? It is possible, of course, that his account was actually based on extensive research. John Schumacher, who has scrutinized another book authored by Artigas, *Los sucesos de 1872* ("The Events of 1872"), has demonstrated that, although Artigas was uncritical in his use of sources and made careless errors in copying texts, he did more than a little digging in the archives and uncovered valuable documents along the way.[32] But, in the case of his Bonifacio biography, we have no hints at all about where he uncovered his data, except for the information about the hero's date of birth. Furthermore, common sense alone suggests that he could not have done a great deal of research on Bonifacio's life. In 1911, the year in which the biography appeared, Artigas published no fewer than four other books, including *Los sucesos de 1872*. In the next year, two more appeared.[33] Artigas simply did not have sufficient time to do extensive research on all the subjects that interested him.

Thus, in the end, our examination of Artigas's oft-cited book does not suggest that we should place absolute faith in its contents. Artigas may have examined documents. He may have talked to some of Bonifacio's surviving contemporaries. He may have based his account on details, possibly untrue ones, that had found their way into the oral tradition. He may also have gotten some data wrong, since, as we know from Schumacher, another of Artigas's books contained "errors and inconsistencies."[34] All we can be certain about is that as an authority Artigas was hardly unimpeachable.

Epifanio de los Santos (1871–1928), who has been described by Gregorio Zaide as "one of the intellectual titans produced by the Philippines," was a man of many talents: a historian, an important government official, a lawyer, a journalist, a writer of fiction, a linguist, a literary critic, a translator, a guitarist, a painter, and a collector of rare Filipiniana.[35] Born in the town of Malabon, not far from Manila, de los Santos was the son of a wealthy landowner. After graduating from the Ateneo Municipal, he entered the University of Santo Tomas, where he studied law and spent much of his spare time reading literature and interacting with men of letters. He played no role in the revolution of 1896, but in 1898, shortly after Dewey's destruction of the Spanish fleet in Manila Bay, de los Santos became a vocal advocate of Philippine independence, eventually joining the staff of the newspaper *La Independencia*. Sometime after the outbreak of warfare between the United States and the newly minted Philippine Republic, however, de los Santos decided to cast his lot with the Americans, and in 1900 he became district attorney for the town of San Isidro in the province of Nueva Ecija. He was later appointed provincial secretary of Nueva Ecija, and in 1902 he became provincial governor. Other official positions followed. In 1904, he served as a member of the Philippine delegation that attended the St. Louis Exposition, and in 1906 he was appointed *fiscal* for the provinces of Bulacan and Bataan, a position he held for almost two decades.

While employed in the insular administration, de los Santos actively pursued other interests. He collected paintings, antiques, furniture, and books. He wrote works of fiction. He conducted research, focusing on Philippine history and literature, and published several books and articles on those subjects, all of which were written in

Spanish. Rafael Palma, himself a well-known historian, described de los Santos as "the foremost Filipino scholar of his time." In 1925, in recognition of the high regard in which he was held, Governor-General Leonard Wood appointed him director of the Philippine National Library and Museum, and he served in that post until his death three years later.

It is not de los Santos's range of interests, nor the fame he achieved in his lifetime, but rather his historical scholarship that concerns us here—in particular, his short biographical study of Andres Bonifacio, which appeared in the *Philippine Review*. Over the years that article has probably been the most frequently cited publication on the early life of Andres Bonifacio. Even today, it commands respect. Corpuz referred to it in his overview of Philippine history, published in 1989; I cited it twice in a 1991 book on the revolutionary period in Batangas.[36]

But, when we place Epifanio de los Santos's article under the magnifying glass, its weaknesses become apparent. Let me start my analysis of de los Santos's treatment of the young Bonifacio by returning to an issue that figured in my discussion of Artigas's book—footnotes (or rather the lack thereof).

Because de los Santos included neither footnotes nor endnotes, it is often next to impossible to figure out his source of information for key factual points. In the second paragraph of the article, for example, he provided a short synopsis of Bonifacio's youth and vocational history, including many of the facts that have subsequently found their way into the textbooks—the poverty, the canes and paper fans, and so forth. Then de los Santos came to Bonifacio's education.

> His parents, whom he is said to have lost at the age of 14 years, gave him some education. The informant from whom we obtained these data does not state of what this education consisted.[37]

What can a reader conclude from such a statement? Who was the informant who furnished the data? Possibly, de los Santos was referring to Artigas, whose book had touched briefly on Bonifacio's education and included no information about its content. But we can't be certain. At several points in his article (but *not* at this point) de los Santos indicated that he derived important data from interviews with some of Bonifacio's contemporaries—among them Clemente J.

Zulueta, Teodoro Gonzales, and Cipriano Pacheco.[38] Any of them might have been the informant referred to by de los Santos, although it might be noted that none was, so far as the documents indicate, especially close to Bonifacio. As with Artigas, therefore, given de los Santos's silence about sources, we can only conclude that much of the author's discussion of Bonifacio's early years rests on shaky evidential foundations.

Yet, even when de los Santos's sources can be identified, one wonders whether his account can be credited. Consider his lengthy treatment of Bonifacio's tastes in literature, a description that clearly forms the basis of similar ones found in subsequent monographs on the revolution (e.g., Zaide's and Agoncillo's) and Philippine history texts. It was based, as we learn from a few of de los Santos's parenthetical remarks, on data from two principal sources. The first was a compilation of documents about the Philippine Revolution by Retana, Artigas's bête noire, who published many books about the Philippines at the turn of the century. Included in that compilation was the testimony of Pio Valenzuela, a ranking member of the Katipunan in the months immediately preceding the outbreak of the revolution, who had surrendered to the Spaniards only a few days after the uprising began and was examined at great length by his former enemies about all manner of things. In the course of that examination, Valenzuela revealed that "Andres Bonifacio [had] read a great deal" ("Andres Bonifacio ha leido mucho") and once possessed a personal library that was destroyed when his home burned. De los Santos accepted all that, and, in addition, he quoted Valenzuela as saying that Bonifacio "went without sleep at night in order to read" ("se pasaba la noche sin dormir por leer").[39] Valenzuela's testimony, it would seem, was the original source for the story about Bonifacio's nocturnal reading habits.

De los Santos's second source—the one that supplied detailed information about the supremo's favorite books—was apparently Valenzuela himself, although it is not clear how the former katipunero transmitted that information to de los Santos. At one point in his article, de los Santos included a list of the books in Bonifacio's library, the titles being the same ones found in the Philippine history surveys: *Les misérables*, *The Wandering Jew*, and so forth. But he was vague about the origins of the list, writing only that "we are indebted to Dr. Valenzuela" ("se la debemos al Dr. Valenzuela") for it. He was also unclear about the languages in which the books were written. Later, discussing Bonifacio's reading preferences, de los Santos was again imprecise: *"The Wandering Jew* by Eugène Sue was one of the favorite books [of Bonifacio], as Dr. Valenzuela tells us" (*"El Judío Errante* de Eugenio Sue era una lectura favorita [de Bonifacio], dícenos el Dr. Valenzuela").[40] Such a list and such information about Bonifacio's tastes did not appear in Valenzuela's testimony to the Spaniards, nor did it appear in his memoir, which was written sometime around 1914.[41] Nor can it be found in other descriptions of the revolution by Valenzuela that appeared in subsequent years.[42] If Valenzuela conveyed those things to de los Santos, he probably did so in a letter, an interview, or a series of interviews.

But if he did—and readers should note the use of the conditional clause—one may reasonably wonder whether Valenzuela's account, and hence de los Santos's, is believable. Valenzuela was, as more than one historian has pointed out, notoriously unreliable about details, often changing his story from one telling to the next.[43] Does it make sense to suppose that this same informant was able to remember correctly the titles of books in Bonifacio's library so many years after the fact? Furthermore, why was it that Valenzuela never included a list of Bonifacio's books in any of his other accounts of the Katipunan and the Philippine Revolution? Why did that information only appear in the article by Epifanio de los Santos?

Hence, on the surface there was something odd about Epifanio de los Santos's account of Bonifacio's reading preferences. Valenzuela may really have conveyed all those things to de los Santos, and it is even possible that the former revolutionary on this one occasion may have gotten the details right. But the opposite is possible, too. De los Santos's discussion of Bonifacio's reading habits and preferences is less than convincing, and his entire treatment of Bonifacio's early years should be viewed skeptically.

If it is true, as I have intimated, that de los Santos's account of Bonifacio's life may have been embellished, what possible motive could he have had for doing so? (The same question could be asked of Artigas, for that matter, since his work had similar qualities.) Here, in raising at last the issue of motives, we find ourselves on very infirm terrain. No questions about the past bedevil historians more than those relating to motives, and, more often than not, our answers amount to little more than informed speculation. It is therefore fitting that in this book, which is more about historians than anything else, motives are again at issue, although on this occasion the motives are not those of the historical actors but of the historians themselves.

In the cases of both de los Santos and Artigas, at least one possible authorial motive can be suggested. Both men were exponents, and to a certain extent formulators, of a brand of Philippine nationalism that was in vogue in certain literary circles after 1908 or so, as the U.S. colonial administration gradually relaxed its controls over the Philippine press. One important characteristic of this nationalism was the tendency of its adherents to laud the revolution of 1896, which they did by retelling anecdotes about the Katipunan, publishing the words of poems and songs, reproducing flags and other symbols, and discussing the lives and exploits of revolutionary leaders. Though on the whole their works were celebratory, they did describe at least some of their heroes' warts. (In fact, while Artigas and de los Santos were favorably disposed toward Bonifacio, both included unflattering information about his personal relations.)[44] Perhaps the best-known literary nationalist of this kind was the former revolutionary Carlos Ronquillo, but Artigas and de los Santos were not far behind.[45] They published their work in several periodicals, among them *Renacimiento Filipino*, which printed the preliminary, abbreviated version of Artigas's biography of Bonifacio, and the *Philippine Review*, which published de los Santos's sketch. In the 1930s, Jose P. Santos was a leading member of a new generation of nationalists.

Artigas and de los Santos were men with clear contemporary missions—to inform Filipinos about their glorious recent past, to promote national pride, and to do some of that by rescuing Andres Bonifacio from obscurity. Those missions, more than any other factors, may ultimately explain why they wrote history as they did. For if, as I suspect, the historical Bonifacio may have mattered less to them than their nationalism—if, that is to say, they cared less about the "documentable" particularities of Bonifacio's life than the contemporary uses to which their reconfigured hero might be put in the present—they might have seen nothing wrong with embellishing a bit. If the ultimate goal was re-creation, the inclusion of footnotes was very much beside the point.

Jose P. Santos (1907–64), the eldest son of Epifanio de los Santos, was himself a historian. For many years, he wrote articles on historical subjects for the Sunday supplements of Tagalog periodicals and was a frequent contributor to the daily *Mabuhay*. In addition, between 1930 and 1938, the younger Santos published at his expense no fewer than twenty books and pamphlets, most of which dealt in one way or another with the revolutionary period. Five of them focused on Bonifacio. True, most of Santos's publications were extremely brief, and none contained more than a modicum of analysis, being primarily compilations of documents. But, in his own day, Jose P. Santos was generally regarded as the leading authority on Bonifacio, and more than a few of today's scholars continue to take his work seriously.[46]

Santos's best-known book on Bonifacio, *Si Andres Bonifacio at ang Himagsikan* ("Andres Bonifacio and the Rebellion"), published in 1935, bore certain obvious similarities to the studies of Artigas and Epifanio de los Santos. Like them, Santos seldom indicated the sources upon which he relied. Like them, he filled his account with lengthy excerpts from documents, invariably omitting to mention where those materials were located. Hence, a reader of Jose P. Santos, like a reader or Manuel Artigas or Epifanio de los Santos, is confronted with two choices: to accept most of what he or she reads on faith or to wonder why other readers over the years have been so willing to accept it.

A great deal of Santos's account of the prerevolutionary Bonifacio is derivative, repeating information found in Artigas, de los Santos, and Kalaw. One finds, for example, the usual litany about parents, schooling, and employment, as well as the data from de los Santos about Bonifacio's library and literary tastes. But there are new details, too—a few tidbits about Bonifacio's siblings, Espiridiona and Troadio, information on the work history of brothers Ciriaco and Procopio, and juicy stories about Bonifacio's love life. Unfortunately, with the exception of an anecdote about the hero's extramarital affair—which is attributed to Dr. Jose P. Bantug, a well-known medical doctor, collector of Philippine artifacts, and author of articles about Rizal—none of the new material is supported by evidence, either documentary or oral.[47] Once again, then, when we probe the origins of the image of the textbook Bonifacio, we find almost nothing of proven substance. Like the young George Washington and Abraham Lincoln found in older popular histories, the young Bonifacio may have been a figment of the mythmakers' imaginations.

III

The principal point made thus far about historians' representations of the young Bonifacio—that the seemingly rock-hard details of his life are unsubstantiated—applies with approximately equal force to Bonifacio's life after the inauguration of the Katipunan. Dates committed to memory by generations of schoolchildren turn out to be based on hazy, after-the-fact guesses of aging revolutionaries. Some well-known details of supposedly important events in the history of the secret society seem to be the inventions of individuals who not only were not there but were not on especially close terms with anyone who was.[48]

In the remainder of this chapter, I do not intend to scrutinize every detail in the traditional account of Bonifacio's role in the Katipunan. Rather, merely to illustrate the deficiencies of that account, I will focus on a single, undoubtedly important part of it—the oft-repeated claim that certain poems, manifestos, and other key texts of the revolutionary period were authored by Andres Bonifacio.

Historians of the Philippines typically credit Bonifacio with composing: four poems—"Pag-ibig sa Tinubuang Bayan" ("Love of Native Land"), "Tapunan ng Lingap" ("Give Your Compassion"), "Katapusang Hibik ng Pilipinas" ("The Last Plea of the Philippines"), and "Ang mga Cazadores" ("The Hunters"); two proclamations; a decalogue; a translation into Tagalog of Jose Rizal's famous poem "Último Adiós"; and a newspaper article entitled "Ang Dapat Mabatid ng mga Tagalog" ("What the Tagalogs Should Be Aware Of").[49] Of those writings, several are today considered Tagalog classics, especially "Ang Dapat Mabatid ng mga Tagalog," which is included in anthologies and has been analyzed by many literary critics.[50] Although Teodoro Agoncillo, Bonifacio's best-known biographer, was somewhat restrained in his assessment of the supremo's literary talents, he and virtually everyone else who has commented on Bonifacio's writings claimed that they had a powerful impact on the hero's followers. Gregorio Zaide's remarks are fairly typical.

> Andres Bonifacio, Emilio Jacinto, and Dr. Pio Valenzuela constituted the triumvirate of Katipunan writers. These three men wrote the revolutionary literature of the society which ignited the people's flaming patriotism.[51]

But what do we really know about the writings attributed to Andres Bonifacio? Where and when did he compose them? How do we know that he actually wrote them? On what evidential foundation do historians base their claims about Bonifacio's authorship?

Again, our search for answers sends us back to the footnotes, endnotes, and bibliographies of an assortment of historical surveys, research monographs, and popular histories. But this time, instead of leading the reader step by step along that circuitous paper trail, I will take a shortcut. As it turns out, to answer our questions about Bonifacio's writings, we need to consider closely the six key sources upon which historians have relied in constructing their accounts of Bonifacio's literary endeavors. Five have already been mentioned: Wenceslao Retana's published compilation of documents relating to the revolution; Manuel Artigas's book; Pio Valenzuela's memoirs; Epifanio de los Santos's article on Bonifacio; and Jose P. Santos's brief biography. The sixth—a collection of the letters and writings of Bonifacio edited by Teodoro Agoncillo (assisted by S. V. Epistola)—will figure prominently not only in the remainder of the present chapter but in every subsequent one. Of the six, the most important are the works of de los Santos and Santos.[52]

Published in 1897, Retana's collection was an amazing grab bag of primary materials. In addition to reproducing the testimony to the Spanish authorities of prominent katipuneros like Valenzuela, Retana included decrees of the governor-general and other Spanish officials, captured Katipunan documents, letters by Marcelo H. del Pilar and other members of the Propaganda Movement, and, most important for our immediate purposes, translations (into Spanish) of several items that appeared in *Kalayaan*, the Tagalog-language newspaper published by the Katipunan. One of those items was "Ang Dapat Mabatid ng mga Tagalog," the title of which was rendered in Spanish as "Lo que deben saber y entender los indios."[53] Retana did not attribute that article to Bonifacio. In fact, he did not know who had written any of the contributions to *Kalayaan* since all of the authors used pseudonyms. The pseudonym of the author of "Ang Dapat Mabatid ng mga Tagalog" was "Agapito Bagum-bayan." In a brief note preceding the translations of *Kalayaan* articles, Retana listed the titles of several items in the newspaper that he had chosen not to include in his compilation. On the list was a poem entitled "Pag-ibig sa Tinubuan[g] Bayan." The pseudonym of the poem's author was "A.I.B."—most likely "Agap-ito Bagum-bayan" again.

Hence, thanks to Retana, we know that both "Ang Dapat Mabatid ng mga Tagalog" and "Pag-ibig sa Tinubuang Bayan" appeared in *Kalayaan*, and we even have a Spanish translation of the former. Thanks to Retana as well, we can be reasonably sure that the same person—"Agap-ito Bagum-bayan"—wrote both of them. Furthermore, given the intriguing fact that Andres Bonifacio's initials (A. B.) are almost the same as those of the pseudonymous author of the two newspaper contributions, we might be inclined to wonder whether that correspondence was merely coincidental. But it must be emphasized that Retana did not know who "Agap-ito Bagum-bayan" was. Retana's compilation alone cannot link Andres Bonifacio to those two writings.

Manuel Artigas's biography of Bonifacio, the second source to be examined, was the first to provide that link. In a brief discussion of the supremo's writing abilities, Artigas pointed out that Bonifacio made several contributions to *Kalayaan*, using the pen name "Agap-ito Bagu*n*-bayan."[54] Although the spelling is slightly different (a typographical error?), there can be little doubt that he was referring to the same pseudonymous author. Typically, though, Artigas did not indicate where he learned that purported fact. So, if we are inclined to believe Artigas, it would appear that Bonifacio was the author of both the article "Ang Dapat Mabatid ng mga Tagalog" and the poem "Pag-ibig sa Tinubuang Bayan"; if we demand more substantial evidence, we might be inclined to reserve judgment.

We come next to Pio Valenzuela. In approximately 1914, as we know, Valenzuela composed a brief memoir focused on his involvement with the Katipunan. Some of the information contained in the memoir corresponded to what he had said in his testimony to the Spaniards eighteen years earlier, but much did not—a fact we will return to in a later chapter. For the moment what interests us is what Pio Valenzuela revealed about the newspaper *Kalayaan*, which he helped publish. According to him, among the items included in the first and only issue of the paper was "a poem by Bonifacio depicting the suffering of the Filipino people under the yoke of the Spanish government run by the Friars and the Civil Guards." That poem presumably was "Pag-ibig sa Tinubuang Bayan." But Valenzuela did not indicate that Bonifacio had written anything else, and, what is more, he stated that the pseudonym used by Bonifacio in signing all Katipunan documents was "Agapito Laong Laan"—not "Agap-ito Bagum-bayan" (or "Agap-ito Bagun-bayan").⁵⁵ That last statement may have been a slip; Valenzuela's accounts are filled with those. In any case, the first name he supplied was the one that appeared in Retana's compilation and Artigas's biography. But, if he was indeed right about Bonifacio's pseudonym, it would follow that he was wrong about Bonifacio being the author of the poem.

To recapitulate: we have learned from Retana than an article entitled "Ang Dapat Mabatid ng mga Tagalog" and a poem entitled "Pag-ibig sa Tinubuang Bayan" appeared in the newspaper *Kalayaan* and that a certain "Agap-ito Bagum Bayan" was the author of both. From Artigas we know that Bonifacio was a contributor to *Kalayaan* and adopted a pen name similar to that used by the author of the two aforementioned works, and from Valenzuela we know that the poem was written by Bonifacio. But some doubt persists about Bonifacio's contributions to *Kalayaan*. Artigas did not reveal his sources. Valenzuela frequently changed his story, and, besides, any reasonable person's confidence in his reliability should have been shaken by his statement about Bonifacio's pseudonym.

Enter, at this point, Epifanio de los Santos. In his influential article in the *Philippine Review*, de los Santos provided translations (into Spanish and English) of three texts, which, he claimed unequivocally, were authored by Bonifacio—the decalogue ("Katungkulang Gagawin ng mga Z. Ll. B."), the poem "Pag-ibig sa Tinubuang Bayan," and the article "Ang Dapat Mabatid ng mga Tagalog." It will be recalled that Retana had previously published a Spanish translation of the third work, but de los Santos's own Spanish version differed so substantially from it that we might justifiably wonder if he had consulted it at all. The other two texts were not included in Retana's compilation, and de los Santos did not reveal where he had located them. Perhaps he based his translation of the poem on the Tagalog original published in *Kalayaan*, but that is nothing more than a guess since we do not know for sure that de los Santos ever saw a copy of that newspaper.⁵⁶ Where he found the text of the decalogue is even more of a mystery. All of the above notwithstanding, the translated texts found in de los Santos's article have been reprinted many times in monographs, textbooks, documentary collections, and literary anthologies.⁵⁷

If questions can be raised about the content and reliability of those texts, so, too, can they be raised about de los Santos's claims that Bonifacio composed them. On what authority did he base his assertions? The answer to that question is, once again, Pio Valenzuela—but not this time the Pio Valenzuela of 1896, the man who had surrendered to the Spaniards and then given testimony to them, nor the Pio Valenzuela of 1914, the former katipunero who had become something of a celebrity and whose memoir described his brave deeds and important contributions to the revolutionary cause, but rather the Pio Valenzuela who, in personal communications of some sort with de los Santos, changed his story one more time and evidently recalled some texts he had neglected to mention before. According to de los Santos, "Dr. Pio Valenzuela tells us that . . . [both] 'Ang Dapat Mabatid ng mga Tagalog' (What the Tagalogs Should Be Aware Of) and 'Pagibig sa Tinubuang Bayan' (Love of Native Land) were written by Bonifacio."[58] De los Santos was silent, though, about how he knew that the decalogue was composed by the supremo.

So, as with his discussion of Bonifacio's early years, de los Santos's treatment of the writings seems problematic. Much of it depends on an informant, Valenzuela, whose reliability is in doubt. Much of it also depends on uncorroborated assertions by the author and on supposedly original texts that were mysteriously rescued from oblivion.

Just as problematic is our fifth key source on Bonifacio's writings—the short biography of the supremo published in 1935 by Epifanio de los Santos's son, Jose P. Santos. Whereas the father had claimed that Bonifacio produced three writings—the decalogue, a newspaper article, and a poem—the son increased the number to eight: the decalogue, a newspaper article, four poems, a translation of a poem by Jose Rizal, and a proclamation.[59] Furthermore, the son provided what he represented to be the original Tagalog versions of the texts of all of those writings except the decalogue. Santos's book has had a major impact on Philippine historiography, primarily because of the inclusion of those texts. All of them have been republished on many occasions, and more than a few scholars, accepting Santos's renderings of them as accurate, have closely analyzed the metaphors, symbols, and tropes found therein.[60]

But, if one reads Santos's biography carefully, it seems clear that neither Santos's claims nor the texts he reproduced deserve the respect that historians have given them over the years. His claims about authorship were at no point supported by documentation, and much of the time he gave no indication of where he had found the putatively original versions of the texts. Consider, first of all, what Santos told his readers about "Ang Dapat Mabatid ng mga Tagalog" and "Pag-ibig sa Tinubuang Bayan." In the paragraph preceding his transcriptions of the texts themselves, he pointed out that the only previously published versions of both had been in translation; that, he, Santos, was the first writer to produce true copies of the Tagalog originals; and that he was doing so "in order to show that our hero also possessed a great gift as a writer and a poet" ("upang maipakilalang ang ating bayani ay nagtataglay rin naman ng malaking katangian sa pagka-manunulat at pagkamakata").[61] But he did not reveal where those originals could be found.

Then, several pages later, immediately following the transcriptions, Santos assured his readers that he had copied them "without making any changes" ("walang anumang pagbabago"). At the same time, he explained that portions of the poem were, unfortunately, unreadable, because they were either torn or obscured, obliging him to insert question marks (???) at those points in the transcriptions.[62] Again, Santos was attempting to convey the impression that the texts he provided were derived from certain originals. But, again, he was uninformative about the exact nature of the originals and their location. Had he based his transcriptions on a copy of *Kalayaan*? Did he or someone else possess a copy of the texts written in Bonifacio's hand? Santos gave no answers.

Another text reproduced by Santos was a translation into Tagalog of Jose Rizal's famous poem "Último Adiós," which he attributed to Bonifacio. According to Santos, the translation had been published numerous times before in newspapers and periodicals.[63] That assertion may be true, but I have come across the translation only twice in earlier publications—in Aguedo Cagingin's brief biography of Bonifacio and in an appendix to the Tagalog-language version of Artemio Ricarte's memoir, published in 1927.[64] In any case, what Santos failed to discuss was how he knew for sure that Bonifacio had translated the poem. In all the newspapers and reviews that reprinted the version attributed to Bonifacio, did any historian or other writer reveal why the translator was thought to be the supremo, or when he had translated it, or where the original text of the translation could be found? Santos did not say.

Only slightly more informative was Santos's discussion of the three new Bonifacio poems he included in his biography: "Katapusang Hibik ng Pilipinas" ("The Last Plea of the Philippines"), "Tapunan ng Lingap" ("Give Your Compassion"), and "Ang mga Cazadores" ("The Hunters"). Santos revealed in his book that copies of all three could be found among the records left by the late Mariano Ponce, an important figure in the Propaganda Movement and subsequently a diplomatic representative of Aguinaldo's government, and that certain unspecified writings in Ponce's papers indicated that they were composed by Bonifacio. He also pointed out that the text of the poem "Ang mga Cazadores" was incomplete because white ants had eaten portions of the paper on which it was written.[65]

While Santos's references to documents and white ants might have given his account some plausibility, his assertions about Bonifacio's authorship cannot be credited for the simple reason that he provided not a scrap of evidence that the poems were authentic. To credit Santos, one must believe claims made by an unspecified person in vaguely described documents found among a dead man's personal papers, themselves residing in an unspecified location.

One last document published by Santos should be mentioned, a proclamation issued by Bonifacio in 1897. Bearing the supremo's signature as well as the symbolic name he used in Katipunan circles (Maypagasa), it detailed the brutality of the Spanish forces, praised the "brothers/sisters" ("mga kapatid") for their bravery and persistence, and called on them to prepare themselves for further struggle. It is worth noting, however, that Santos was himself uncertain about whether Bonifacio had written the proclamation. As he admitted, the author may have been Emilio Jacinto.[66]

In the end, therefore, not a single one of the eight writings Santos attributed to Bonifacio can definitively be shown to have been composed by him. Santos's claims about Bonifacio's authorship of the three new poems, the translation of Rizal's poem, and the proclamation are not convincing. His father's earlier assertion that Bonifacio authored the newspaper article and another poem has already been called into question (although there is, it must be conceded, at least a possibility that the father's claim was true, since it is supported to some extent by other sources). As for the decalogue, there is no evidence at all that Bonifacio was the author.

And so we must conclude that Andres Bonifacio the literary master, the unschooled genius, the creator of timeless Tagalog prose, and the gifted poet whose verses have been anthologized and explicated by scholars and memorized by millions of schoolchildren may have been a myth. We do not know, nor will we probably ever know, exactly how all the writings allegedly composed by Bonifacio came to be attributed to him. We will probably never know for sure whether any of those writings were authored by him. What we do know is that the two key players in the process of creating the image of the literary Andres Bonifacio were the historians de los Santos and Santos, father and son, both makers of unproven claims, translators and transcribers of possibly bogus texts, and much respected experts on the revolutionary period.

We come finally to our sixth source on the supremo's literary output—the collection of the supremo's writings edited by Agoncillo. Despite the fact that this collection has been cited often by scholars, it is surely the least important of the six since it is obviously derivative.[67] In that slim volume, Agoncillo (and his collaborator S. V. Epistola) did little more than reproduce verbatim the Tagalog texts found in Santos's book and the English translations of a few of them found in de los Santos's article, to which they added their own translations of some of the writings heretofore untranslated into English. Aside from Bonifacio's correspondence, which will be discussed in the next chapter, and the record of his trial, a total of nine texts were included—the decalogue, the newspaper article, four poems, the translation of Rizal's poem, and two proclamations. The only new item was a proclamation dated August 28, 1896. Why Agoncillo included it is puzzling, since, according to Santos's book, upon which he relied extensively, that proclamation was actually written by someone named Sinforoso San Pedro with the assistance of Florencio Inocentes. (Typically, Santos did not indicate how he knew that.)[68]

Since the value of Agoncillo's collection depended ultimately on the scholarly judgments of Santos, and since Santos's judgments were, as we have seen, far from trustworthy, we would be justified in concluding that this source, too, like the other five discussed here, is of doubtful reliability. As far as I can determine, not a single one of the nine texts attributed by Agoncillo to Bonifacio can be conclusively shown to have been composed by him. Indeed, it is not beyond the realm of possibility that every one of them was written by someone else.

IV

Thus far, I have not discussed the content of the prose and poetry attributed to Bonifacio, and, given the possibility that he was not the author of most of those works, it might be wondered why I would even consider doing so. Yet a brief treatment of it appears to be in order, not for what it might reveal about the national hero but for what it tells us about the image of Bonifacio conveyed to Filipinos.

My discussion of these writings will strike some readers as pedestrian and theoretically innocent. I intend it to be exactly that. More than a few literary critics and even a historian or two have subjected these same writings to close, theoretically informed, textual analyses, and I see no point in attempting to duplicate their efforts. My sole objective here is to describe as straightforwardly as I can the most obvious themes developed in those texts. A single belief guides me in adopting this approach—the conviction that, over the years, many (if not most) readers of those writings have understood their basic messages but not necessarily the "deeper" meanings that the literary critics and historians have identified.[69]

Three principal themes surfaced repeatedly in the Tagalog texts attributed to Bonifacio. The first, and clearly the most prominent, was the wickedness of the Spaniards. It was developed at some length, for example, in the newspaper article "Ang Dapat Mabatid ng mga Tagalog" in which Bonifacio (or whoever authored the text) argued that, dating from the first contacts between Spaniards and Tagalogs, the former had conspired to subjugate the latter: "We [the Tagalogs] have been providing a bountiful existence to the race of Legazpi, [and] they have enjoyed abundance and satiated themselves, even though we have suffered privation and starvation" ("Ang lahi ni Legazpi ay ating binubuhay sa lubos na kasaganaan, ating pinagtatamasa at binubusog, kahit abutin natin ang kasalatan at kadayukdukan").[70] The poem "Katapusang Hibik ng Pilipinas," which was addressed to "Mother Spain," elaborated on the abuses suffered by the Tagalogs at Spanish hands.

> Binding the Tagalogs tightly with ropes,
> Weakening them with kicks, blows from gun butts, and fists,
> Torturing and hanging them like animals—
> Mother, is this, then, your love?

> To be imprisoned by you and thrown into the sea,
> To be shot, poisoned, in order to exterminate us—
> Is this the sentence you have rendered on us Tagalogs,
> On all your subjects, merciful Mother?
>
> ([Gapusing] mahigpit ang mga tagalog
> hinain sa sikad, kulata at suntok,
> makinahi't ibiting parang isang hayop
> ito baga, Ina, ang iyong pag-irog?
>
> Ipabilanggo mo't sa dagat itapon
> barilin, lasunin nang kami'y malipol,
> sa aming tagalog ito [baga'y] hatol,
> Inang mahabagin sa lahat ng kampon?)[71]

In addition, several of the poems and both of the proclamations specifically condemned the conduct of the Spanish forces during the revolution. Their sins included "the burning of children, abusing and staining the honor of women, whose weakness was not respected, cutting short the lives of old people who weren't able to get out of the way and of babies who were still sucking the mother's breast" ("yaong pagpapasunog nito sa mga bata, yaong paglapastangan at pagdungis sa kapurihan ng mga babae na di na pinakundanganan ang kanilang kahinaan, yaong pagputol ng buhay ng mga matatandang hindi na makausad at sanggol na sumususo pa").[72]

A second major theme of the Bonifacio texts was love of country. In the "decalogue," one of the ten stated "duties" of katipuneros was "love of one's native soil" ("ang pag-ibig sa lupang tinubuan"), which was equated with faith in God and love of one's fellow human beings. The decalogue went on: "Imprint in your heart [the hope] that the height of honor and good fortune is to die in struggling to deliver the country from servitude" ("Ykintal sa puso ang pagasa na malabis na kapurihan at kapalaran na kung ikamamatay ng tawo'y magbubuhat sa pagliligtas sa kaalipinan ng bayan").[73] This second theme figured, too, in the famous poem entitled, appropriately enough, "Pag-ibig sa Tinubuang Bayan" ("Love of Native Land"). It reads in part:

> What love can be better,
> Purer and more sublime

> Than love of native land?
> What other love? Surely, no other love. None.
>
> . . . . .
>
> There is nothing that a person with a noble heart
> Will not give to defend the country;
> Blood, riches, knowledge, suffering,
> Even if life itself is cut off.
>
> (Alin[g] pag ibig pa ang hihigit kaya
> sa pagka dalisay at pagkadakila
> gaya ng pag ibig sa tinubuang lupa?
> alin[g] pag ibig pa? wala na nga, wala.
>
> . . . . .
>
> Walang mahalagang hindi inihandog
> ng may pusong mahal sa Bayang nagkupkop
> dugo yaman dunong katiisat pagod
> buhay may abuting magkalagot lagot.)[74]

A third theme, related to the previous two, was the texts' repeated appeals to Tagalogs to persevere in the struggle against Spanish tyranny. In one of the proclamations, after discussing the horrible things done by the Spaniards, the author urged his Filipino followers to be willing to give their lives for the cause of "Liberty" ("Kalayaan"):[75]

> You should know that the reason for our ever more costly
> and dangerous efforts is to obtain the hoped-for Liberty
> of our native Land, which will bring us great prosperity
> and will restore our honor, which has been consigned by
> the yoke of slavery to the pits of incomparable disgrace.
>
> (Dapat naman ninyong mabatid na ang kadahilanan ng
> ating paggugugol ng lalong mahalaga sa loob at sampu
> ng ingat na buhay ay nang upang tamuhin at kamtan
> yaong nilalayong Kalayaan ng ating Bayang tinubuan na
> siyang magbibigay [ng] buong kaginhawahan at magbabangon ng kapurihan na inilugmok ng kaalipinan sa
> hukay ng kadustaang walang katulad.)[76]

Similar sentiments were expressed in the poems "Pag-ibig sa Tinubuang Bayan" and "Tapunan ng Lingap."[77]

Such, then, were the most obvious messages in the assorted writings attributed to Bonifacio. The man who presumably wrote them seemed to be a model patriot—a dogged opponent of Spanish domination and a denouncer of Spanish abuses, a loyal son of the motherland and an eloquent advocate of sacrifice in its defense. Yet, I should reemphasize that this Bonifacio—the noble Bonifacio, the committed Bonifacio, the persistent Bonifacio, the sublimely patriotic Bonifacio—was also, quite possibly, a historically constructed Bonifacio. As with the details of his biography, the writings, none of which can be shown to be Bonifacio's creations, contributed to the posthumous remaking of the man. This re-created Bonifacio, unlike the revolutionary leader excoriated by foreign writers and homegrown enemies, was someone who could be admired by his countrymen, his exploits lauded, his famous writings committed to memory. Here was a worthy national hero, an attractive revolutionary alternative to the reform-oriented Rizal.

V

Close to the beginning of this chapter, I posed three questions about the traditional picture of the early Bonifacio: where did it come from, can it be supported by evidence, and what was the prerevolutionary Bonifacio really like? The time has come to summarize what I found.

First, it should be obvious by now that three long-dead historians, Artigas, de los Santos, and Santos, collectively sketched the traditional picture. The broad outlines of Bonifacio's youth were drawn by Artigas, who cited no sources to document his assertions. De los Santos fleshed out the sketch with new details and also published texts that were supposedly written by the supremo, but he was either silent or vague about how and where he discovered all of that. Santos added still more data, produced still more Bonifacio texts, and was similarly elusive on the matter of sources.

My response to the second question is implicit in the answer to the first: very little of the traditional account of Bonifacio's life before the revolution can be supported by reliable evidence. We can be certain about his date of birth, the names of his parents and possibly those of his siblings, his membership in the Liga Filipina, his marriage to Gregoria de Jesus, and even some aspects of his involvement with the Katipunan, but beyond those scant particularities the historical record is extremely unclear. Furthermore, as I have suggested, much of what has been claimed about the prerevolutionary Bonifacio may have been extracted from the oral tradition or even invented. The latter possibility cannot be proven—not, in any case, beyond a shadow of a doubt. But it should be recognized that the three historians who created the idealized image of the young Bonifacio all adhered to a nationalist program in which a re-created Andres Bonifacio played a crucial part.

That brings me to the third question. If the traditional picture of Bonifacio cannot be automatically credited, what was the early Bonifacio really like? My answer is both uninformative and somewhat depressing. I have not the faintest idea what he was like. I have no idea how educated he was, how much or what he read, what sort of a relationship he had with his siblings, why he became a revolutionary, or whether he believed any of the ideas found in the writings attributed to him. What is more, I am doubtful that we will ever learn such things about him.

That is not to say that we are unlikely to learn more about certain aspects of Bonifacio's life. To my knowledge, no historian has yet made an effort to examine systematically any surviving parish records or the mammoth collections of the Philippine National Archives for data about the prerevolutionary Bonifacio. Such research would certainly be tedious and time consuming. Discoveries would come infrequently. And, at best, the sort of things discovered would be mere tidbits of detail—information about the location and assessed value of his house, perhaps, about his income, the women he married, or the businesses for which he worked. But at least those details would be supported by sources; as matters now stand, we have precious few of those.

Having disposed of those three questions, I want, at this juncture, to pose a final one. If the accounts of Artigas, de los Santos, and Santos are as problematic as I maintain they are, why did later historians not see their deficiencies? As it happens, a few of them did—or, to be more precise, a few of them did question *aspects* of those accounts. One was Nick Joaquin, the brilliant writer of novels, short stories, plays, poetry, political commentary, and occasionally history, who discussed Bonifacio in his book *A Question of Heroes*. Joaquin's most intriguing comments related to Bonifacio's economic status at the time he joined the Liga Filipina and the Katipunan. Although he referred to Bonifacio as "proletarian," seemingly endorsing the notion conveyed by the mythmakers that Bonifacio's origins were humble, Joaquin also demonstrated that, as a sales agent for Fressell and Co., he clearly was a man on the make. The fact that he "dabbled in dramatics" suggested as much, as did his clothes and his membership in the Masonic Order and the Liga Filipina, which brought him into the "dazzling company" of Jose Rizal and other luminaries.[78]

An even more explicit challenge to aspects of the traditional picture could be found in a book coauthored by Jonathan Fast and Jim Richardson, *Roots of Dependency: Political and Economic Revolution in the 19th Century Philippines*. Primarily a study of the major social and economic transformations that occurred in the nineteenth-century Philippines as a result of the development of cash cropping, the book also included a discussion of the revolution of 1896, an uprising the authors saw as issuing from tensions generated by the aforementioned changes. One of their key arguments was that traditional scholarship overemphasized the lower-class orientation and radicalism of the Katipunan. They claimed that, despite the fact that Bonifacio was often described as plebeian, "the Katipunan Supremo was not of the 'lowest class' of Philippine society." They intimated, for instance, that his parents may have had at least modest means by emphasizing the fact that they "were able to send Andres to private tutors in the locality and provide him with a sound elementary education." In their view, the jobs Bonifacio held before the outbreak of the revolution also indicated that he was anything but poor. "Whatever the exact duties involved, . . . employment in the capital's foreign houses offered good opportunities for advancement, and was much sought after." They pointed to his marriage to Gregoria de Jesus, the child of a prominent man from Caloocan, as further "circumstantial evidence that Bonifacio's fortunes were indeed on the rise." Like Nick Joaquin, they pointed, too, to his membership in the Masonic Order and the Liga Filipina. They concluded:

> The foregoing discussion is not intended to [imply] that Bonifacio belonged to the same social stratum as men

like Rizal. Educationally, he was excluded from true *ilustrado* status by his unfinished schooling, and financially he was probably one of the least affluent of the original Liga members. But the *relative* modesty of Bonifacio's circumstances in this company should not disguise the fact that he occupied a position closer to the centre of the social pyramid than to its base, closer to the petty-bourgeoisie than the proletariat.[79]

But Joaquin, Fast, and Richardson were definitely exceptions. Most historians who wrote about the prerevolutionary Bonifacio depicted him essentially as he had appeared in the studies of Artigas, de los Santos, and Santos. Many no doubt did so—and here I return to my last question—because they were too trusting. Artigas, de los Santos, and Santos were highly regarded scholars. What reason did anyone have to doubt the seemingly hard data they provided? Yet, I suspect that more than a few historians had an additional reason for being inclined to credit their accounts: that, like the three pioneer mythmakers before them, they found that a re-created, idealized Bonifacio suited their ideological objectives far better than an unknowable Bonifacio did. If one looks closely, for example, at the modern historians I have discussed in this chapter—Agoncillo, Constantino, Corpuz, and so forth—one finds that they had two important things in common: their nationality and their nationalism. All are or were members of what has been dubbed the "nationalist school" of Philippine historiography.

The term *nationalist school* is fairly imprecise. Furthermore, some of the scholars I might be inclined to place in it might object to being so included. (Zaide, for one, were he still alive, might object strongly.) Even so—conceding that the term is vague and the size of the school in some doubt—it is still possible to identify three distinctive, common characteristics of its membership. By and large, nationalist historians have tended to glorify the past exploits of native Filipinos, especially Filipinos of humble origins, and they have criticized severely the policies and actions of both Spanish and American colonial overlords. They have also tended to be critical of Philippine elites, often portraying such people as insufficiently patriotic, too interested in promoting their own economic interests, and much too willing to collaborate with the colonial powers. From the nationalist perspective—pro–lower class, anticolonial, and anti–upper class—the re-created Bonifacio, the humble proletarian who read by the lamplight, organized an anticolonial uprising, and was eventually overthrown by upper-class usurpers, was almost made to order.

For at least four decades, the nationalist school has dominated the Philippine historical establishment. It is not surprising, therefore, that the only challenges to the existing orthodoxy have come from outside the establishment. Joaquin does not hold an academic post in the Philippines, having supported himself for most of his career as a reporter and writer. Fast and Richardson are foreigners. Nor is it surprising that such challenges have been studiously ignored by the establishment. The observations of the dissenting scholars have not been incorporated into textbooks or historical syntheses.[80]

So the formulations of Artigas, de los Santos, and Santos persist in the historical literature and continue to shape popular perceptions of the early Bonifacio. Old myths die hard, particularly if, as in this case, they serve vital ideological and political functions.

Perhaps the most famous statue of Bonifacio, sculpted by Guillermo Tolentino, located in Grace Park, Caloocan, Metro-Manila

(Credit: Glenn May)

CHAPTER TWO

The Mysterious Letters of Andres Bonifacio

Thus far, we have focused on Bonifacio's life before the outbreak of the Philippine Revolution—which is to say, on the first thirty-two years and eight months of it. But most of what has been written about Bonifacio deals with his final nine months, the period between August 1896, when the uprising began in Manila and its immediate environs, and May 1897, when the former supremo of the Katipunan was executed by fellow revolutionaries in the nearby province of Cavite. Some of the events of that final phase of Bonifacio's career have been chronicled in elaborate detail—his meetings with fellow revolutionaries in the early days of the rebellion, his disastrous initial battles with the Spaniards, his efforts to rally his forces in the aftermath of those defeats, his subsequent decision to transfer to Cavite, his arrival in that province, the emerging conflict between him and various revolutionary leaders in Cavite, the election at Tejeros, his refusal to accept the Tejeros verdict, his trial, and his death. Philippine history textbooks devote many pages to these events because they are seen to be crucial in the development of the Philippine nation. Zaide's account runs to ten pages, Agoncillo and Guerrero's to fifteen, Constantino's to seventeen, and Corpuz's to thirty-two.[1]

But it should be recognized that all the narratives of all the historians who have written about this phase of Bonifacio's life are based on a very narrow evidential base—not so narrow, perhaps, as that on which the monument to the prerevolutionary Bonifacio was built, but narrow all the same. The sources they mention most include a few memoirs by revolutionary leaders (in particular, those of Artemio Ricarte, Emilio Aguinaldo, and Santiago Alvarez), the records of Bonifacio's trial, interviews with a few surviving revolutionaries (a type of source that was, of course, only available to researchers studying the subject many decades ago), a smattering of records generated by Spanish generals and government officials, and a handful of letters ostensibly written by the national hero himself.

In this chapter, I subject the last source, the letters of Andres Bonifacio, to extended scrutiny, and in the end I find them wanting. In the course of my research on the life of Andres Bonifacio, I have been confronted time and again with highly problematic texts—poems supposedly written by the supremo that were almost certainly composed by other people and memoirs seemingly intended to cover up more than they reveal. But none is as patently untrustworthy as the famous Bonifacio letters.

I

Six Bonifacio letters have surfaced over the years—two brief communications to Mariano Alvarez, a major revolutionary figure in Cavite who was also a relative of Bonifacio's wife, and four considerably longer and seemingly more revealing ones written to his close friend and associate Emilio Jacinto. The letters to Jacinto—all of which, historians tell us, were composed in March and April of 1897—describe in considerable detail the factional rivalries that led to Bonifacio's ouster as leader of the revolutionary movement and ultimately to his trial and execution a short time later. Their length alone would seem to insure their importance. In the collection of Bonifacio's writings edited by Teodoro Agoncillo, which is 132 pages in length, only 25 pages are devoted to the texts of writings and correspondence attributed to Bonifacio. (The remaining pages consist of the proceedings of Bonifacio's trial and English translations of all the Tagalog texts.) The writings take up 14 of those 25 pages, and the letters to Alvarez occupy a single page. The remaining 10 pages are devoted to the Bonifacio-Jacinto correspondence.[2]

Let me begin by providing a general idea of the contents of those letters to Jacinto, so that readers unfamiliar with them can get a sense of the issues discussed therein. My summary is based on the Tagalog versions of the letters found in Agoncillo's collection. As later sections of this chapter will demonstrate, those versions should not necessarily be viewed as definitive. But they suffice for the limited purpose of identifying the topics addressed in the Bonifacio-Jacinto correspondence, and they have the added advantage of being included in a book that is accessible to interested readers.[3]

All four of Bonifacio's letters to Jacinto were apparently composed at a time when Bonifacio was residing in the province of Cavite, taking part in the heavy fighting between the Filipino revolutionaries and the recently reinforced Spanish Army and simultaneously struggling to remain in control of the revolutionary movement. His principal antagonist in the latter struggle was Emilio Aguinaldo, the former municipal official from the town of Kawit who had emerged as one of the leading field commanders of the Filipino forces in Cavite. Jacinto was directing Filipino military operations somewhere to the north. Of the four letters, three bear dates—March 8, 1897; April 16, 1897; and April 24, 1897. One does not, but, according to Agoncillo, internal evidence suggests that it was composed in mid-March of 1897.[4] All four are reportorial in nature, and the writing style in each is discursive.

The letter of March 8, 1897, the shortest of the four, is also the least interesting, principally because no subject is developed in depth. Bonifacio[5] began with a few specific news items, among them the news that a certain "Capitan Mariano" had perished in a recent battle. He next advised Jacinto to use a code ("ang clave de segunda clase") if he had any secret information to convey because when Jacinto's letters reached him they invariably had been opened. Finally, Bonifacio broached the subject that became a recurrent theme in his correspondence with Jacinto—the revolutionaries' shortage of weapons and ammunition. Evidently responding to Jacinto's request for ammunition, Bonifacio reported regretfully that he had been able to provide only eight hundred cartridges for the simple reason that the forces in Cavite were engaged in nonstop fighting and were themselves suffering from serious shortages. All in all, the letter is somewhat disappointing, adding little to our understanding of Bonifacio and the Philippine Revolution. It has the general characteristics of a communication hastily composed, a brief update written during a respite in the ongoing military struggle against the Spanish forces.

The undated letter—which, it would appear, was written a week to ten days later—is both longer and meatier. It deals with more than a dozen different issues, but two in particular are developed most fully. First of all, Bonifacio returned to the subject of matériel shortages, urging Jacinto to gather up as many weapons as possible, commenting on the recurring need for more cartridges, and conveying to his friend some information about the Filipinos' efforts to obtain arms in Hong Kong. Second, he described the growing tensions within the revolutionary camp in Cavite, placing all of the responsibility for that state of affairs on the "brothers from the Magdalo region" ("[ang] mga kapatid na taga Magdalo")—which is to say, on the revolutionaries from Kawit, Imus, and other towns in eastern Cavite who were led by Emilio Aguinaldo and his cousin Baldomero Aguinaldo. Bonifacio intimated that the Magdalo people may have been to blame for the disappearance of a sizable amount of silver sent to Hong Kong to pay for needed weapons; claimed that those same people wanted to govern the entire Tagalog area ("Katagalugan") and planned to place Emilio Aguinaldo at the head of the revolutionary government, relegating members of the rival Magdiwang provincial organization to subordinate positions (a plan that, according to Bonifacio, the Magdiwang group "detested"); and opined that the bullying tactics of the Magdalo men had resulted in many "failures" ("kabiguan"), no doubt a reference to the military reverses suffered by the Philippine Army.

The letter of April 16, 1897, was written in Naik, in western Cavite, following a series of defeats suffered by the revolutionary troops at the hands of the Spanish forces. Yet, significantly, Bonifacio focused far more on developments within the revolutionary ranks than on the battles against the Spaniards. He attributed the Filipinos' difficulties in warfare in large measure to dissension within the revolutionary leadership, once again blaming the Magdalo men for the trouble and singling out for criticism his rival Emilio Aguinaldo, the man who in March 1897 had been elevated over Bonifacio to the presidency of the Filipino government. Bonifacio discussed at some length a peace overture that the Spaniards had made to Aguinaldo, inviting the revolutionaries to lay down their arms in exchange for a general pardon. Aguinaldo had attached several conditions to the offer, including the expulsion of the Spanish religious orders, and passed it on to Mariano Alvarez, the Magdiwang leader, advising him to agree. The Magdiwang chiefs refused to go along. Then Aguinaldo, at the urging of his own Magdalo group, wrote secretly to the heads of the Magdiwang towns, calling on them to disregard the Magdiwang leadership. When Mariano Alvarez learned of that, he called a general meeting and asked the assembled revolutionaries what they wanted to do ("sila'y tinanong kung ano ang kanilang niloloob"). At that gathering, it was agreed to establish a revolutionary government, but, in the end, because certain political shenanigans of the Magdalo group were discovered, "the convention achieved nothing" ("ang combencion ay walang nagawa").

Here was Bonifacio's first reference to the Tejeros assembly, the famous meeting of revolutionaries held at the Tejeros estate house in Cavite on March 22, 1897, which resulted in the election of Emilio Aguinaldo to the highest position in the revolutionary movement. Bonifacio's discussion of that gathering was unique in at least two respects: unlike every other first-person account of the events, it attributed the calling of the assembly to the Spanish peace overture. Furthermore, it implied that Aguinaldo had strongly favored an end to hostilities—that, in other words, he was a lukewarm revolutionary. Clearly, since Bonifacio and Aguinaldo were enemies, one might suspect that Bonifacio's account was tainted with bias and that he was attempting to prejudice Aguinaldo in the eyes of his friend and supporter Jacinto.

Also worth noting about Bonifacio's account is his claim that the Tejeros meeting "achieved nothing." The obvious implication of that remark is that the elections elevating Aguinaldo to the presidency had not been valid. If that was so, then Bonifacio was still in charge. Again, it is incumbent on us to be aware that Bonifacio would have had practical reasons for making such a claim, even if it was incorrect.

A second important subject discussed in the letter is the activities of the revolutionaries in Batangas, the province immediately to the south of Cavite. According to Bonifacio, the Batangueños had placed themselves under the authority of the "Supreme Council" ("Consejo Supremo") of the Katipunan, the implication being that they still recognized Bonifacio as their leader. Bonifacio also reported that the revolutionaries in Batangas had plans to invade eight towns, that he had provided them with support for their operations, and that if they succeeded in taking the important town of Lipa they wanted him to transfer his government to Batangas in order to carry the fighting into the Bikol region to the south. As with his treatment of the Tejeros meeting, Bonifacio's discussion of developments in Batangas suggested that, despite his problems with Aguinaldo and the Magdalo men, he still had substantial support.

The fourth letter, written at Limbon (in the jurisdiction of the town of Indang in Cavite Province) on April 24, 1897, deals primarily with the growing rift in the revolutionary ranks. Bonifacio focused initially on the Tejeros assembly. Once again, he indicated that the meeting issued directly from a Spanish peace proposal supported by Aguinaldo, but this time he added a key detail to the account provided in the April 16 letter: one reason for the Magdiwang refusal to endorse the proposal was that, at the time it was passed on to them, Bonifacio was absent from Cavite, having gone to the province of Batangas. He went on to provide a blow-by-blow account of the Tejeros meeting, which includes several intriguing assertions: that the convention had rejected the idea of a compromise with the Spaniards because of Bonifacio's arguments against it; that, even before the assembly began, he had learned that the Imus people ("taga Imus") had been lobbying secretly for the elevation of Emilio Aguinaldo to the leadership of the revolutionary government; that at the end of the session Mariano Alvarez, the Magdiwang chief, had declared that the elections were invalid; that Bonifacio refused to recognize the results as well; that following the meeting Aguinaldo had been prevailed upon to resign his position; and that subsequently a circular had been published in Cavite to the effect that the elections held at Tejeros had been nullified.

As it happens, many of the details provided by Bonifacio differ markedly from those found in other descriptions of the Tejeros assembly, although it is worth mentioning that none of those accounts—or at least none that has been used extensively by historians (the memoirs of Artemio Ricarte, Santiago Alvarez, and Emilio Aguinaldo)—had been published in 1917 when the first versions of Bonifacio's letters appeared in print. Bonifacio's version of the events clearly implied that Aguinaldo's elevation to the presidency had been brought about by the improper actions of his followers and that, in the end, the results of those elections had been voided. As in the earlier letter, the author conveyed the impression that he was still recognized as the head of the revolutionary movement.

Bonifacio's dissatisfaction with Emilio Aguinaldo's supporters again surfaced toward the end of his letter of April 24. He denounced a number of the Magdalo chiefs who had surrendered to (and received pardons from) the Spaniards. Furthermore, he revealed that in the past week he had ordered the arrest of one of Aguinaldo's ministers, Cayetano Topacio, because he was about to release some Spanish prisoners. To his disgust, a military commission had let Topacio go free. Because of developments like these, Bonifacio was coming to the conclusion that he should leave Cavite. "A majority of the leaders here are bad" ("mga namumuno dito na ang karamihan ay masama"), he wrote.

Such, then, were the kinds of things discussed by Andres Bonifacio in his letters to Jacinto. Perhaps predictably, the story they told was one-sided. More graphically than any other source of the revolutionary period, they made the case for Bonifacio and against Emilio Aguinaldo and his Magdalo followers. The Bonifacio that emerged from those letters was honorable and patriotic; he was, in other words, very similar to the idealized prerevolutionary Bonifacio created by the mythmakers. The Magdalo men, on the other hand, were pictured as dishonest, dangerous, greedy for power, guilty of shady political tactics, and willing to compromise with the enemy. In Bonifacio's eyes, they alone were responsible for the growing dissension in the revolutionary ranks and the declining fortunes of the Filipino forces on the battlefield. By promoting conflict between the factions in Cavite, Aguinaldo and his supporters had made it virtually impossible for the revolutionaries to resist the Spanish advance.

II

Given the central place occupied by Bonifacio in Philippine history, the limited number of surviving sources concerning his life, and the widely recognized historical value of the Bonifacio-Jacinto correspondence, one might expect that the four letters are safely preserved behind bullet-proof glass or deep inside a theft-proof vault in one of the Philippine Republic's official manuscript repositories.

But they are not. Nor have they ever been. The Bonifacio papers—or, to be more precise, what appear to be the Bonifacio papers—have had a bizarre and checkered past, every bit of it in the private sector. It is to the papers' history that we now turn.

A central player in that history is Epifanio de los Santos. In late 1917, as we already know, de los Santos published a Spanish-language sketch of Bonifacio's life in the *Philippine Review*, one of the principal forums of Philippine literary nationalism. A few months later, an English-language version of the article appeared in the same periodical. In the body of both versions of the article, de los Santos included translations of the entire Bonifacio-Jacinto correspondence along with several other documents bearing on the conflict between Bonifacio and Aguinaldo—among them the so-called Acta de Tejeros (a document signed by Bonifacio and more than forty others protesting the results of the elections) and a letter by Artemio Ricarte concerning irregularities in the elections.[6]

Curiously, Epifanio de los Santos never published transcriptions of the original Tagalog-language documents upon which the Spanish- and English-language versions that appeared in his sketches were based. It should be noted, though, that in *both* the Spanish- and English-language versions, for reasons never fully explained by the author, he inserted Tagalog words and phrases in parentheses at certain points in the text. According to Teodoro Agoncillo, who edited a published collection of Epifanio de los Santos's historical writings, the Tagalog insertions were included by the translator, who "was merely trying to 'play it safe' by putting into parentheses words or phrases he feared he might have translated wrongly."[7] But even a superficial examination of the texts of those translations reveals that such an explanation is incorrect, since in some cases the item in parentheses is a proper name or place name (Magdalo, Magdiwang, Hong Kong, Malabon) that merely repeats, letter for letter, the word or words that precedes it. Actually, there is a much simpler explanation—one that, if one reads de los Santos's article very closely, the author alluded to, albeit cryptically, in the text. Discussing his reasons for composing his sketch of Bonifacio, de los Santos wrote:

> Our object is more limited: to hear and read what he has said and present him to our readers by means of his private correspondence, *which is partly in cipher* and

therefore of a sincerity that makes it worthy of much credit; and then to compare it with other explanatory and clarifying testimony, in order to make our deductions concerning the character of the man, his work, and the consequences of the same. [Emphasis added.]

(Nuestro propósito es más limitado: oirle, leerle y presentarle a los lectores por medio de su correspondencia privada, cifrada en parte y por lo mismo, de una sinceridad muy digna de crédito; y luego colacionarlo con otros testimonios aclaratorios y depuradores, para poder deducir nuestras lecciones acerca del carácter del hombre, de su obra y de las consecuencias de la misma.)[8]

In other words, the parenthetical Tagalog words and phrases are ones that had appeared in some sort of code in the actual letters.

Where did those Bonifacio letters come from? Epifanio de los Santos did not indicate in his sketch of Bonifacio where, when, or how he had located the letters, nor did he do so in his subsequent writings. Two other historians discussed the matter, however. In the introduction to his edited collection of Epifanio de los Santos's writings, Teodoro Agoncillo claimed that the author had come upon the Bonifacio documents in the first decade of the twentieth century, shortly after he had been serving as governor of the province of Nueva Ecija.

Meanwhile, in 1906 [de los Santos] was relieved of his gubernatorial post and appointed provincial fiscal of Bulakan and Bataan. This marked a turning point in his career, for it was during this period that he discovered Andres Bonifacio's letters to Emilio Jacinto, the so-called Acta de Tejeros, and the Naik military agreement in, of all places, a hen's nest in a Bataan town. How those documents, so important in assessing Bonifacio's actions in Cavite at a crucial moment, came to roost in a hen's nest has no historical value except to the matter-of-fact people whose uniqueness lies in their wasting so much valuable time on matters of no consequence. Insofar as

> [de los Santos] was concerned, the discovery of the
> Bonifacio documents may be said to have aroused his
> interest in history writing. The history of the Revolution
> of 1896 would have been the poorer had not [his]
> inquisitiveness, which led him to go under a nipa house to
> peek into a hen's nest, [taken] the better part of propriety.[9]

Unfortunately, Agoncillo did not disclose his source for the story about the hen's nest.

A very different explanation was provided by Epifanio de los Santos's son, Jose P. Santos. After de los Santos's death in 1928, the Bonifacio papers came into the hands of the son, who, in several historical writings he published in the mid-1930s, alluded to the fact that they were in his possession.[10] Then, slightly more than a decade later, in a lengthy study entitled "Si Andres Bonifacio at Ang Katipunan," a manuscript he submitted to a Bonifacio biography contest conducted by the newly independent Philippine Republic in 1947-48, Jose P. Santos provided a detailed discussion of the history of the Bonifacio papers.[11] Santos was assisted in preparing that manuscript, never published, by his eldest daughter Teresita Santos (who became Teresita Pangan when she married).[12]

Santos's account, which appeared in a chapter of the manuscript entitled "Mga Hiwaga at Kabalaghan ng Kasulatan ng KKK" ("Mysteries and Wonders of the Papers of the Katipunan"), began with the revelation that in 1904 a meeting was held by a number of Filipino intellectuals, including his father, to discuss the history of the Katipunan and the Philippine Revolution of 1896. The people in attendance agreed that, in order to prepare a valid history of the revolutionary period, it was vitally important to locate documents about Bonifacio and Jacinto. Following that meeting, Epifanio de los Santos made an effort to unearth such materials, enlisting the help of Bonifacio's widow, Gregoria de Jesus, as well as people who had been acquainted with Bonifacio when he was a child. After investing a great deal of time and energy in this project, de los Santos located a man in the Tondo district of Manila who was in possession of the Bonifacio-Jacinto correspondence, the Acta de Tejeros, and various other documents. Epifanio de los Santos purchased the lot for a substantial sum.

According to Jose P. Santos, the man who sold his father the Bonifacio materials also had some information about their recent past. Initially, it seems, they were held by Emilio Jacinto, who placed them in a vase and buried them under the ground floor of his house. But followers of General Aguinaldo, Bonifacio's rival, learned of their existence and set fire to Jacinto's home in order to destroy the documents. Although Jacinto's residence was razed, the Bonifacio papers escaped unscathed because the vase in which they were lodged had been buried so deeply in the ground. Some time later, apparently after the documents had been consigned to the man who sold them to Epifanio de los Santos, they barely escaped destruction again when a large fire leveled much of the Tondo district.

Jose P. Santos's account did not end there. Over the next forty years or so, while the Bonifacio papers were in the custody of the Santos family, they had at least a dozen more narrow, seemingly incredible escapes. In 1907, when they were being held in the de los Santos home in San Isidro, Nueva Ecija, virtually every other house in the town was destroyed by fire. In subsequent years, the letters survived floods, white ants, the Japanese occupation, and fires set by the Huk rebels. As Santos's account of the history of the Bonifacio papers was doubtless intended to show, the trials to which the documents were subjected were akin to those endured by the most sacred of religious relics, and he commented at one point that their survivability was nothing short of miraculous ("ang mga kasulatan ukol kay Bonifacio ay parang himalang muling nakaligtas").[13]

Obviously, both accounts of the history of the Bonifacio papers have a fantastic quality. Agoncillo's version has the ring of an uncorroborated anecdote many times repeated; Santos's calls to mind the text of brochures distributed at major religious shrines in the Philippines. This is not to say that the accounts should be disregarded, but they do raise justifiable concerns—about how the Bonifacio papers survived the revolution; how they came into the possession of the Santos family; and, beyond all that, how we can be certain that they are authentic.

III

It will be recalled that Epifanio de los Santos did not provide a transcription of the Tagalog originals of the Bonifacio letters. His son Jose P. Santos, who produced numerous books and articles about the revolutionary period and wrote almost exclusively in Tagalog, intended to publish a transcription in the 1930s. At the end of a number of his books—for example, one entitled *Mga Kasulatang Lumiliwanag sa Pagkakapatay kay Andres Bonifacio* ("Documents Shedding Light on the Killing of Andres Bonifacio"), with a publication date of 1935—one finds a lengthy notice about a book "soon to appear" ("malapit nang lumabas") with the title *Ang Sigalot ni Bonifacio at ni Aguinaldo* ("The Quarrel between Bonifacio and Aguinaldo"), which was to include "letters from Andres Bonifacio to Emilio Jacinto describing their quarrel with General Aguinaldo" ("mga sulat ni Andres Bonifacio kay Emilio Jacinto na naglalarawan ng kanilang sigalot ni Heneral Aguinaldo").[14] But apparently that book was never published, except perhaps in a limited vanity-press edition, since there is no copy of it in any research library in Manila or the United States and no reference to it in any of the standard bibliographical guides to Filipiniana or the specialized bibliographies on the revolutionary period.[15] But Santos *did* include the Tagalog transcriptions in "Si Andres Bonifacio at Ang Katipunan," the manuscript he submitted in 1948 to the Bonifacio biography contest, a copy of which can be found in the stacks of the University of the Philippines Library. So, some thirty years after the publication of the Spanish and English translations by Epifanio de los Santos, a version of what appeared to be the original Bonifacio letters at last surfaced, even if in unpublished form.[16]

Since translations are not always faithful to the original, I thought it useful to compare the Tagalog transcriptions furnished by Jose P. Santos with the Spanish-language versions in his father's 1917 article. A few simple observations emerged from that examination. First, while the Spanish translation generally conveys the meaning of the Tagalog text, there are a number of strange discrepancies between the two. For some reason, various words and phrases in the Tagalog version are not translated at all, and, on occasion, the Spanish translation seems to distort the sense of the Tagalog text. The Spanish version also includes a few passages that do not correspond to anything at all in the Tagalog text.[17]

Perhaps there are reasonable explanations for these anomalies. In light of the manifest difficulty and vagueness of the Tagalog text, some mistranslation could have been predicted. Furthermore, the inclusion of words in the Spanish text that did not appear in the Tagalog one might have been the result of transcription errors (that is, possibly the person who prepared the Tagalog transcriptions, presumably Jose P. Santos, inadvertently left certain passages out). All the same, one cannot escape the conclusion that both the Spanish translation and the Tagalog transcriptions are flawed in certain ways.

That conclusion is reinforced by comparing the Tagalog-language parenthetical insertions in the Spanish translation with the corresponding passages in Jose P. Santos's transcriptions. One might have expected that the two would be identical, or that at most there would be only a few minor differences. Curiously, there are more than a few, and a number of them are anything but minor. Words, word order, and sometimes even verb forms were altered. Hence, "mga tao" ("people") in the father's text was rendered as "mga kabig" ("male followers," "servants," "vassals") in the son's; "lalong malaki ang pagkaalit ng dalawang Sb. [sangguniang bayan]" in the father's became "malaki ang pagaalit ng dalawang Sb." in the son's; and "[ang] Magdalo ay hinihiling na sila ng mamahala sa lahat at sa buong Katagalugan" in the father's became "hiniling ng mga taga Magdalo ay mananihala sa buong Katagalugan" in the son's.[18] In the last example alone, the parenthetical clause in de los Santos's article contains a different sentence structure, different verb forms, and two additional words.

Such discrepancies cannot be attributed to mistakes in transcription alone—the differences between the two versions are too great. It seems likely, then, that Jose P. Santos made a conscious decision to edit the prose of the Bonifacio documents. Why? What possible motive could Santos have had for producing transcriptions that varied so radically from the "originals"?

Readers should be assured that I will answer those questions in time. But, for the moment, I merely want to underline a point that may be obvious—that once again, as with our examination of the historical construction of the prerevolutionary Bonifacio, it would appear that there was something strange about the scholarship of Epifanio de los Santos and his son Jose P. Santos. Already, as we have seen, doubts have been expressed about their use of evidence, the validity of their claims, and the authenticity of writings they attributed to Bonifacio. I have discussed the possibility that they may have been more interested in promoting a nationalist agenda than in recapturing the past. Is it possible that once again de los Santos was doing odd things with the past? Or Santos? Or both? And what precisely was being done?

Let us review at this juncture the questions that have been raised, both explicitly and implicitly, about the famous Bonifacio letters. First, we have no satisfactory explanation of their origins—unless, that is, the reader is inclined to credit the stories that they were found in a hen's nest or invested with miraculous powers of survival. Second, we have no hard proof that they were written by Bonifacio, since the only scholars who apparently had seen them as of 1948 were the two men who owned them and used them in their publications, Epifanio de los Santos and his son. The documents had not, in other words, been submitted to independent academic specialists for authentication. Third, we do not have an accurate idea of their contents, given the manifest differences between Jose Santos's transcriptions and his father's translations. At the very least, therefore, it is clear that the transcriptions provided by Jose Santos in his manuscript biography of Bonifacio cannot be considered trustworthy.

IV

The next sighting of the Bonifacio letters occurred in 1956, when another version of what seemed to be the complete Tagalog text of those documents was published in an appendix to Teodoro Agoncillo's *The Revolt of the Masses*.[19] Actually, Agoncillo's book was a somewhat revised version of the winning entry in the same Bonifacio biography contest to which the younger Santos submitted his manuscript "Si Andres Bonifacio at Ang Katipunan." The publication of Agoncillo's study had been delayed because Emilio Aguinaldo, who was still alive, objected to certain parts of it.[20] Since I have never had the opportunity to examine the manuscript Agoncillo submitted in 1948, I cannot be certain that the transcriptions of the letters found in 1956 book were included in the earlier version. But at least two important points can be made with reasonable certainty about the documents relating to Bonifacio that ultimately appeared in print: (1) by the time *The Revolt of the Masses* was published, Agoncillo had managed to see a copy (and possibly the original) of at least *one* document in Jose P. Santos's personal collection; and (2) the versions of the Bonifacio letters published by Agoncillo bear a strikingly close resemblance to the Tagalog transcriptions made by Santos.

Evidence on the first point was provided by Agoncillo himself. In the bibliography of *The Revolt of the Masses*, he listed, under "Primary Sources," a number of the documents in the possession of Jose P. Santos, including the Bonifacio-Jacinto correspondence, the Acta de Tejeros, and Ricarte's letter of protest after the Tejeros meeting.[21] Curiously, he did not indicate, at that point in the text, that the materials were in Santos's hands, nor did he, in the introduction to the book, acknowledge that Santos had permitted him to consult those sources. But a muted acknowledgment of a sort can be found elsewhere in Agoncillo's book. Facing page 239, one finds a photographic copy of the first page of the Acta de Tejeros, and below that copy and the caption describing it, Agoncillo added the words "Courtesy of Jose P. Santos."[22]

My second point—that Agoncillo's version of the Bonifacio letters closely resembles Santos's transcriptions—can be confirmed by comparing the two. That laborious task yields the following findings: (1) a total of 125 discrepancies, large and small, can be found between the two versions (4 in the March 8 letter, 41 in the undated one, 18 in the April 16 letter, and 62 in the one dated April 24); but (2) if one discounts from that total minor spelling differences—the use of the single *g* instead of the double *g* in certain words (e.g., *natangap* instead of *natanggap*), use of contractions instead of complete words, and so forth—the number of discrepancies is reduced to only 20. Furthermore, if one compares those 20 instances of significant discrepancy in the Agoncillo text with the equivalent passages in Epifanio de los Santos's *Spanish-language* text, one finds that in fully 11 of them the Agoncillo version corresponds exactly to the wording in the parenthetical insertions in the elder Santos's article. Of the remaining 9 discrepancies, 3 obviously resulted from copying mistakes by Agoncillo and the other 6 appear to be Agoncillo's editorial changes.

The clear implication is that Agoncillo did not have to examine the Bonifacio letters in order to produce the transcriptions he included in *The Revolt of the Masses*; in fact, as we shall see in the next section, he did not. What Agoncillo did examine was Jose P. Santos's transcriptions, which he edited for style and altered somewhat based on what he found in Epifanio de los Santos's earlier article.

But, if Agoncillo was able to see and even photocopy the original version of at least one rare document owned by Santos, the Acta de Tejeros, why was Agoncillo obliged to rely on transcriptions of the Bonifacio letters rather than the letters themselves? Why, that is, did Santos not allow Agoncillo or anyone else to consult those documents? Ambeth Ocampo, a talented young historian and journalist who came to know Agoncillo well in the final months of Agoncillo's life, suggested in a controversial public lecture that there may have been some tension in the Santos-Agoncillo relationship, since the two men were rivals—both authorities on the revolutionary period and competitors in the Bonifacio biography contest.[23] That may explain why Agoncillo was so clearly disinclined to acknowledge Santos's assistance in his book. Santos's daughter, Teresita Santos Pangan, on the other hand, claims that the two men were friendly and that Agoncillo often came to her father's house to use the books in his library.[24] My own suspicion—which is based on information to be revealed later—is that Santos prevented Agoncillo from using the Bonifacio letters not only because the two men were rivals but because he either had doubts about their authenticity or knew they were not authentic and feared that Agoncillo might come to the same conclusion.

It should be noted that the foregoing discussion of Agoncillo's transcriptions of the Bonifacio letters directly contradicts other statements made by Ocampo in the lecture referred to above. A great admirer of Agoncillo, Ocampo had come to realize in the years following the celebrated historian's death that his mentor's historical efforts were not without serious faults. In this public presentation, after having had the opportunity to examine photocopies of the original Bonifacio letters (or what appeared to be the originals), he made at least two astounding announcements: that the transcriptions found in *The Revolt of the Masses* differed from the originals in many significant ways; and that Agoncillo's transcriptions had not been based on the originals but rather were Agoncillo's *retranslations* into Tagalog of the English-language versions of the Bonifacio letters found in Epifanio de los Santos's *Philippine Review* article. Indeed, according to Ocampo, Agoncillo's translations were three stages removed from the originals. The originals had first been translated into Spanish, the Spanish translations had then been translated into English, and finally Agoncillo had translated the English text back into Tagalog. The manifest differences between the originals and Agoncillo's versions resulted, in Ocampo's view, from the multiple retranslations of the texts.[25]

But, while Ocampo was correct in concluding that Agoncillo did not have access to the manuscripts, he was unaware of Santos's transcriptions, the actual source of Agoncillo's own version of the Bonifacio-Jacinto correspondence. Agoncillo may have had failings as a historian, but he was not guilty of something so serious as passing off as transcriptions his retranslation of a translation of a translation.

Seven years after the appearance of *The Revolt of the Masses*, in conjunction with the Bonifacio centennial celebration, Agoncillo (in collaboration with S. V. Epistola) published *The Writings and Trial of Andres Bonifacio*, a collection of primary sources, which included transcriptions of the Bonifacio letters. In the volume's introduction, the editors claimed that the Tagalog texts were "published ... exactly as they appear in the original"—a statement they could not know to be true since Agoncillo never saw the original letters.[26] In fact, the transcribed letters were virtually identical to the ones that appeared in *The Revolt of the Masses*. Only seven discrepancies between the two texts can be found, and every one of them appears to be either a minor editorial change or a spelling error. Furthermore, obvious mistakes that had somehow crept into the 1956 version—for example, Agoncillo's substitution of "dalawang gulukan" ("two bolomen") for "dalawangpung gulukan" ("twenty bolomen") in the April 16 letter and his omission of an eight-word passage in the one dated April 24—were repeated in the volume published in 1963. That book also included English translations of all four of Bonifacio's letters to Jacinto, but, as the editors acknowledged in a footnote, they merely duplicated the ones published in the *Philippine Review* in early 1918.[27]

V

Teodoro Agoncillo was not the only historian of the post–World War II era to pay serious attention to the mysterious letters of Andres Bonifacio. Indeed, as I intimated at the beginning of this chapter, virtually every scholar who has written about the Philippine Revolution has been obliged to take them into account. So, for instance, Carlos Quirino, in an important 1963 study of Emilio Aguinaldo's early years, included a lengthy quotation from Bonifacio's letter of April 24, 1897, and, in a more recent biography by Alfredo Saulo, one finds two different excerpts from the Bonifacio-Jacinto correspondence. John Schumacher cited one of Bonifacio's letters in his suggestive article on the Philippine Revolution in Cavite Province, and, in his textbook on modern Philippine history, Renato Constantino quoted a passage from the April 24 communication to support his contention that Bonifacio's defeat at Tejeros resulted from the political machinations of his opponents. O. D. Corpuz relied on Bonifacio's letters, among other sources, in piecing together his account of the conflict between Bonifacio and Aguinaldo; Gregorio Zaide reproduced an English translation of an excerpt of the April 24 letter in his multivolume collection of primary sources, *Documentary Sources of Philippine History*; and I cited the Bonifacio papers on three different occasions in documenting my account of the Philippine Revolution in Batangas Province.[28]

Significantly, not a single one of these historians had access to the original documents. Quirino and Zaide relied on the English translations in Epifanio de los Santos's article in the *Philippine Review*; I cited Agoncillo's collection of Bonifacio's writings; Corpuz based his narrative on both de los Santos's article and Agoncillo's collection; and Saulo, Schumacher, and Constantino used the versions of the letters found in *The Revolt of the Masses*.[29] In constructing our accounts of the revolutionary period, all of us operated on two assumptions: that Bonifacio's letters to Jacinto were, as previous historians had represented them to be, authentic sources; and that the readily accessible published transcriptions and translations we used were reliable. In other words, lacking evidence to the contrary, we believed that the scholars who had published those versions of the Bonifacio papers—Epifanio de los Santos and Teodoro Agoncillo— were acting in good faith and deserved our trust. In our collective defense, I might add that historians of all nationalities, shapes, colors, and sizes typically make such assumptions, but, in retrospect, I cannot shake the notion that all of us failed to pay enough attention to certain warning signs, not the least of which was the fact that the documents were not available to be consulted.

As historians of the Philippines continued to base their narratives of the revolution on published versions of the Bonifacio papers, the original documents, still in the private sector, passed out of the hands of the Santos family. In the early 1980s, with her husband in poor health and the family in need of cash, Teresita Santos Pangan, the daughter of Jose P. Santos, who had collaborated with him in writing "Si Andres Bonifacio at Ang Katipunan," decided to sell a collection of rare manuscripts given to her by her father, which included the Bonifacio papers. According to Pangan, she first offered the manuscripts to the Philippine National Library, but Director Serafin Quiason, himself a historian, claimed that his institution had insufficient funds to purchase them. He encouraged Pangan to donate the documents instead, but she refused. Sometime later, Quiason came to her house with a well-known antique dealer, Severina "Viring" de Asis, who offered to purchase the manuscripts. Pangan maintains that she initially refused the offer, but de Asis was persistent. Finally, in either 1983 or 1984, she sold the lot to the dealer. A few years later, a collector of Filipiniana by the name of Emmanuel Encarnacion purchased a portion of the collection, including the Bonifacio letters, from de Asis. Since that time they have remained in Encarnacion's possession.[30]

In 1989, as related above, photocopies of the Bonifacio papers, along with some other documents in Jose P. Santos's former collection, came into the hands of Ambeth Ocampo. Ocampo, relying on those photocopies, composed his public lecture of November 1989 in which he charged Agoncillo—incorrectly—with passing off a translation of a translation of a translation as transcriptions of the original documents. But incorrect though Ocampo may have been in some of his conclusions about Agoncillo, his lecture made at least three major contributions to scholarship.

First, in a lengthy appendix to the mimeographed typescript of his lecture, Ocampo provided transcriptions of a portion of the Bonifacio-Jacinto correspondence (as well as certain other sources relating to Bonifacio's life). Out of forty-three pages of transcribed documents, fourteen were devoted to the Bonifacio letters. Fully transcribed were the undated letter and the one dated March 8, 1897, and partially transcribed were those of April 16 and April 24. Somewhat hastily done, due to the fact that Ocampo wrote the lecture under time pressure and evidently did not intend it for publication, the transcriptions contained a few obvious typographical errors and misspellings, and on one occasion Ocampo felt obliged to insert a parenthetical question mark in the text following a word he could not decipher. Still, the appearance of these incomplete transcriptions, even in a mimeographed lecture text, was an event of no little importance in the historiography of the Philippine Revolution. For the first time, members of the scholarly community were able to examine a reasonably accurate version of the "original" Bonifacio letters.

Second, by comparing the supposed originals with Agoncillo's published transcriptions, Ocampo demonstrated that the latter could not be trusted. Needless to say, that simple finding, made by a scholar known to be sympathetic to Agoncillo, was a blow to the reputation of the most famous Philippine historian of the twentieth century as well as a shock to a generation of academics who had used the versions found in Agoncillo's books in their research.

Third, Ocampo finally provided a full explanation for the presence of parenthetical Tagalog words and phrases in the English and Spanish translations of the Bonifacio letters in Epifanio de los Santos's seminal article. Rather than marking passages in the Tagalog text that the translator had difficulty in rendering in another language, as Agoncillo had surmised, those parenthetical phrases called attention to passages in the original documents that were written in a code occasionally used by Bonifacio in his correspondence—passages that had subsequently been deciphered into Tagalog by Epifanio de los Santos. So, for example, the coded word *Vzgdzje* actually meant *Magdalo*, and *llzvzty* meant *namatay* ("died" or "dead," in English).[31] One obvious implication of that finding was that it demonstrated, beyond a shadow of a doubt, that Agoncillo could not have seen the supposed "originals." If he had, his explanation of the presence of those parenthetical insertions would not have been so wide of the mark.

To verify Ocampo's findings about the parenthetical insertions, I compared his transcriptions—which rendered the coded words in italics, followed by the decoded version (written in bold letters and placed within brackets)—with the text of the Bonifacio letters provided by Epifanio de los Santos in his 1917 article. I focused on the communication of March 8, 1897, and the undated one, the two letters fully transcribed by Ocampo. In all, there were forty-five coded passages in those letters (two in the March 8 letter, forty-three in the other), and in thirty-three cases the parenthetical Tagalog words in de los Santos's texts corresponded exactly to the decoded ones in Ocampo's. Of the remaining twelve, eleven were virtually identical, with only a letter or two of difference (e.g., "Rizal" in one text and "Risal" in the other; "humihingi" in one and "homihingi" in the other), such discrepancies issuing no doubt either from editorial changes or transcription errors. In only one case was there a significant difference between the two versions, but even it could be easily explained. At that point in the text, Ocampo simply neglected to decipher a coded word—an understandable omission, perhaps, in light of the fact that his transcriptions were something of a rough draft not intended for publication. The unambiguous result of my comparative exercise was a finding that Ocampo was absolutely right; the parenthetical Tagalog words in Epifanio de los Santos's article did indeed correspond with the passages of the original that were rendered in code.

As we know, Ocampo compared the photocopies in his hands with the transcriptions in Agoncillo's books and found radical discrepancies between the two. It should not be surprising, then, that, given the established fact that Agoncillo's transcriptions were based on Santos's, one finds equally radical discrepancies between Santos's version and the "originals." Let us consider, for instance, the first paragraph of Bonifacio's undated letter to Jacinto. Santos's transcription reads:

> Sumakamay kong lahat ang ipinadala mong sulat na kasama sampu ng salapi, poder at salitre na lubos na ikinatuwa ng ating mga kapatid na tumitingin ng utang na loob dahil sa iyong ipinadala na kailangan sa pakikilaban, at gayun din naman ang sinasabi mong tulong na iyong naibigay.[32]

> (All the letters sent by you along with ten *salapis* [fifty-centavo coins], powder[?], and saltpeter came/have come

into my hands. Our brothers/sisters are thoroughly pleased and filled with gratitude as a result of your having delivered the things needed for the campaign and also for the assistance that you say you have given.)

Ocampo's, on the other hand, runs as follows.

> Tinangap kong lahat ang mga sulat na inyong ipinadala sa akin at gayon din naman ang kalakip na salapi, polvora at salitre. Ang ating mga kapatid dito ay malabis ang tua at pasasalamat sa inyong ipinahatid ditong mga kailangang mahigpit sa pakikipaglaban, at gayon din sa balitang tulong na inyong ginagawa diyan.[33]

> (All the letters sent by you to me and also the accompanying salapis, gunpowder, and saltpeter were/have been received by me. Our brothers/sisters are very happy and grateful for your having delivered here the things so much needed for the struggle and also for the reported assistance that you have given there.)

A Tagalog speaker would quickly see that, although there are slight differences in the details, the general sense conveyed in the two versions is similar. Yet one would not need to know even a word of Tagalog to recognize that the ways in which the two texts express their meanings are strikingly different. Only about half of the root words found in the first text are present in the second. Furthermore, if one compares the two versions of the entire letter, one will observe the same kinds of discrepancies in every line of text. True, most of the time, the meaning of the two versions is more or less the same, but invariably the vocabulary, sentence structure, and verb forms are different.

Again, a number of questions come to mind. How can such bizarre differences be explained? Why would Santos, who presumably had the originals in front of him when he was transcribing them, have altered the text of those documents so fundamentally?

VI

Of course, Santos is no longer around to answer these questions. But fortunately the documents he guarded closely for so many years still exist, and, while they do not provide complete and certain answers, they furnish some stunning clues. In November 1993, during a brief research trip to the Philippines, I had the opportunity to examine photocopies of the famous Bonifacio letters at the office of Ramon Villegas. The owner of a jewelry business, the author of an excellent book on Philippine jewelry, and a well-known collector, Villegas was in possession of those photocopies because at the time he was collaborating with Emmanuel Encarnacion, the owner of the Bonifacio papers, and Milagros Guerrero, a respected academic historian who had earlier coauthored *History of the Filipino People* with Agoncillo, on a book about Bonifacio. Villegas was aware at the time of our meeting that I had concerns about the authenticity of the Bonifacio-Jacinto correspondence, and I had even shared with him some of my preliminary conclusions about the scholarship of Epifanio de los Santos, Jose P. Santos, and Teodoro Agoncillo.

I have never received any training as an authenticator of historical documents, but one did not have to be an expert to see that there was something odd about the photocopied correspondence I perused in Villegas's office. Clearly, one of the letters was written in a very different hand from the others. The writing slanted in a different direction. The writer formed all of his letters differently. The only thing that appeared to be similar was Andres Bonifacio's signature at the end.[34]

When I pointed out that obvious fact to Villegas, he was taken aback and hesitated to concede my point. I asked him if he had a magnifying glass. Naturally, being in the jewelry business, he had an assortment of loupes available. The two of us proceeded to compare the handwriting of the one letter with that of the other three, closely observing the way the writers formed each of their letters. We started with the lower-case *a*, then moved on to the capital *A*, and made our way through the alphabet.[35] By *h* or so, Villegas's protests became muted. My unsurprising conclusion—which I communicated to Villegas at the end of our meeting—was that it seemed highly doubtful that the Bonifacio "originals" owned by Encarnacion were authentic. I urged him to submit the manuscripts to scientific experts to verify their authenticity. As best as I could determine from examining the photocopies, the famous Bonifacio letters were, in all likelihood, forgeries.[36]

In retrospect, I realize that this conclusion was reached too hastily. I failed to consider certain other possibilities. Even though my scrutiny of the photocopies indicated that Andres Bonifacio did not *write* all the letters, that finding does not preclude the possibility that he was their *author*. He might have dictated one or more of them or instructed a subordinate to make copies of the originals. In either case, the resulting documents would have been composed and signed by Bonifacio even if the penmanship of the text was not his own. Any scholar familiar with nineteenth-century Philippine bureaucratic documents knows that a large percentage of them were written by scribes. A document does not have to be a complete holograph in order to be authentic.[37]

Thus, while the bizarre accounts of the provenance of the Bonifacio letters and the fact that more than one hand penned the documents currently owned by Encarnacion raise reasonable doubts about their historical value, none of this proves that they are forgeries. Scientific analysis might narrow the possibilities. I would like to know whether the paper on which the putatively original letters were written and the ink used by the writers will stand up to scientific testing and whether the Bonifacio signatures on the letters match those on other documents presumed to have been signed by the supremo.[38] But, of course, I have no control over whether those documents are submitted to such analysis; the owner of the documents alone has the authority to do that, and to my knowledge he has made no effort to authenticate them.

All of this would seem to suggest that no firm, or somewhat firm, conclusions can be reached at present about the authenticity of the Bonifacio letters. But one additional type of evidence has not been taken into account: the bizarre transcriptions of Jose P. Santos. Up to this point, I have made no effort to explain the younger Santos's apparently inexplicable actions. However, in light of what we now know about the physical appearance of the supposed originals, a simple explanation suggests itself: Santos may have known, or strongly suspected, that the documents in his possession were bogus and wanted to cover up that fact.

Let us try to reconstruct the scene. Santos could have developed suspicions about the supposed Bonifacio letters in any one of several ways. His father or other family members might have told him of their doubts about the documents' historical value. He could also have reached the same conclusion on his own. If I, with my untrained eyes, could easily detect major defects in those documents in only a few hours, surely Santos, who had the manuscripts in his possession for several decades, must have been able to do the same. But, however he learned about the documents' possible inauthenticity, it is clear—in my view—that he did.

Because he did, and because, for one reason or another, he preferred not to reveal that to others (perhaps he did not want to tarnish the image of Bonifacio that he and his father had worked so hard to create; or he did not want to diminish the scholarly value of his father's historical writings; or he did not want others to entertain the possibility that his father was aware that the letters may have been bogus or had somehow been involved, unwittingly or not, in the circulation of forged historical documents; or he did not want to diminish the monetary value of manuscripts he owned) he may very well have been inclined to do what I believe he did: disguise, as best he could, all traces of the documents' deficiencies. Hence, while Santos was willing to allow a page or two of the Acta de Tejeros to be copied, he was not prepared to show Agoncillo—or anyone else—the complete Bonifacio-Jacinto correspondence. He no doubt feared that Agoncillo, who prided himself on his close examination of primary sources, would see the inconsistencies in penmanship.[39] Hence, while he did produce transcriptions of the Bonifacio letters, he did not execute faithful ones because he probably realized that the defects of the "originals" *were not limited to penmanship.*

That last statement is, I admit, somewhat speculative. All the evidence on the matter is either circumstantial or textual. But here it is. First, let us assume, merely for the sake of argument, that Santos either knew that the Bonifacio letters were forgeries or had strong doubts about their authenticity. Second, let us recall that Santos was an accomplished Tagalog stylist. He wrote primarily in that language, and, more than most educated Tagalogs of his generation (or ours), he would have been able to spot stylistic hints in the Bonifacio letters that they were not the bona fide literary creations of the Philippine national hero. Third, let us look more critically at both the "originals" and Santos's transcriptions to see whether there is any pattern in the changes made by Santos.

As it turns out, it is possible to observe two principal differences between the texts. First, Santos consistently made an effort to personalize the letters more. Consider, for example, the second paragraph of the undated letter. Whereas in the "original" the letter writer used the phrase "sa mga kapatid dito" ("to the brothers here"), Santos changed the text to read "sa mga kapatid natin dito" ("to our brothers here"); similarly, in the next clause, "ang mga kalaban dito" ("the enemies here") became "ang ating mga kalaban" ("our enemies").

Second, the verb constructions used in the two texts are very different. Tagalog verbs consist of two principal components—the base, which expresses the core meaning of the verb, and a verbal affix. The affixes include prefixes (e.g., mag-), infixes (-um-), suffixes (-in), and complex affixes consisting of both a prefix and a suffix (pag- . . . -an). In addition, Tagalog verbs can roughly be divided into two categories: actor-focus (or actor-topic) verbs and goal-focus (or goal-topic) verbs. Actor-focus verbs signal that the topic (subject) of the sentence is the actor, agent, or doer of the action. Goal-focus verbs indicate that the focus of the sentence is the goal or the receiver of the action. Whether a verb is goal-focus or actor-focus is determined by the verbal affix. Certain affixes (ma-, mag-, mang-, -um-) typically occur in actor-focus verbs, while others (an-, i-, in-) occur in goal-focus verbs.[40]

A simple example may help to clarify this for readers unfamiliar with the Tagalog language. Let us construct two simple sentences using the verb base *abot*, which can be translated into English as "to reach for":

1. "*Um*abot siya ng baso." ("He reached for the glass.")
2. "*In*abot niya ang baso." ("The glass was reached for by him.")

Whereas the two sentences appear to have more or less the same meaning (as the English translations I have provided suggest), there is actually an important difference between them. In the first, the focus of the sentence is on the actor, *siya* ("he" in English), but in the second it is on the object, *baso* ("glass"). The difference in focus is conveyed by the verb—*umabot* in the first case, an actor-focus verb, and *inabot* in the second, a goal-focus verb.

If we turn now from this hypothetical example to the texts under examination, the Ocampo and Santos transcriptions of the

Bonifacio letters, what we observe is that the verbs used in the former, the presumed "originals," tend to be goal-focus verbs, while those in the second tend to be actor-focus verbs. Consider, for instance, the extended excerpts of the undated Bonifacio letter quoted previously in this chapter. The first word of the excerpt from the original—*tinangap* ("was/were received")—is a goal-focus verb; in Santos's version, however, the first word is *sumakamay* ("came into [my] hands"), an actor-focus verb. A subsequent paragraph of the original contains the clause "tinangap ko ang isang sulat" ("a letter was received by me"), which uses a goal-focus verb; Santos changed it to "tumanggap ako ng sulat" ("I received a/the letter"), an actor-focus verb construction.[41] A few sentences later, *tatangapin*—a goal-focus form of the verb *tangap* ("to receive")—was changed to *tatanggap*, an actor-focus construction. Indeed, time and again, goal-focus verbs in the "original" text were replaced by actor-focus ones in Santos's transcriptions.

What Santos was doing was, in my judgment, fairly obvious. Aware that one striking characteristic of older Tagalog was that it tended to be more actor focused, and no doubt sensing that the Bonifacio letters used far more goal-focus verbs than a man of Bonifacio's era would have been expected to use, Santos attempted to rewrite the letters to make them seem more authentic.[42] One noteworthy, and probably foreseen, result of Santos's selective rewriting of the text of the letters was to change their style in ways that made them resemble more closely the other writings allegedly composed by Bonifacio—the poems, the proclamations, the decalogue, and the newspaper article, all but one of which Santos included in his short biography of the national hero published in 1935 (see chapter 1). In all of them, actor-focus verbs predominate and possessive pronouns are used frequently to personalize the expression. Had Santos not made the changes, the stylistic differences between those writings and the mysterious Bonifacio letters would have been glaring.[43]

In the end, therefore, the accumulated weight of the evidence—the unbelievable stories about the provenance of the documents, the inconsistencies in penmanship, and the defects in the prose—seems to indicate that the Bonifacio letters are probably fabrications. Admittedly, if they are forgeries, they are not as crudely executed as the ones that can be traced to Jose E. Marco; that is, they are not riddled with striking anachronisms, fantastic details, obviously forged signatures, and the like. The author of the Bonifacio letters, if it was not Bonifacio, was obviously well acquainted with the events of the revolutionary period—a historian, a participant in the events, or someone familiar with the major players. That is ultimately why the letters have been taken so seriously over the years; had their contents been nonsensical, scholars would have been more skeptical.

VII

What can we conclude about the Bonifacio letters? Obviously, much about them remains very mysterious. Although it seems probable that the documents are forgeries, we do not know who created them or what motive he or she may have had in doing so. We do not know how they came into Epifanio de los Santos's hands. Nor do we know what role, if any, that famous man—the one for whom the best-known thoroughfare in Manila, EDSA, is named—played in the production of these probably fabricated documents.

Still, there is much we do know. De los Santos, it now seems clear, added little of consequence to our knowledge of Bonifacio and, far more significantly, placed into circulation a number of documents of dubious historical value. Did he know or suspect that they were spurious? That cannot be proven, but, when we take into account the clear inconsistencies of penmanship in the documents, it seems highly unlikely that he would not have had some reservations about their authenticity. Jose P. Santos, on his part, produced seriously flawed transcriptions, probably because he was trying to cover up the fact that the Bonifacio letters published by his father appeared to be forgeries. Teodoro Agoncillo used Santos's flawed transcriptions to produce his own, never indicating that he had failed to consult the originals. All three of these historians—de los Santos, perhaps knowingly; Santos, definitely knowingly; and Agoncillo, almost certainly unknowingly—helped to foster the notion that the Bonifacio-Jacinto correspondence was authentic. By doing so, all three contributed to the view conveyed in those letters—that of Bonifacio the patriotic, Bonifacio the honorable, Bonifacio the misunderstood. All three, in other words, played a role in reinforcing the image of Bonifacio found in the accounts of his youth and his involvement with the Katipunan.

So where do we go from here? If the famous letters are probably bogus, as I suggest they are, what does that do to our understanding of Andres Bonifacio and the revolution he led? On one level, of course, it appears to diminish our understanding more than a little and raises troubling questions about existing scholarship concerning Andres Bonifacio and the Philippine Revolution, since so many scholars—myself included—have given credence to those documents and based some of their conclusions on them. It now appears that, with the possible exception of Bonifacio's two brief letters to Mariano Alvarez (neither of which I have been able to locate), not a single document or text heretofore thought to be composed by Bonifacio can be shown conclusively, or even convincingly, to have been actually written by him. Without the Bonifacio letters, the picture of the national hero that emerges is very different and much less heroic. Without them, we also have a different picture of the tensions between Bonifacio and the Magdalo group, of the Tejeros assembly, and of Bonifacio's efforts to rally support in the aftermath of that meeting. Clearly, historical studies that have leaned heavily on those problematic texts will have to be reconsidered. But, in the end, I believe that all of us are better off without the Bonifacio-Jacinto correspondence. However thin the surviving documentary evidence about the life of Andres Bonifacio and the internal dynamics of the Philippine Revolution may be, it is not so thin that we must use dubious sources to flesh out the story.

Reunion of katipuneros, in front of Balintawak monument, on Bonifacio Day in the early post-independence period. This monument by Ramon Martinez, first unveiled at Balintawak in 1911, was actually a memorial to the heroes of 1896 but subsequently became known as a monument to Bonifacio. It has been relocated to the front of Vinzons Hall at the University of the Philippines, Diliman.

CHAPTER THREE

Ricarte's Bonifacio

The Bonifacio we know is not the creation of historians alone. In the decades following the supremo's death, a number of his contemporaries wrote memoirs that have heavily influenced our understanding of Bonifacio's role in the revolution of 1896. Perhaps the most influential one was composed by Artemio Ricarte, a man celebrated as a hero of both the struggle against Spain and the subsequent war with the United States. Filled with data about Bonifacio's activities in the first days of the uprising, the liberation of Cavite by Filipino forces, the emerging tensions within the revolutionary ranks, the growing challenges to Bonifacio's authority, the supremo's fall from power, his trial, and his eventual death, Ricarte's account has been used by many scholars over the years. In his biographical study of Bonifacio, Agoncillo cited it more often than any other source, and other leading students of the revolutionary period—Zaide, Quirino, and Saulo, for example—have themselves placed considerable weight on data provided by Ricarte.[1]

But is Ricarte's memoir a trustworthy source? Unfortunately, it is not. In this chapter, I subject to extended scrutiny a small, albeit undeniably important, portion of Ricarte's narrative—his description of the famous Tejeros assembly of March 22, 1897, and a meeting held on the following day at the parish house of Tanza (a town also known as Santa Cruz de Malabon), only a short distance from Tejeros.[2] I focus on the Tejeros gathering not only because it is regarded by many historians as a seminal event in the Philippine past but because it is the most frequently described event in Andres Bonifacio's life.³ At Tejeros, the assembled revolutionaries replaced Bonifacio as their leader, Bonifacio became enraged, and a process was set in motion that led in less than two months to Bonifacio's execution.

In this chapter, I show that Ricarte's narrative of those events—a source on which existing secondary accounts of both the Tejeros assembly and Bonifacio's fall from power are largely based—cannot be given automatic credence. Ricarte's version is contradicted by a number of documents, some of which have been ignored by historians. At some points, the differences between Ricarte's version and others might be considered minor; at others, they are substantial. Taken together, they indicate that the real events at Tejeros did not closely resemble those described by Ricarte. I also suggest that Ricarte consciously dissembled in telling the story of the Tejeros assembly and that he had a practical reason for doing so. This much-praised hero of both the revolution against Spain and the war against the United States wanted to disguise his own role in bringing about Bonifacio's fall from power. Finally, I make an effort to determine what really happened at Tejeros and Tanza on those two days in March 1897. Even with the deeply flawed sources we have at our disposal, I believe it is possible to perceive, however dimly, some documentable truths about key events in Andres Bonifacio's life. One of those events—in some ways, the most significant one, since it marked the beginning of the end for the Philippine national hero—is the Tejeros assembly.⁴

I

Artemio Ricarte—the author of the memoir that has shaped our view of the Tejeros assembly—was one of the few non-Tagalog leaders of the uprising of 1896. Ricarte was born in October 1866 in Batac, Ilocos Norte. Educated at the Colegio de San Juan de Letran and subsequently at the Escuela Normal, both in Manila, he came to Cavite as a schoolteacher, taking a position in the town of San Francisco de Malabon (now General Trias). After joining the Katipunan, Ricarte became associated with the Magdiwang organization (Sangguniang Magdiwang), based in Noveleta, which had jurisdiction over western Cavite. At the time of the Tejeros meeting, Ricarte held the position of brigadier general in the Magdiwang forces.⁵

Ricarte composed his account in either 1908 or 1909, at a time when he was an inmate in Bilibid Prison in Manila, having been incarcerated by the Americans for his ongoing resistance to the colonial regime.[6] According to Armando Malay, who prepared one version of the memoirs for publication, Ricarte wrote them in pencil in his cell where he had no access to diaries, notes, or documents that might have jogged his memory. The language of composition, Malay tells us, was Tagalog, despite the fact that the original title of the narrative—"Apuntes Históricas de la Insurrección por los asociados [de] 'Kamahalmahala't Kataastaasang Katipunan nang manga Anak ng Bayan' Contra el Gobierno Espanol en las Islas Filipinas"—suggests that it was written in Spanish. In any case, the original, which was at one time appendix 136 in the Watson Collection (a compilation of documents assembled by the British writer William Brecknock Watson and later housed in the Philippine National Library), has disappeared, as has the rest of the collection.[7] Four versions of the memoirs were eventually published: an English-language version in 1926, one in Tagalog in 1927, another in Ilocano in 1929, and a second English-language version in 1963.[8] A comparison of the texts reveals that, while there is much overlap from one edition to the next, there are also significant differences. The first English-language edition, for instance, does not include large amounts of material found in the others. In writing the present chapter, I have relied on the Tagalog-language version; all English translations included in the text are my own.[9]

A number of scholars who have scrutinized Ricarte's memoirs have pointed out that they suffer from signal defects. Teodoro Agoncillo, for one, was extremely critical.

> In studying Ricarte's memoirs of the Revolution I found several obviously unreliable statements that documents, discovered later on, belied. His strong personal prejudices, so apparent in his delineation of characters, are too pronounced to escape the attention of even a casual reader.[10]

But that did not stop Agoncillo or other historians from basing their accounts of the Tejeros assembly on Ricarte's narrative.

Let us turn to that narrative.[11] According to Ricarte, the Tejeros meeting was called by the leaders of the Magdiwang organization for the principal purpose of discussing how to defend the area under its control. At that point in the conflict, the Spanish Army, having earlier lost control of the Tagalog-speaking provinces south of Manila, was in the process of winning back the territory, and the Magdiwang leadership realized that a Spanish invasion of its jurisdiction was imminent. Ricarte claimed that the Magdiwang issued invitations to "all the rebel leaders within its jurisdiction" ("ang lahat ng mga pinunong naghihimagsik sa sakop niya"). But when the assembly began,[12] the Tejeros estate house was filled not only with the Magdiwang chiefs "but also many of the Magdalo" ("kundi pa naman sa maraming taga Magdalo"), the revolutionary organization in charge of eastern Cavite.

> Included among the Magdiwang chiefs in attendance, aside from the Supreme Chief of the Katipunan [Bonifacio], were the following gentlemen:–
> Mariano Alvarez, Pascual Alvarez, Santiago Alvarez, Luciano San Miguel, Mariano Trias Closas, Severino de las Alas, Santos Nocon, and others; among those affiliated with Magdalo were included Baldomero Aguinaldo, Daniel Tirona, Cayetano Topacio and Antonio Montenegro and other gentlemen.
>
> (Sa mga pang-unang pinuno ng Magdiwang na nagsidalo, bukod sa Ktt. Pang-ulo ng Katipunan, ay kabilang ang mga ginoong sumusunod:–
> Mariano Alvarez, Pascual Alvarez, Santiago Alvarez, Luciano San Miguel, Mariano Trias Closas, Severino de las Alas, Santos Nocon, at iba pa; at sa mga kaanib ng Magdalo naman, ay babilang sina GG. Baldomero Aguinaldo, Daniel Tirona, Cayetano Topacio at Antonio Montenegro at iba pang mga ginoo.)

The person who initially presided over the gathering was Jacinto Lumbreras, a member of the Magdiwang.

Shortly after the session commenced, Severino de las Alas of the Magdiwang organization suggested that, before dealing with the question of defensive preparations, the assembly "should first discuss the kind of government that should exist in the archipelago in the present circumstances" ("dapat munang pag-usapan ang uring pamahalaang dapat pairalin sa Kapuluan sa loob ng kasalukuyang kalagayang yaon"). Lumbreras and Bonifacio dissented, maintaining that the revolutionaries already had a government—the system of consultative bodies (such as the sangguniang bayan) that had been established by the Katipunan. The discussion became heated. Antonio Montenegro, a Manileño and an adherent of the Magdalo group, vociferously supported de las Alas's proposal, using somewhat intemperate language. In a loud voice, he declared that unless some definite understanding were reached about the nature of the government the revolutionaries were nothing more than a group of "bandits" ("mga tulisan") or, even worse, "beasts who are unable to reason" ("mga hayop na walang mga katuwiran"). According to Ricarte, Montenegro's words "wounded the feelings" ("nasugatan ang damdamin") of Santiago Alvarez, the Magdiwang leader, and he directed insulting remarks of his own toward Montenegro. Weapons were drawn, and the session broke up in disorder. An hour passed, allowing time for the tempers of the adherents of Alvarez and Montenegro to cool.

When the meeting resumed, Lumbreras was no longer in charge. He had decided to step down, he explained, because the assembly was discussing a subject that had not been mentioned in the invitations issued to the delegates, which "concerned the establishment of a General Government for the Revolution" ("natutukoy sa pagtatatag ng isang Pamahalaang Pangkalahatan ng Panghihimagsik"). In Lumbreras's place was Andres Bonifacio, who was asked by all to preside over the meeting. Ricarte assumed the position of secretary.

Bonifacio began the new session by stating somewhat magnanimously that he would not object to a reorganization of the revolutionary government. "But," he added, "I must first invite you all to join us in acknowledging a principle that should be the basis of our decisions at this meeting, and at other ones, and said principle is the following:– that we respect and obey the decision of the majority" ("Datapwat dapat munang anyayahan ko kayo na tayong lahat ay kumilala sa isang simulaing mapagbabatayan ng ating mga pasya sa pulong na ito, o sa iba man, at ang nasabing simulain ay itong sumusunod:– Na, ating igalang at sundin ang pasya ng nakararami"). The audience agreed unanimously, and the Philippine Republic was proclaimed (although Ricarte did not explain what the delegates meant by a "republic" nor how it was expected to function in the absence of a document describing its workings). Then the delegates prepared to conduct an election for the officials of the new government. Before the voting began, Bonifacio returned to the theme of his earlier remarks, reminding the delegates that any person elected by a majority vote should be respected and obeyed, "whatever his status in society and whatever level of education he has achieved" ("maging anoman ang kanyang kalagayan sa loob ng kapisanan at maging gaano man ang naabot na taas ng pinag-aralan"). Again, everyone agreed.

Initially, the electors voted by written ballot. In the contest for president of the government, Emilio Aguinaldo, who was not present at Tejeros since he was conducting military operations elsewhere, was elected, defeating Bonifacio and Mariano Trias. Trias won the election for vice president, prevailing over Bonifacio, de las Alas, and Mariano Alvarez. Ricarte was elected "captain general"—the top military position—over Santiago Alvarez. (Ricarte wrote in his memoirs that he protested that result, claiming that he lacked the ability to do the job, but the electors would not accept his protest.)

By now, night was falling. In an effort to speed up the election of other officials, the assembly agreed to dispense with written ballots. Thereafter, delegates who favored a particular candidate were obliged to stand on one side of the room, and those who favored another had to assemble on a different side. By the new procedure, Emiliano Riego de Dios was elected director of war, defeating Ariston Villanueva, Daniel Tirona, and Santiago Alvarez.

Then came the ill-fated election of director of the interior. After losing twice before, Bonifacio was finally victorious, besting Mariano and Pascual Alvarez. But, as the revolutionaries were acclaiming Bonifacio, Daniel Tirona, a member of the Magdalo group, voiced his dissent.

> Compatriots:– The position of director of the interior is almost as important as that of leader or president; hence that department should not be managed by a person who does not possess a lawyer's credentials. We have in our province a certified lawyer, and his name is Jose del Rosario; we must protest against the person elected and praised.
>
> (Mga kababayan:– Ang tungkuling pagka-Direktor del Interior ay halos kasinglaki rin nang sa Pang-ulo o Presidente; kaya't ang Kagawarang iya'y di dapat

pamanihalaan ng isang taong di nagaangkin ng isang
katibayan ng pagka-abogado. Mayroon tayo dito sa ating
lalawigang isang abogadong may sadyang katibayan, at
ito'y si G. Jose del Rosario; dapat nga tayong tumutol
laban sa nahalal at pinapurihan.)

Tirona urged the assembly to choose Jose del Rosario.

Ricarte's narrative tells us that Bonifacio was deeply hurt by Tirona's words. Bonifacio reminded all that they had agreed to accept the will of the majority, regardless of the social status of the person chosen, and he demanded that Tirona retract what he had said and apologize for his insulting remarks. While Tirona tried to hide in the crowd, Bonifacio drew his revolver, but Ricarte prevented him from firing. As the electors prepared to leave the room, Bonifacio announced:

I, as presiding officer of this assembly, and also as head of
the Supreme Sanggunian of the Katipunan . . . announce
the dissolution of this meeting and nullify everything that
has been done and decided herein.

(Ako, sa aking pagka-Pang-ulo ng kapulungang ito, at sa
pagka-Pang-ulo rin naman ng Ktt. Sanggunian ng
Katipunan . . . ay ipinahahayag kong lansag na ang
kapulungang ito at pinawawalaan ng kabuluhan ang
lahat ng sa loob niya'y pinagkayarian at pinagpasyahan.)

At that point, Bonifacio left, followed by his supporters.

Shortly after the disruption, Baldomero Aguinaldo, cousin of the newly elected president, came to an understanding with Ricarte that the meeting would resume on the following day. Their aim, Ricarte implied, was to effect a reconciliation. The next day, Ricarte, Bonifacio, Mariano Alvarez, and other Magdiwang leaders showed up, but the adherents of the Magdalo organization did not. Ricarte and the others waited until 5 p.m. and then dispersed. An hour later, Ricarte received an invitation from the Magdalo leadership to attend a meeting at the parish house of the nearby town of Tanza.

In his narrative, Ricarte claimed that he was unaware of the purpose of the Tanza meeting. Still, he went. Initially, he hid in the crowd and learned that the people were waiting for the newly elected officials to take their oaths of office. Emilio Aguinaldo, the elected president, who had just arrived from the battlefield, and Mariano Trias, the elected vice president, eventually emerged from a room, along with Daniel Tirona (the insulter of Bonifacio), Severino de las Alas (the man who had suggested that the revolutionary government be reorganized), the parish priest, and many others. They proceeded to the reception hall, in which there was a crucifix and a candelabra with lighted candles. Aguinaldo and Trias knelt before the crucifix and took their oaths. Shortly thereafter, Ricarte tried to leave, but he was spotted by several men, among them Jacinto Pulido, a revolutionary from Tanza. Aguinaldo and his followers tried to convince Ricarte to take his oath as well, but he resisted, asserting that if he did so there would be great "resentment" ("samaan") among the rebels. Finally, around midnight, "merely in order to be able to get away from that group" ("upang siya'y makalayo na lamang sa pulutong na yaon"), he relented, but on the condition that his resignation would be accepted immediately after he took his oath. He took it and left.

According to Ricarte, Emilio Aguinaldo and the others continued to meet at Tanza until March 25, dispersing after the nearby town of Imus was captured by the Spanish Army and Crispulo Aguinaldo, Emilio's brother, was killed. He concluded his discussion of the Tanza meeting with the following arresting paragraph.

> When the assembly [in Tanza] dissolved, . . . the members agreed to announce that everything done and decided in that meeting had no force, since they believed that in this way they would check the angry feelings against them that were felt by many.
>
> (Nang malansag ang pagpupulong na ito [sa Tanza], . . . ay pinagkaisahan ng mga nagpulong na ibalitang walang naging bisa ang lahat ng ginawa at pinagpasyahan na naturang pulong, sa pag-aakalang sa paraang ito'y masasawata ang mainit na simbuyong laban sa kanila'y naghahari sa loob ng marami.)

If Ricarte's memory was correct, it would appear that Aguinaldo was no longer the president of the new government.

At this juncture, a number of points should be made about Ricarte's narrative of the Tejeros assembly. First, he indicated that the men who called the meeting did not intend to change the revolutionary government or hold elections. The decision to do these things came only after the assembly had begun, when de las Alas and Montenegro pressed for a reorganization of the revolutionary government.

Second, Ricarte presented his own involvement in the proceedings in an extremely favorable light. Elected captain general by the delegates, he modestly protested that he was unworthy of the honor. When Bonifacio, aroused by Tirona's words, drew his pistol, it was Ricarte who managed to stop him from firing. After the breakup of the Tejeros meeting, it was Ricarte, along with Baldomero Aguinaldo, who decided to effect a reconciliation between the hostile parties. At the subsequent gathering in Tanza, Ricarte refused to take his oath of office, believing that it was impolitic to act so hastily. Hotheads there may have been at the Tejeros assembly, but, according to Ricarte, he was not one of them.

Third, his account is distinctly critical of the members of the Magdalo group. Montenegro, a Magdalo, used provocative language. Daniel Tirona insulted Bonifacio and called into question the will of the majority. Having agreed with Ricarte to resume the Tejeros meeting, Baldomero Aguinaldo did not appear at the appointed time. If the Tejeros assembly produced a fatal split in the revolutionary movement, the people chiefly responsible for the split were, in Ricarte's view, members of the Magdalo organization.

Finally, a few members of the Magdiwang also played roles in bringing about changes in the revolutionary government. At the Tejeros meeting, de las Alas originally proposed that the government be reorganized, and he subsequently participated in the oath-taking ceremony at Tanza. Mariano Trias took his oath of office at Tanza. Jacinto Pulido was present at that ceremony as well. Ricarte implied, however, that after the breakup of the Tejeros assembly an overwhelming majority of the Magdiwang membership remained loyal to Bonifacio and that the meeting at Tanza was essentially a Magdalo affair.

There can be no doubt that Ricarte presented a colorful account of the Tejeros meeting, full of the sort of details—the names of about two dozen participants, the results of several elections, the speeches given by Bonifacio, Tirona, and others—that lend an air of authority to his voice. Why, then, should we question his version of events?

Four answers, some more obvious than others, come to mind. First, as I have indicated, he wrote his account several years after the revolution, without access to records or people who could have corrected factual mistakes. Can we really accept at face value all the details he presented in his narrative? In fact, the same particularities that appear to lend authority to his account—the names, the speeches, the play-by-play—are the ones we should view most skeptically. Even though Ricarte was at Tejeros (and though, according to him, he served as secretary during part of the meeting), it is unlikely that he could have remembered so much, so clearly, so many years after the event.

Second, his description of his actions at Tejeros is self-congratulatory. Memoirists of all nationalities have been known to misremember the past in order to influence the way future generations might assess their role in it. Is it not likely that Ricarte was guilty of the same sort of creative misremembering?

Third, Ricarte's narrative is almost certainly tainted by bias, both personal and political. Like all of us, he had his favorites and his enemies, and no doubt he was inclined to be protective of the former and critical of the latter. As a member of the Magdiwang organization and a close associate of Bonifacio, moreover, he might have been expected to place responsibility for the conflict at Tejeros on the members of the rival Magdalo group.

Fourth, as the remainder of this chapter will show, other accounts of the Tejeros assembly contradict Ricarte's. They call into question many, if not most, of the factual details in Ricarte's description of the meeting, and they suggest that he may have had ulterior motives for providing a factually inaccurate narrative.

The time has come to direct our attention to those sources.

II

A total of eleven additional documents provide information about the Tejeros meeting. Four are memoirs, two of which have been published (the narratives of Santiago Alvarez, which first appeared in print in 1927, and Emilio Aguinaldo, which bears the publication date of 1964 but was obviously penned several decades earlier) and two of which have not (the reminiscences of Carlos Ronquillo, Aguinaldo's secretary, written in 1898, and Telesforo Canseco, a lay employee of the Dominican Order, penned in 1897).[13] Like other sources of this genre, all four memoirs are problematic in one way or another, although not necessarily as problematic as Ricarte's. Two of the authors—Alvarez and Aguinaldo—wrote so many years after the events they describe that their accounts are probably filled with factual errors. Furthermore, like Ricarte, three of the memoirists (all but Canseco) had reasons to misremember, either because they held grudges or because they wanted to sanitize their own images or those of close associates or family members.

The other seven sources are a decidedly mixed bag. Five of them must be classified as unreliable or of dubious reliability. They include two of Bonifacio's letters to Jacinto (those of April 16 and April 24, 1897), which have already been exposed as probable forgeries and do not merit our serious attention, and three documents that surfaced in either Epifanio de los Santos's 1917 biographical sketch of Bonifacio or Jose P. Santos's 1935 biography. These are the declaration known as the Acta de Tejeros, signed by Bonifacio, Ricarte, and other revolutionary leaders, dated March 23, 1897; a statement written by Artemio Ricarte on March 24, 1897; and a brief note by Bonifacio to Mariano Alvarez dated April 27, 1897.[14] Questions about the historical value of these three documents are raised not only by the fact that de los Santos and Santos first published them but by the following considerations: (1) the first document, according to Jose P. Santos, was part of the collection of Bonifacio materials allegedly purchased by his father from the unidentified man in Tondo;[15] (2) the second source, too, has long been in the possession of the Santos family; and (3) the only historian who apparently has ever seen the third document is Jose P. Santos. Despite my perhaps understandable concerns about the evidential value of all three documents, I will, on occasion, allude to their contents in the following pages, but readers should be assured that my conclusions about the Tejeros assembly are at no point dependent on information found therein.

The final two sources are a letter from Baldomero Aguinaldo to Felix Cuenca and Mariano Noriel written on March 21, 1897, and the testimony of Andres Bonifacio at his trial in early May of 1897.[16] Both the letter and the trial records differ from the five sources discussed in the previous paragraph in two important respects: both appear to be genuine historical documents and both can be found in archives and are therefore available for inspection by scholars. Unfortunately, though, the fact that the trial records are held by a well-known manuscript repository—the Philippine National Library—has done nothing to insure their safety. Only a short time ago, it was discovered that thousands of rare documents had been stolen from the library, including the transcript of Bonifacio's trial. In the end, portions of the trial records were returned in installments, but it is unclear whether all of them were finally delivered. Other stolen documents apparently remain in private hands.[17]

In the remainder of this chapter, I do not intend to list all the points of difference between Ricarte's description of the Tejeros meeting and those found in the other sources. Suffice it to say that some of the accounts—those of Ronquillo and Alvarez, for example—differ from Ricarte's on dozens of particulars (the names of participants, the date and sequence of events, the results of the election, and so forth). On nearly as many occasions, they also disagree with each other. The discrepancies are so numerous that it strikes me as virtually hopeless to attempt to produce an accurate, blow-by-blow narrative of the Tejeros assembly. Instead, I will focus on the ways in which those other sources (especially the six that can be given a certain amount of credence) challenge key elements of Ricarte's account of the Tejeros assembly—that is, I hope to show how they, taken singly or in conjunction, provide a very different slant on those momentous events. Even though we may never know exactly what happened at Tejeros, it is possible, at least, to gain a better general understanding of that meeting and its aftermath. From my reading of the sources, I have concluded that they call into question at least five key elements of Ricarte's narrative.

III

Finding 1. The elections at Tejeros may have been—and probably were—rigged.

It should come as no great surprise to students of the Philippines that one of the most important elections in the country's past was marred by irregularities. Such was the norm in Philippine local elections during the final decades of the Spanish regime and such is often the case in Philippine elections today.[18] On the other hand, it is surprising that, with a single exception, historians of the revolutionary period have ignored that possibility as well as the evidence about it.[19] One can only speculate that scholars have been reluctant to attribute to the nation's founding fathers the sins of its sons and grandsons.

But the evidence is fairly compelling. Consider the narrative of Telesforo Canseco. At the time of the Tejeros meeting, Canseco was residing in San Francisco de Malabon, a few miles from the meeting place. What he knew about the assembly he learned from a friend, the concierge of the Tejeros estate house. According to Canseco, the voting at Tejeros was hotly contested and there were "many disturbances and intrigues to get votes for oneself in the elections" ("muchos disturbios e intrigas al buscar para si votos en las elecciones").[20]

Canseco's comment is significant. Whereas Ricarte's account indicates that disturbances occurred at Tejeros, it is silent about "intrigues." According to Ricarte, the delegates were invited to the meeting solely to discuss defensive preparations and it was after they had assembled that the subject of elections was broached. If he is to be believed, there was no possible reason for the attendees to intrigue beforehand, and, except for the one hour recess period when Alvarez and Montenegro were cooling off, there was no opportunity to win over voters during the meeting itself. Hence, Canseco's statement hints that Ricarte was not telling the whole story.

How can Ricarte's failure to discuss such intrigues in his memoirs be explained? One possibility, of course, is that faulty memory was to blame. Several years after the event, even important details can be forgotten by anyone. A second possibility is that the intrigues did not occur. As I have pointed out, Canseco was not present at Tejeros and his informant could have been mistaken. A third is that Ricarte failed to mention the intrigues because to do so might have tarnished his image. One thing we know for sure about Ricarte is that his public image was very important to him. In the first decade of the twentieth century—the same one in which he composed his memoirs—he was hard at work crafting it. By 1905 or so, the onetime schoolteacher had been transformed into Ricarte the defiant, the man who not only had fought against Spanish and American armies but had refused to take an oath of allegiance to the United States even after the Philippine-American War was over, the unreconstructed revolutionary who had continued to plot against the U.S. colonial regime and had landed in prison for his efforts. Surely, it is possible that such a man, now writing his memoirs alone in his prison cell, might have wanted posterity to think that his own elevation at Tejeros to the position of captain general had been due to the high regard in which he was held by his fellow revolutionaries, not to disturbances, intrigues, or any other kind of electoral impropriety.

There is still another possibility, but, for the moment, let us defer our discussion of it.

Even more informative about electoral improprieties at the Tejeros meeting are the memoirs of Santiago Alvarez. After listing the leading members of the Magdiwang and Magdalo organizations who were in attendance at the Tejeros estate house, Alvarez wrote the following passage.

> It must also be mentioned that, before the meeting began, the secretary of war of the Magdiwang government Mr. Ariston Villanueva received the secret news that the meeting would not to able to complete what it had invited [us] to accomplish, but [would do] only what the Magdalo people wanted to do, and that the secret leader [who was orchestrating all that] was Mr. Daniel Tirona, who had been able to persuade many Magdiwang leaders.
> Secretary of War Villanueva remained silent and secretly informed General "Apoy" [Santiago Alvarez] to prepare the soldiers for any unexpected development.
>
> (Dapat ding mabanggit na bago nagbukas ng pulong, ang kalihim-digmang G. Ariston Villanueva ng Pamahalaang Magdiwang ay tumanggap ng lihim na balita, na ang pulong ay di mayayari sa ipinag-anyaya, kundi sa kagustuhan ng mga taga Magdalo, at ang lihim na lider ay si G. Daniel Tirona, saka maraming nahikayat na mga Puno ng Magdiwang. Gayon man, ang kalihim-digmang Villanueva ay nagwalang kibo at sukat ang lihim na pagbibigay-alam sa pangulung-digmang "Apoy" sa paghahanda ng Kawal sa alinmang biglang pangangailangan.)[21]

Read in isolation, this excerpt from Alvarez's narrative seems vague. How exactly did Tirona expect to achieve his objectives? Was Alvarez perhaps referring to the decision by the delegates to reorganize the revolutionary government, to Tirona's provocative remarks about Bonifacio's qualifications for office, or to something else? And who among the Magdiwang leaders had purportedly come to an understanding with Tirona? Some of those questions are answered a few pages later when Alvarez discusses the elections of government officials.

> General Artemio Ricarte, who was appointed secretary of the Supremo Bonifacio, with the assistance of Mr. Daniel Tirona, then distributed pieces of paper on which the votes were to be written; and when said election papers had been collected on a table, Mr. Diego Mojica, the Magdiwang secretary of the treasury, advised the Supremo A. Bonifacio that "many pieces of paper [that had been] given out had writing on them beforehand, and they weren't filled out by the voters." The Supremo didn't say anything, and did not indicate that anything improper had occurred and did not stop what he was doing.
>
> (Si hral. Artemio Ricarte ang inilagay na Kalihim ng Supremo Bonifacio, saka pagtatapos ay ipinamahagi ang mga tilas ng papel na susulatan ng boto, katulong si G. Daniel Tirona; at nang naiipon na sa hapag ang mga sinabing papel ng botohan, si G. Diego Mojica, Kalihim-Yaman ng Magdiwang, ay nagpagunita sa Supremo A. Bonifacio "na maraming tilas na papel na kumalat na may sulat na, at di na sinulatan ng Manghahalal." Ang Supremo ay di kumibo, hindi nagpakita ng anumang kaselangan at patuloy sa kanyang mga gawain.)[22]

Significantly, Alvarez suggested that the delegates' ballots may have been subject to tampering. He also named two individuals who, as the distributors of the ballots, were in an ideal position to learn about, or take part in, the supposed tampering that resulted in Aguinaldo's election to the presidency: Ricarte, the secretary, and Daniel Tirona, the man who reportedly had conspired with others. Was Alvarez not implying that the tactic adopted by Tirona to manipulate the proceedings was ballot tampering and also that Ricarte, who would later be elected to the post of captain general, may have been one of the Magdiwang leaders who had reached an accommodation with Tirona? In fact, if there was ballot tampering, how could Ricarte not have been aware of it?

Alvarez's memoir thus provides us with a vital clue to the reason for Ricarte's silence on the question of electoral improprieties. Merely by alluding to the charge of ballot tampering, he would have raised the possibility that he, as the secretary of the meeting, had been responsible for the tainted results. And if he had been complicitous—if, for example, he had been party to a deal about who would be elected to positions in the government (a common practice in elections for municipal posts in the late Spanish period)—posterity might hold him partly responsible for an act that it would not be likely to judge charitably: a political arrangement intended to remove Bonifacio from power and to put Caviteños in control of the revolutionary organization. To admit that—or even hint at it—would have done serious damage to Ricarte's reputation.[23]

A few other sources also contain hints about electoral irregularities at Tejeros, but, since all of them are documents of demonstrated or likely unreliability, I will not dwell long on their contents. Consider briefly the Acta de Tejeros—literally, the "Tejeros minutes," although they were not minutes at all but rather a lengthy letter of protest (similar to the letters of protest typically filed in the aftermath of disputed municipal electoral contests during the Spanish regime). It was written at Tejeros on the day after the historic meeting and signed by Bonifacio, Ricarte, Mariano Alvarez, Jacinto Lumbreras, and forty-one other revolutionaries.[24] The signers of the Acta explicitly repudiated the results of the recently held election because of electoral abuses allegedly committed by members of the Magdalo organization. Among other things, they claimed that ballot tampering had occurred and unqualified people had voted. This document—which, it should be emphasized, bears Ricarte's signature—presents a view of the Tejeros meeting strikingly similar to that found in Alvarez's memoirs.

Let me underline the point that the Acta (as well as Ricarte's declaration of March 24, 1897, which also touches on the question of electoral improprieties) is a somewhat dubious source, so we should not place a great deal of weight on the accusations found in it. But even without the Acta there is sufficient evidence—Canseco's statement,

Alvarez's narrative—to suggest that Ricarte's description of the election at Tejeros was misleading, that irregularities occurred behind the scenes, and that Ricarte was well aware of their existence. Beyond that, if we recall that Philippine elections of that day were typically rigged, it would have been downright shocking if some kind of electoral shenanigans had not taken place.

Hence, common sense, as well as the documentary record, suggests that something at Tejeros must have been amiss. The problem we face is to determine the extent of the electoral improprieties. Canseco's narrative alludes to "disturbances and intrigues to get votes for oneself." Alvarez's account indicates that the ballots were tampered with and that Ricarte and Tirona may have been involved. None of that seems implausible, but it must be acknowledged that neither source is absolutely unimpeachable: Canseco got his information second hand, and Alvarez wrote his memoir long after the event. In the end, then, whatever conclusions we reach about the Tejeros assembly must be tempered with qualifications. It is unlikely that we will ever know how widespread the electoral improprieties were, but we may feel reasonably certain that there were some.

There is one thing more about which we can be reasonably certain—that Ricarte's description of the Tejeros elections cannot be trusted. At best, it is seriously flawed; at worst, it is a lie. Ricarte knew more than he revealed and kept silent because, in all likelihood, he had something to hide—his own complicity in a preelectoral agreement. Ricarte the defiant was, in reality, Ricarte the deceitful.

Finding 2. The decision to hold elections was made before the delegates assembled at Tejeros.

If electoral improprieties did occur at Tejeros, it follows logically that at least one other aspect of Ricarte's account must be considered misleading—his implications that the delegates came to Tejeros to discuss the danger posed by the advancing Spanish forces and that they decided to change the revolutionary government and hold elections only after the meeting had begun. It would have been almost impossible for interested parties to influence or manipulate the elections—to lobby eligible voters and prepare tainted ballots—if they had no advance warning that elections were going to be held. They needed time to do that.

One source demonstrates unambiguously that they did have advance warning: a letter written by Baldomero Aguinaldo, the head of the Sangguniang Magdalo, to two prominent members of that organization, Felix Cuenca and Mariano Noriel, on March 21, 1897, the day before the Tejeros assembly.[25] In that arresting document, Aguinaldo informed his colleagues that he had just received a letter from the Magdiwang president, Mariano Alvarez, inviting him to a meeting at Tejeros on the following day when elections would be held for officials in the central and provincial revolutionary governments. Aguinaldo asked Cuenca and Noriel to consider which men were deserving of such posts and urged both to attend the proceedings at Tejeros (which were scheduled to begin at 6 a.m.) and "inform the heads of other towns [about the meeting] and to tell them not to be absent" ("pagsabihan mo po ang mga G. Plo ng taga ibang bayan di[y]an at ipag[p]auna na huag mag culang").[26]

Baldomero Aguinaldo's letter reveals that at least some of the delegates attending the Tejeros meeting were aware that elections were going to take place and that they had had an opportunity to think about and discuss the candidates. We learn, too, that the idea of making changes in the revolutionary government was proposed by Mariano Alvarez, the Magdiwang leader who was supposedly Bonifacio's biggest supporter. There can be little doubt that Ricarte was aware of all that. As a leading figure in the Magdiwang organization, he would have been given as much information about the upcoming elections as the Magdalo president Baldomero Aguinaldo had. But why, then, did Ricarte convey the impression that the decision to reorganize the government was something of an afterthought?

By now, it should be apparent that there is a pattern to Ricarte's omissions. As in so much else, Ricarte was trying to avoid self-incrimination, and his inclusion of the not insignificant detail that the delegates knew, before their arrival at Tejeros, that there would be elections would have raised understandable questions about whether there had been preelectoral shenanigans. More intriguing is another question. Why did other memoirists—Santiago Alvarez, Carlos Ronquillo, and Emilio Aguinaldo—omit that detail as well? Santiago Alvarez had to know beforehand that his father planned to hold elections; Emilio Aguinaldo and Ronquillo might have been privy to the information sent to Emilio's cousin. Perhaps the memoirists, like Ricarte, had no interest in calling attention to wrongdoing that they had either participated in or benefited from. They, too, may have had something to hide.

So, all things considered, the meeting at Tejeros bore more than a superficial resemblance to the kind of elections with which Filipino political influentials of the day were familiar. Rather than an afterthought, the elections were one of the chief reasons—possibly, *the* chief reason—for convening the meeting in the first place. Under those circumstances, the men who took part would have been expected to conduct themselves as they normally did in electoral contests. That is to say, they probably consulted with each other, lobbied, cajoled, threatened, conspired, drew up slates of candidates, and made deals. Some may have engaged in ballot tampering. In the aftermath of the voting, as might have been expected, too, the defeated or dissatisfied cried foul, charging their opponents with all sorts of nasty behavior.

It is understandable that historians of the Philippines, writing decades after the fact, might wish that the heroes of the anticolonial struggle had conducted themselves at Tejeros with the sort of dignity that, in their view, such a moment deserved. Historians of all countries have been known to entertain such thoughts about presumed heroes, particularly in the early years of a nation's independence when the study of history typically serves the vital function of building pride in the accomplishments of the past. But the evidence suggests that the revolutionary leaders who attended the Tejeros meeting were inclined to operate as they always had. They did not know that historians would one day expect a higher standard of behavior. The elections at Tejeros were, after all, only elections.

Finding 3. Non-Caviteños, and especially delegates from the nearby province of Batangas, played a decisive role in the Tejeros assembly.

Ricarte's narrative seems to suggest that, with the exception of Bonifacio and Montenegro, the principal players in the Tejeros meeting were the members of Cavite's two sangguniang bayan: Mariano Alvarez, Ricarte, de las Alas, and various others. Most secondary accounts, which rely heavily on Ricarte, convey the same impression. But it is clear that large numbers of non-Caviteños took part in the meeting and that the role of some of them—in particular, a delegation from Batangas led by Santiago Rillo—was crucial.

The prominent role played by Batangueños in the events of March 1897 is not, I think, terribly surprising when we consider the strength of Batangas's military columns at that point in the conflict. Throughout the recent offensive by Spanish forces in the southern Tagalog region, substantial numbers of troops from Batangas had taken part in operations in Cavite. One of the principal Batangueño commanders, Miguel Malvar, had fought near the Zapote Bridge in February 1897, and by the end of March several thousand Batangueño soldiers could be found in Cavite. Understandably, the commanders of such a huge military force were bound to be influential in the revolutionary councils, and the groups vying for control of the revolutionary government were also bound to realize that their chances of success depended on gaining the support of those men.[27]

The Batangueño commander who had the most significant impact on the Tejeros meeting—the leader of the Batangueño delegation, Santiago Rillo—was actually a transplanted Caviteño, a fact that doubtless contributed to his influence. Rillo was born in Maragondon, Cavite, and he had spent his childhood and part of his adult life in that town. Rillo had relocated to the town of Tuy in Batangas, eventually entered municipal politics, and in 1890 became gobernadorcillo of Tuy. When the Philippine Revolution broke out in August 1896, Rillo held the post of Tuy's justice of the peace, and in the subsequent months of warfare, he emerged as the commander of an armed force numbered in the thousands.[28]

The source that tells us most about the part played by Rillo and the Batangueños at the Tejeros assembly is the narrative of Carlos Ronquillo.[29] According to Ronquillo, it was Rillo—not, as Ricarte asserts,[30] the Caviteño Severino de las Alas—who, shortly after the beginning of the meeting, put forward the idea of using the occasion to reorganize the revolutionary government (an idea that, as I have intimated, had likely been discussed beforehand by many delegates). Rillo's stated motive for suggesting the change in government was to unify the feuding regional factions "so that in this way they become united in purpose, in administration, and in any actions and decisions concerning our defense" ("upang sa ganito'y magkaisa sa lakad, sa pamamahala, sa ano mang pagkilos at pagpapasiya tungkol sa pagtatang[g]ol"). Through unification, Rillo hoped, the Filipinos' performance on the battlefield would improve. Ronquillo indicated, furthermore, that when certain members of the Magdiwang organization objected to his motion Rillo continued to press for governmental reorganization, insisting on the principle of popular sovereignty.

> Brothers, . . . What everybody wants shall prevail, and the will of the People shall be the only priority. Well, brothers, do you want us to elect, right now, officials who shall be obeyed by every place and town in rebellion?

> (Mga kapatid, . . . Kung ano ang ibig ng lahat, ay siyang maghahari, at kung ano ang loob ng Bayan, ay siyang tanging masasamba. Ano, mga kapatid, nais ninyo ang maghalal tayo ngayon din ng isang pamunuang dapat sundin ng tanang pook at bayang naghihimagsik?)

After hearing Rillo's words, the delegates cried: "Yes, let us do it, let us do it right now. Nothing else can satisfy the will of the people" ("Oo, gawin natin, gawin natin ngayon din. Walang makapangyayaring iba sa loob ng bayan").[31]

One additional piece of evidence, questionable though it may be, touches on the role of Batangueños at Tejeros: a passage in Emilio Aguinaldo's memoirs. Aguinaldo did not, of course, attend the Tejeros assembly; at the time, he was in the vicinity of Imus, involved in military operations against the Spanish forces. His account of the meeting was based on information provided to him by Vicente Riego de Dios, a member of the Sangguniang Magdiwang, and other men who had come directly from Tejeros to tell him that he had been elected president. Aguinaldo asserted, in any case, that, after the incident involving Bonifacio and Tirona and Bonifacio's announcement that the elections were null and void, Rillo—whom he described as "the representative of about 2,000 rebels" ("na kumakatawan sa may 2,000 manghihimagsik")—had stood up and attempted to stop the supremo from leaving the meeting hall, pointing out to him that he had been fairly elected director of the interior and that no one had seconded Tirona's offensive motion. After Bonifacio had departed, moreover, Rillo urged the delegates to continue the meeting and appoint him presiding officer. They agreed, and Rillo presided over the remainder of that meeting as well as the one at Tanza the following day.[32]

The clear implication of this evidence is that the agenda as well as the outcome of the Tejeros assembly was determined in no small measure by Rillo and his fellow Batangueños—that is, by people other than the members of the Magdiwang and Magdalo organizations. Rillo had committed himself to the idea of unification and by doing so had overcome the objections of some to reorganization of the revolutionary government. And, having produced that result and witnessed the elections that led to the elevation of Emilio Aguinaldo to the presidency, Rillo and the other Batangueño delegates were not inclined to support Bonifacio's objections to the assembly's decisions. The Tejeros assembly may have taken place in the province of Cavite, but Caviteños were not the only important participants in it.

Finding 4. Bonifacio probably had very little support after the Tejeros meeting.

We will never know for sure whether a majority of the delegates at Tejeros wanted Bonifacio to be president of the new government. On the one hand, the results of the elections suggest that they did not: Ricarte's narrative tells us—and other sources confirm—that Bonifacio was defeated in two electoral contests and the one he finally won was for the comparatively minor post of director of the interior. On the other hand, as we have learned from various sources, foul play may have occurred in the balloting, so Bonifacio's defeats in the presidential and vice presidential contests may not have been fair reflections of the delegates' preferences. Perhaps, then, the best measure of their support for the supremo was Bonifacio's seemingly insignificant victory in the election for director of the interior, since, in that case at least, the delegates were able to state their preferences openly. As the matter now stands, it is unclear whether the elections held at the Tejeros assembly can really be interpreted as a rejection of Bonifacio's leadership. Valid arguments can be made on both sides of the question.

What, then, can be said about the level of support for Bonifacio in the immediate aftermath of that meeting? The evidence discussed thus far hints that it may have been high. Ricarte's narrative implies that few members of the Magdiwang organization took part in the Tanza meeting. The possibly bogus Acta de Tejeros bears the signature of forty-five individuals, including Bonifacio and Mariano Alvarez, who swore to oppose the government established at Tejeros. All of this might lead us to believe that, in the days immediately following the Tejeros assembly, there was a substantial amount of dissatisfaction with the electoral results. But additional (and, in my view, far more convincing) evidence tells us otherwise.

We need first to address the question of numbers. Let us assume, for the sake of argument, that the Acta is a trustworthy source and that forty-five delegates actually filed a letter of protest against the elections at Tejeros. What does that number show? While it indicates that there was indeed dissatisfaction with the proceedings, it tells us nothing about the level of dissatisfaction. In addition to knowing the number of protesters, we need to have some idea of the total number of delegates who participated in the Tejeros meeting. If there were seventy or eighty people in attendance, a protest by forty-five might be interpreted as a strong vote of support for Bonifacio. If the number of delegates was much greater, such an interpretation would be unwarranted.

The best-known sources do not provide much help in determining how many people attended the Tejeros meeting. In his memoir, Ricarte did not estimate the number of delegates, although he did include the names of twenty-three individuals who were present either at Tejeros or Tanza. Santiago Alvarez provided no head count, nor did Aguinaldo.

More helpful is the narrative of Telesforo Canseco, which furnishes two important clues. First, Canseco asserted that the Tejeros meeting was attended by virtually all of the katipuneros in the region; second, he provided the ballot count of the three candidates for president: Emilio Aguinaldo, 146; Bonifacio, 80; and Mariano Alvarez, 30. Canseco's account tells us, in other words, that a total of 256 votes were cast.[33] Of course, given the fact that Canseco relied on data provided by someone else, we might wonder whether those figures are accurate. And, even if those tallies were correctly reported, we cannot assume, given the strong probability that electoral irregularities occurred, that the numbers truly reflected the level of support for the candidates. Still, this source suggests that at least 256 delegates took part in the Tejeros assembly.

If Canseco's figures lead us to think that the meeting at Tejeros was well attended, so do a few other scraps of evidence. The letter from Baldomero Aguinaldo to Cuenca and Noriel reveals that the Magdalo leadership made a strong effort to turn out its supporters. Ronquillo's narrative also hints that the turnout was high. "That meeting was attended by all the town leaders of the two Sanggunian" ("Dumalo sa pulong na yaon ang tanang pangulong-bayan sa dalawang

Sang[g]unian"), he wrote at one point. Then, after listing a number of the Magdalo and Magdiwang officials who were present, he commented: "Many other people attended. The place was absolutely filled to capacity" ("Maraming iba't iba pang tao ang dumalo. Siksikan magkabikabila").[34] Some of those "other people" were the members of the Batangas delegation led by Santiago Rillo and men from Tagalog-speaking provinces to the north. All things considered, then, Canseco's total of 256 ballots does not seem improbable. What is more, if we take into consideration the fact that eligible voters do not always cast ballots, the number of people in attendance at Tejeros may have been considerably in excess of 256.

Hence, even if the Acta de Tejeros can be shown to be a genuine source, it cannot be interpreted as proof of strong support for Bonifacio. If anything, it shows the opposite: that only a relatively small number of the original participants in the Tejeros assembly—possibly 15 percent or so—decided to join Bonifacio on March 23 to protest the electoral results. The signers of the Acta—if they did sign such a document—would then appear to be merely a rump group, ostensibly the diehard Magdiwang supporters of Bonifacio and Mariano Alvarez who had been outmaneuvered and outvoted in the previous day's balloting. And not all of them supported Bonifacio completely. Recall that one of the apparent signatories was Ricarte, whose commitment to Bonifacio is in doubt.

If the Tejeros meeting was as well attended as Canseco's narrative and other sources indicate, what happened to all those people after the meeting? Some, of course, may have met with Bonifacio and protested. Some may have returned to their communities. But most of the delegates, including more than a few from the Magdiwang ranks, probably went to the meeting at Tanza where the newly elected officials were administered their oaths of office. Judged by their actions alone, these people appeared to accept the verdict of the Tejeros assembly.

One source—the memoir of Aguinaldo's secretary Carlos Ronquillo—provides us with hints about the size of the Tanza gathering and contradicts the notion conveyed by Ricarte that it was attended primarily by members of the Magdalo organization. According to Ronquillo, when the proceedings began at the parish house of Tanza on March 23, "no one was missing except for one or two among those who attended the meeting at Tejeros" ("walamang kulang, maliban sa isa o' dalawa, ang tanang nagsipagpulong sa Tejeros"). His account refers at several points to the large size of the gathering. "Every corner of the large parish house was packed tightly with people. No one could drop a needle" ("Siksik na siksik ang lahat nang sulok ng malaking convento. Walang hulugang karayom"). It tells us, too, that the participants included a huge delegation of Batangueños under the leadership of Santiago Rillo and that, as on the previous day, the Batangueños were extremely enthusiastic about the governmental reorganization. So it was then that, when Emilio Aguinaldo arrived at the meeting to take his oath of office, Rillo greeted him warmly and pledged his support. When Aguinaldo wavered about accepting the presidency because of the opposition of Mariano Alvarez and others, Rillo implored him to take the job. And, when Aguinaldo finally agreed, Rillo stood up, faced the Batangueño delegation, and cried: "People, we have a Leader! That's why I can now hold my head high, Batangueños; it is no longer bowed" ("Bayan, may isang Puno kana! Kaya ngayo'y taas na ang noo ko, mga batangueño, at hindi na yuko").[35]

Thus, in the intermediate aftermath of the Tejeros assembly, whether or not irregularities had occurred, the principal decisions made at that meeting—the reorganization of the revolutionary government and the elevation of Aguinaldo to the presidency—seemed to have considerable support. The Magdalo group was doubtless pleased that Aguinaldo was now in charge. Some members of the Magdiwang organization were satisfied that ranking positions in the government had gone to Ricarte, Trias, and Riego de Dios. Above all, non-Caviteños like Rillo and the members of his delegation from Batangas could take satisfaction in the fact that a union of the revolutionaries in Cavite had at last been effected. For all intents and purposes, Bonifacio's leadership of the revolutionary movement had ended.

Finding 5. It is unlikely that, when the Tanza meeting was dissolved, Emilio Aguinaldo and the other delegates who had met there decided to announce that they had nullified everything they had done.

One of the most intriguing details in Ricarte's account of the Tejeros meeting and its aftermath—and one of the few that historians tend to ignore—is his assertion that at the conclusion of the meeting the delegates agreed to announce that they had voided their decisions "since they believed that in this manner they would check the angry feelings against them that were felt by many" ("sa pag-aakalang sa paraang ito'y masasawata ang mainit na simbuyong laban sa kanila'y naghahari sa loob ng marami"). That is a stunning claim, for it seems to imply that Aguinaldo and his supporters had decided not to insist that the verdict of Tejeros be respected. If that was so, then the Philippine "republic" had ceased to exist, Aguinaldo was no longer the president, and Bonifacio, as leader of the Katipunan, was once again the leading figure in the revolutionary movement. Furthermore, Bonifacio's refusal to acknowledge Aguinaldo's authority in the weeks following the Tejeros and Tanza meetings was anything but treasonous, and many of the charges made against him in his subsequent trial were without foundation. For, if Bonifacio was still the leader of the revolutionary movement, the people who should have been brought to trial for treasonous conduct were Aguinaldo and his followers.

Common sense alone should tell us that there is more to this story. Ricarte's description of the meetings at Tejeros and Tanza has been shown to be unreliable. Furthermore, given the strong likelihood that Bonifacio did not have widespread support at this stage in the proceedings, why would Aguinaldo and his followers have decided to undo the results that so many of their fellow revolutionaries evidently found satisfactory?

It is not surprising, therefore, that other evidence tells us that the delegates at Tanza did not nullify the verdict of Tejeros. In his memoir, Aguinaldo wrote that, at noon on March 24, he received the news at Tanza that on the previous day members of the Magdiwang organization had passed a resolution (the Acta de Tejeros?) declaring the Tejeros meeting null and void. His response, he stated, was simply to ignore the resolution. He decided not to prosecute Bonifacio at this point, since he did not want to create further ill feeling. But that was the limit of his conciliatory conduct; he did not agree to give up his office or overturn the decisions of the previous days.[36]

True, if Aguinaldo and his followers had done what Ricarte claimed, Aguinaldo would have been unlikely to admit it in his memoirs, since to do so would have raised the embarrassing issue of whether, in the following month, he actually had the authority to bring Bonifacio to trial. So, by itself, Aguinaldo's account is not convincing. But Santiago Alvarez, who was one of Bonifacio's strongest supporters, provided a similar discussion of the events. Referring to the Tanza gathering, he wrote:

> The following morning, . . . even though many refused to admit the fact that a meeting was held at said Parish House, there were also many people who had spied [on that meeting] and who confirmed that the decisions of the Leader of the Assembly, Supremo A. Bonifacio, regarding the election at the estate house of Tejeros, San Francisco de Malabon, were not respected.
>
> (At kinabukasan ng umaga, . . . bagaman itinanggi ng marami ang katotohanan ng pulong na ginanap sa nabanggit na Kumbento, ay marami naman ang nanubok na nagpatutoo na di iginalang ang naging kapasyahan ng Pangulo ng Pulong, Supremo A. Bonifacio, tungkol sa ipinasya nito sa kinawian ng Paghahalalan na idinaos sa bahay asyenda ng Teheros, S. F. de Malabon.)[37]

In addition, it is worth noting that no other memoirist mentioned a decision by Aguinaldo's camp to nullify the decisions made at Tejeros and Tanza. If that had actually occurred, Canseco, who was keenly interested in developments within the revolutionary camp, might have been expected to comment on it. He was silent on the matter.[38]

All of this leads me to conclude that, on this particular point as on so many others, Ricarte's account is probably incorrect. Having won the presidency, by fair means or foul, at Tejeros, having taken his oath at Tanza, and still enjoying the strong support of a large number of revolutionary leaders, Aguinaldo would not have been the least bit inclined to undo what had been done. Bonifacio was unhappy, but that was to be expected: electoral contests in the Philippines invariably led to bad feelings. If things had gone differently, members of the Magdalo organization might well have been the ones complaining about the result. But they had not, Aguinaldo was president, and there was no good reason to make concessions to Bonifacio.

IV

Over the years, a highly distorted picture of the Tejeros assembly has been produced by historians of the revolutionary period. One cause of the distortions has been the excessive reliance of scholars on the narrative of Artemio Ricarte—an account that, as this chapter has shown, is not an accurate representation of historical reality. But the mere existence of Ricarte's text—as well as its accessibility—cannot alone explain the prominent place it has assumed in the footnotes of scholars. In some measure, Ricarte's version of events has also been accepted so readily because it, like most of the other problematic texts that have contributed to the Bonifacio myth, has had particular appeal to nationalist historians, who have been inclined to view the nation's heroes in a favorable light. By sanitizing the past in the way he did— by removing all references to his own role in Bonifacio's fall from power and, in the process, all references to the tawdry details of Philippine electoral politics—Ricarte provided a description of Tejeros that fit neatly into the interpretive framework of nationalist historiography.

The result has been the creation of a mythical Tejeros assembly. To believe Ricarte's narrative—and the historians' accounts that are based on it—we must accept the notion that local political influentials like Baldomero Aguinaldo, Mariano, Santiago, and Pascual Alvarez, Mariano Trias, Artemio Ricarte, Emiliano Riego de Dios, Santiago Rillo, and many others who attended the Tejeros meeting suddenly, and for no apparent reason, began to conduct themselves in an uncharacteristic way: that is, we must accept the notion that they refrained from electoral politicking, arm twisting, and dirty tricks. In reality, those founding fathers did some, if not all, of the above. In reality, the Tejeros meeting more closely resembled a typical Philippine election than a constitutional convention. In reality, Artemio Ricarte, the national hero who was primarily responsible for the creation of the myth, was a dissembler. He may even have been a plotter.

If there is a lesson to be learned from this reexamination of the Tejeros assembly, it is that the best-known, most readily available primary accounts may at once decisively shape our view of an event and serve as barriers to our understanding of it. The most unfortunate thing about Ricarte's version of the Tejeros meeting is that the sanitizing process has removed not only all traces of the author's complicity but almost all indications of the true character of the events being described. For too many years, readers of Ricarte's narrative—and of historians' accounts based on it—have been obliged to suspend belief, to accept the notion that the astute Filipino political operatives who assembled at Tejeros did not act like astute Filipino political operatives. Isn't it time for the history books to provide a credible account of that seminal event?

Rally by Federation of Free Farmers at Liwasang Bonifacio, August 2, 1971.

CHAPTER FOUR

Agoncillo's Bonifacio

The historian Teodoro Agoncillo has been mentioned on numerous occasions in the preceding pages, and it is understandable why that it is so. Author of the famous book *The Revolt of the Masses: The Story of Bonifacio and the Katipunan* and editor of the only published collection of Bonifacio's writings, Agoncillo was long considered the foremost academic authority on the national hero and, indeed, on the entire revolutionary period. Thus far, I have expressed several concerns about Agoncillo's scholarship—about his heavy reliance on the publications of the mythmakers (Artigas, de los Santos, and Santos) in crafting his own account of the early Bonifacio; his use of Santos's doctored transcriptions of Bonifacio's letters; his statements implying that he had consulted original texts when he had not; and his unjustified faith in Ricarte's narrative of the Tejeros assembly. But, while none of those criticisms should be seen as quibbles, they do not necessarily call into question the larger picture of the Philippine national hero presented in Agoncillo's books. The present chapter looks closely at that picture.

Specifically, it focuses on *The Revolt of the Masses*, a book that has influenced our view of Bonifacio more than any other. Based on both documentary evidence and interviews with his contemporaries, it contains not only the fullest account ever written of Bonifacio's role in the revolution of 1896 but the first detailed study of the national hero's personality. For more than a generation, historians have cited Agoncillo's data, repeated his arguments, and adopted his conclusions, although it is worth noting that by the mid-1970s a few of them—Renato Constantino, Milagros Guerrero, and Reynaldo Ileto—had raised doubts about certain aspects of his study.[1] To a great extent, the historical Bonifacio one finds in the scholarly literature is the Bonifacio depicted in Agoncillo's book.

Actually, Agoncillo created two Andres Bonifacios in *The Revolt of the Masses*. One is the heroic Bonifacio of the Manila underground, the humble, quiet, honorable supremo of the Katipunan who commanded respect. The other is the demon of the Cavite battleground, a man who seemingly underwent a psychological change in late 1896 once he left the city for the countryside. Whereas the first Bonifacio was calm and even tempered, the second was hotheaded; whereas the first was widely admired, the second alienated his followers. But, as I show in this chapter, Agoncillo's reconstruction of Bonifacio's personality, which relied on questionable data derived from his interviews with the supremo's contemporaries, is seriously flawed. There was no mysterious personality change; rather, the bizarre duality was invented by Agoncillo for personal and political reasons. My aim here is not to discredit Agoncillo, for I believe that he made major contributions to Philippine historiography. But, if we are ever to understand Andres Bonifacio and the revolution he led, we must first jettison prevailing views of the man's personality—views influenced in large measure by the historical writings of Teodoro Agoncillo.

I

Born in 1912 in Lemery, Batangas, Agoncillo received both his B.A. (1934) and M.A. (1935) from the University of the Philippines. For many years, his field of specialization was Tagalog language and literature. Agoncillo served as head of the Division of Research and Translation at the Institute of National Language, and he also taught Tagalog literature at Far Eastern University and Manuel L. Quezon University. But, as time passed, it became apparent that Agoncillo's true calling was as a historian. In 1956, he published *The Revolt of the Masses* and overnight gained an enormous amount of attention. Two years later, he joined the History Department of the University of the Philippines, remaining there until his retirement in 1977.

Agoncillo served as department chair from 1963 to 1969 and, in his final year of teaching, held the Rafael Palma professorial chair in Philippine history.[2]

Considered by many to be the leading historian of the Philippines in the twentieth century, Agoncillo was extremely productive. In addition to several surveys of Philippine history and his seminal book on Bonifacio, he wrote mammoth research monographs on the Philippine-American War and the Japanese occupation of the Philippines in World War II, a somewhat shorter book on collaboration during World War II, and numerous articles. He edited several books, including a volume of documents related to Filipino nationalism and the aforementioned collections of Bonifacio's writings and Epifanio de los Santos's articles.[3] Agoncillo was also controversial. An outspoken nationalist, he was critical of both colonial rule and colonial historiography. His writings had a Marxist tinge, featuring a certain amount of class analysis.[4] But his was a Marxism of a decidedly soft-core variety. Agoncillo's discussion of class formation and conflict was impressionistic at best, and his assertions about the attitudes of lower-class actors were rarely supported by hard evidence.[5]

As we know, the book that launched Agoncillo's career as a historian, *The Revolt of the Masses*, was originally submitted as an entry in a Bonifacio biography contest. But Agoncillo's study was not, as the author himself acknowledged in the introduction to the published volume, a complete biography of Bonifacio, primarily because the documentary record concerning his life was so limited. Instead of writing a classic life and times, therefore, Agoncillo was obliged to produce something closer to a times and life. In some chapters, Bonifacio figured prominently, but in many the reader's attention was directed to other actors about whom more was known, or to the Katipunan, or to the course of the revolution itself. The thread connecting all the included episodes was, of course, Bonifacio—which is to say, all of them were included because of their relevance to his life—but, given the limitations of the sources, Agoncillo was often unable to tell us much about his actions and thoughts during crucial periods of his life.

Let us turn to the content of the book. According to Agoncillo— who based some of his key claims on information provided by Artigas, de los Santos, and Santos—Andres Bonifacio was, at bottom, a man of the people: an individual of humble origins (65), limited intellectual attainments (283), and "rugged simplicity" (284). Lacking wealth and connections, he rose to prominence thanks to his common sense (284, 287) and ability to motivate his followers (91–95, 284–85). Bonifacio had other winning personal characteristics: he was "calm and composed" (73), "persevering and humble" (74), "tolerant and broadminded" (75), "patient" (286), and "tight-lipped and usually given to meditation" (286).

Agoncillo saw Bonifacio's role in the development of the Katipunan as crucial. The secret society was, he wrote, "the idea of the plebeian Andres Bonifacio" (45). As leader of the society, Bonifacio directed his appeal to the common people (91), and as time passed more and more of them joined its ranks (91, 94–97, 284). Agoncillo also maintained that, by and large, "middle class" Filipinos were unsympathetic to the revolutionary objectives of the Katipunan. Jose Rizal—the leading figure in the Propaganda Movement—advised the katipuneros not to launch an uprising against the Spaniards because they were short of weapons, and other men of means joined the revolutionary ranks only after the uprising had begun and then attempted to wrest control of the revolutionary government out of the hands of the original leadership (98–127).

Agoncillo divided Bonifacio's career as a revolutionary into two distinct periods. In the first, lasting from the founding of the Katipunan in 1892 up to (and slightly beyond) the outbreak of the revolution in August 1896, Bonifacio was successful. He led the Katipunan effectively, inspired his followers, attracted new members, and acted decisively in times of crisis. In the second, from late 1896 until his death in May 1897, Bonifacio's record was much less impressive. After arriving in the province of Cavite in December 1896, he became embroiled in a series of disputes with members of the Magdalo organization. Gradually his support began to dissipate, and at Tejeros in March 1897 he was replaced as leader of the revolutionary movement (203–16). In the following weeks, Bonifacio refused to recognize the authority of Aguinaldo's new government and conspired to undermine it. Aguinaldo, convinced that Bonifacio represented a threat, ordered his arrest (217–42). A trial was held, the court found Bonifacio guilty of subversion and other crimes, and he was sentenced to death. Aguinaldo initially intended to commute the sentence to exile, but a number of revolutionary leaders prevailed on him to do away with Bonifacio. The pardon was withdrawn, and in May 1897 Bonifacio was executed (242–75).

Here, then, is Agoncillo's Bonifacio—a basically good man, an effective organizer, and a charismatic leader in the period leading up to the revolution; a difficult, intolerant, hypersensitive, politically inept, subversive character in the final months of his life. How can the apparent transformation be explained? One significant cause, in Agoncillo's view, was changing surroundings. Bonifacio's successes had occurred in Manila, his birthplace. Once he entered the unfamiliar province of Cavite, he lacked a solid base of support—with the exception of the Alvarez family of Noveleta, which was related to Bonifacio's wife, Gregoria de Jesus. He also failed to understand provincial realities. When, therefore, he sided with one provincial group, the Sangguniang Magdiwang (which was also, incidentally, the organization headed by Mariano Alvarez, his wife's uncle), at the expense of the Magdalo, his popularity began to wane. According to Agoncillo, once it became clear that the revolutionaries in Cavite would not accept his authority without question, Bonifacio seemed to undergo a personality change: "From here on, Bonifacio's personality suffered modifications that were in direct contrast to the character that had made him the unchallenged organizer and leader of the early Katipunan" (293; also see 308 and 310).

One striking characteristic of Agoncillo's version of events is that on balance it is extremely favorable to Emilio Aguinaldo, Bonifacio's principal rival. On the battlefield, Aguinaldo was brave and decisive (172–86). A modest man, he was reluctant to assume the presidency of the revolutionary government (205, 219). An admirer of Bonifacio, he sought to work out an accommodation with the former supremo in the period following the Tejeros assembly and adopted a harder line only after he became convinced that Bonifacio's conduct was traitorous (226–35). Whereas Agoncillo criticized the actions of some of Aguinaldo's followers—for example, the officials involved in Bonifacio's trial who did not give the accused a fair hearing (310)—he did not reproach Aguinaldo himself. As we shall see, Agoncillo may have had personal as well as political reasons for dealing with Aguinaldo so favorably.

II

In writing his account of Bonifacio, the Katipunan, and the revolution of 1896, Agoncillo had to wrestle with a problem I have alluded to repeatedly—the meager number of sources relating to Andres Bonifacio's life. A perusal of Agoncillo's footnotes tells us that, in addition to the probably forged Bonifacio letters and the assorted writings attributed to the supremo that cannot be shown to have been composed by him, Agoncillo relied heavily on the "minutes" of the Katipunan, a document written in code and filled with so many factual inaccuracies that former katipuneros doubted its authenticity;[6] several memoirs, in particular, those written by Pio Valenzuela and Artemio Ricarte (both very unreliable former katipuneros), Gregoria de Jesus (Bonifacio's widow), and Pantaleon Garcia and Francisco Carreon (soldiers in the Filipino Army); the testimony given by a few katipuneros (especially Jose Dizon, Domingo Franco, and Pio Valenzuela) to the Spanish authorities shortly after the outbreak of the revolution; the documentary record of Bonifacio's trial; and interviews with about half a dozen men and women who either participated in or observed the events described in the book—among them Emilio Aguinaldo,[7] Pio Valenzuela, Marina Dizon (the secretary of the women's chapter of the Katipunan), and Guillermo Masangkay (who described himself as Bonifacio's neighbor).

Significantly, Agoncillo did not use—probably because he lacked the time and resources to do so—the so-called Philippine Insurgent Records, the mammoth collection of documents confiscated by the U.S. Army during the Philippine-American War, which included files of Philippine records relating to the earlier revolution against Spain.[8] Nor did he examine the records of the religious orders in the Philippines (which would have been difficult to access but were not entirely inaccessible), the collections of the Philippine National Archives (which may have been unavailable to researchers at the time), or any records in Spain. Nor did he cite the memoirs of the leading revolutionary Santiago Alvarez, which had been published several decades earlier in the magazine *Sampagita*. Thus, while Agoncillo uncovered a number of new sources, his research was far from exhaustive.

In addition to having relatively few sources at his disposal, Agoncillo faced another problem, one that confronts all historians who write about the revolutionary period—the flawed nature of those sources. As we have seen, the memoirs were filled with factual errors, and most also bore distinct traces of bias, since the writers were themselves participants in controversial events. Other documents were no less troublesome. The aforementioned "minutes" were of dubious value. The testimony of katipuneros to the Spaniards was evidently extracted by force (321, 324, 327) and could not be accepted at face value. The record of Bonifacio's trial included many statements about the former supremo's wrongdoings, but most of them came from supporters of his enemies. The interviews were clearly just as problematic, although Agoncillo expressed no concerns about their deficiencies. All were conducted in the late 1940s, half a century after the events, and it might reasonably have been expected that they would include mistakes on points of detail as well as conscious distortions on touchy issues.

Agoncillo was aware of the questionable nature of many of his sources, and the lengthy endnotes in his book (56 pages in all, following a text of 312 pages) tell us about his efforts to assess their usefulness. Often faced with conflicting accounts of events, he had to decide which version to believe. On more than a few occasions, the only available evidence was a document tainted by bias or factual error, and he had to determine how much weight to place on it. From Agoncillo's notes, one can learn a great deal about his mind as well as his methods, and it is necessary at this point to focus on them.

It should be emphasized that we are able to examine Agoncillo's use of sources so closely only because he was an extraordinarily revealing scholar. Rarely does a historian devote as much space as Agoncillo did to a discussion of the evidence. Most of the time, footnotes or endnotes in historical studies merely indicate the documents that authors rely on in arriving at their conclusions; they rarely tell us anything about the historical value of the evidence, the biases of the people who produced it, or the author's reasons for accepting one account of events rather than another. It would be unfair, then, to conclude from the analysis that follows that Agoncillo's methods were more deficient than those of most other historians. The simple truth is that, since most historians are much less informative than Agoncillo about their use of sources, their scholarly deficiencies cannot be so easily demonstrated.

Still, it is clear that Agoncillo's methods, as revealed in his notes, were downright strange. While he often made insightful comments about the reliability of documentary evidence, his assessments of the sources were even more frequently marked (and marred) by inconsistencies, lapses in logic, and unwarranted assumptions. At one point, Agoncillo might dismiss a particular source as untrustworthy, and at another he might cite the same one as hard proof. Furthermore, while he manifested a healthy skepticism toward written evidence, he relied without question on the interviews he conducted, even though his interviewees were far from unimpeachable—and even though the documents he consulted often contradicted data derived from the interviews. In fact, whenever an interviewee and a document presented conflicting versions of events, Agoncillo accepted the one found in the oral source. These are significant methodological deficiencies, to be sure, and ones that could have been expected to skew the book's findings. Let us first look at the author's methods in some detail. Then let us attempt to explain, albeit somewhat speculatively, Agoncillo's reasons for doing what he did.

Two concrete examples provide some insight into Agoncillo's approach to his sources. In the fourth chapter of *The Revolt of the Masses*, we learn that the Katipunan was founded on July 7, 1892, at 72 Azcarraga Street in Manila (43). That statement is supported by a note (320), which informs us that in reality the evidence on the matter is somewhat ambiguous. In a letter to Jose P. Santos, Ladislao Diwa, a charter member of the Katipunan, asserted that the founding occurred on July 6, 1892, at 734 Elcano Street.[9] Agoncillo believed that Diwa was mistaken about the date and place. The meeting was called, as Diwa himself pointed out in his letter to Santos, as a direct result of Jose Rizal's arrest. Rizal was arrested on July 6, but "nobody, except perhaps the immediate members of the family, knew of Rizal's 'arrest' on July 6 and certainly, the event could not have been known to the bulk of the population on that day." On the other hand, a decree announcing Rizal's deportation was published in the *Gaceta de Manila* on July 7, 1892, and that public announcement "must have induced Andres Bonifacio and his men to meet at once on the very night that the decree became known." Agoncillo opined that Diwa was "confused in his dates as his testimony was given about thirty years after the event." Discounting Diwa's account, Agoncillo based his conclusion about the date on the statements of Jose Dizon and Pio Valenzuela, both katipuneros, who discussed the founding in their testimony to the Spaniards in late 1896.

Was Agoncillo justified in challenging Diwa's account? How did he know for sure that word about Rizal's arrest would not have spread quickly to an associate like Bonifacio, who himself might have been a candidate for arrest? And why was he inclined to believe Dizon and Valenzuela rather than Diwa? In the next paragraph of the note, Agoncillo pointed out that Dizon, the presumably more believable source, was actually wrong about the place at which the meeting occurred. Dizon claimed that the founders met at a house on Ilaya Street in Manila, whereas a "majority of the Katipuneros" (whom Agoncillo credited on this point) contended that the correct location was a house on Azcarraga Street. Furthermore, in a subsequent note (320), Agoncillo raised troubling questions about the validity of the testimony of both Dizon and Valenzuela. Discussing an interview he conducted with Valenzuela in 1947, Agoncillo wrote:

> The Doctor emphasized that many of his statements before the Spanish authorities were not true. Asked why it was so, he answered that he had to save his life. Moreover, the statements were extracted from him by force. The reader is hereby warned that in consulting Retana's *Documentos Políticos*, [the source in which the testimony of the katipuneros appeared,][10] care should be taken not to give weight to some statements contained therein. *As to which statements should be taken seriously and which to be taken with more than a grain of salt depends on the critical faculty of the reader.* [Emphasis added.]

In light of Agoncillo's own skepticism concerning this source, we can only wonder why, on this occasion, his "critical faculty" told him to give more credence to the testimony of Dizon and Valenzuela than to that of Diwa.

The second example relates to the "minutes" of the Katipunan. Here Agoncillo was dealing with a document about which profound doubts had long existed. Purchased by the Philippine National Library in 1927 from David Cortes, the son of a deceased katipunero, the minutes had been declared spurious by a number of surviving members of the secret society. They pointed out that the code found in the minutes was different from the one usually used by the society, that Bonifacio's signature on the document was not genuine, and that it contained numerous incorrect or fictitious details.[11]

Agoncillo, however, believed that the minutes had historical value, and in a lengthy note (323–24), he attempted to justify his reliance on them. He claimed, first of all, that the katipuneros who questioned the document's authenticity were mistaken about the code: in fact, the code used in the minutes was a new one, adopted in 1896 by Bonifacio and his trusted lieutenant Emilio Jacinto, and it was consequently unknown to most katipuneros. As for the forged signature of Bonifacio, Agoncillo speculated that the actual signer was Jacinto, who (he again speculated) transcribed the minutes into the new code. As for the fictitious details, Agoncillo maintained that they were included in order to broaden the base of the Katipunan. Pointing to passages in the minutes about large financial contributions by wealthy Filipinos to the secret society, he argued that these were written to "persuade the wealthy and the middle-class intellectuals to side with the *Katipunan*, by showing them that So-and-So had already contributed to the organization for the purpose of buying arms. It was a trick to persuade the lukewarm Filipinos to subscribe to the aims and purposes of the Katipunan." Agoncillo concluded:

> First, that the so-called Pinagtatalunang Akta [Controversial Minutes] is genuine in so far as the code in which it was written is concerned. Second, that some of the contents of the minutes were purposely exaggerated to make it appear, for the benefit of the doubting and reluctant wealthy Filipinos, that the *Katipunan* was being financed by some wealthy Filipinos. And third, *there is no doubt that where a document has no element of exaggeration, it is genuine and the events narrated therein actually took place.* [Emphasis added.]

With the possible exception of the first point, Agoncillo's arguments are unconvincing. His discussion of Bonifacio's signature is obviously conjectural, and his explanation of the factual errors in the document seems illogical. If the details about the financial contributions of the well-to-do were intended to gain further support, why were they included in a document not intended for public reading and written in a code that only Bonifacio and Jacinto could understand?

A few pages later, Agoncillo returned to the question of the minutes' historical value, and again he decided in their favor (327). He also produced corroborating evidence, pointing out that, in an interview he conducted with Pio Valenzuela in October 1947, the former katipunero had confirmed certain details found in the minutes. "Some of the documents in the Akta are reliable," he wrote. "But care should be taken in referring to them."

One point worth noting is that, in his analysis of the minutes, as with his discussion of the founding of the Katipunan, Agoncillo showed an inclination to discount the evidential value of certain after the fact testimony. In the present example, the evidence discounted was the skeptical statements of surviving katipuneros about the minutes; in the earlier one, it was Ladislao Diwa's letter to Jose P. Santos, probably written about 1930.[12] And let us remember Agoncillo's words about that letter: "It is not improbable that Diwa was confused in his dates as his testimony was given about thirty years after the events" (320). But, if Diwa and the other katipuneros were deemed to be unreliable, why was Agoncillo so willing to believe Dr. Valenzuela, whom he interviewed more than fifty years after the events described? One cannot escape the conclusion that, in these instances as in many others, Agoncillo's standards for assessing the reliability of sources were shifting and seemingly arbitrary. Why was one admittedly problematic written source trustworthy on one point of detail but not on another? Why was one long after the fact statement reliable and another unreliable? The answer to those questions was provided by Agoncillo himself in the passage italicized above: "As to which statements should be taken seriously and which to be taken with more than a grain of salt depends on the critical faculty of the reader."

I do not mean to suggest here that Agoncillo was the only historian who ever used "shifting and seemingly arbitrary" standards in assessing the sources at his disposal. His judgment was not uniquely flawed. Indeed, if the works of most historians were subjected to sufficient scrutiny, instances of equally questionable judgment would doubtless be exposed. But there is, as I have indicated, one important difference between Agoncillo and the rest: he, unlike the others, provided his readers with much hard evidence about his standards.

III

Thus far, I have focused on Agoncillo's documentation of particularities—the date and place of a meeting, the code of the Katipunan. But Agoncillo's peculiar treatment of sources affected not only his recounting of minor details but the basic thesis of his book—his argument that Bonifacio underwent a personality change after his arrival in Cavite in late 1896.

As we saw in chapter 1, Agoncillo's account of Bonifacio's early years—like all other accounts of that phase of the national hero's life—depended heavily on the writings of Artigas, de los Santos, and Santos, three authors who did not indicate where they derived the bulk of their information. But, in addition, he cited frequently the memoirs of Gregoria de Jesus, the memoirs and testimony of Pio Valenzuela, and three interviews Agoncillo conducted in 1947 with Bonifacio's contemporaries—Valenzuela, Marina Dizon, and Guillermo Masangkay. So, for example, on the question of Bonifacio's intelligence, he quoted Valenzuela's sometimes dubious testimony of 1896: "He was astute and intelligent and spoke Tagalog fluently and those who did not know him would not think he was a *bodeguero* [warehouse employee]" (67, 328). And in describing Bonifacio's assumption of the presidency of the Katipunan he cited an interview with Valenzuela (71, 328–29).

Even more important, Agoncillo's discussion of the early Bonifacio's personality was shaped by the same sources. In an endnote documenting his assertion that Bonifacio was "always calm and composed" (73), he explained:

> In my separate interviews with Marina Dizon, Dr. Valenzuela and Guillermo Masangkay, I asked them what they knew of Bonifacio's personality, temper, etc. It was their unanimous opinion that Bonifacio was "calm and composed" and had never been seen in an angry mood. Marina Dizon confided to me: "Emilio Jacinto was more irascible and emotional than Bonifacio. The latter was quiet and tight-lipped." Jacinto was Marina Dizon's first cousin. (330)

Further evidence about Bonifacio's calmness came from an anecdote related to Agoncillo by Valenzuela in October 1947 (75, 331):

> At another time when Bonifacio and Daniel Tirona were in Dr. Valenzuela's house, the two exchanged opinions on the subject of revolution. Tirona became heated, though Bonifacio remained calm and showed no signs of excitement. Dr. Valenzuela, who was putting on his coat, approached Tirona and said: "I know, Don Daniel, that you are more educated than Don Andres, but when it comes to the history of revolutions, I think you have yet to read all the books that he has read on the subject before you can successfully defend your side." The discussion was immediately stopped. Tirona left a few minutes later.

In documenting his assertions about Bonifacio's humility and lack of interest in positions of authority (74–75), Agoncillo cited another anecdote by Valenzuela, this one derived from the doctor's then unpublished memoirs:

> Before the voting, Bonifacio worked for my election as President of the Supreme Council, but as soon as I learned of this I started working in his behalf, and I begged him not to work for me, explaining that it was not possible for me to be in Manila permanently as I had to go to the provinces. I pointed out that it would be better and more appropriate if he continued to be the President, and in fact it resulted that way. (330)

In other words, Agoncillo's description of the early Bonifacio's personality was derived almost exclusively from his long after the fact interviews with Bonifacio's contemporaries. And, in each case, Agoncillo appeared to accept the statements of those interviewees without the slightest reservation. In the fifty-six pages of notes in Agoncillo's book, which contain more than fifty citations of interviews, Agoncillo did not contradict, or even question, a single statement made by his interviewees. There is no suggestion that the passage of time might have dulled their recollections, no warning that their relationship with Bonifacio might have affected their memories of the man.

Once again, let us defer discussion about why Agoncillo might have adopted such an approach and focus on the consequences of his doing so. By seemingly operating on the assumption that his interviewees could be trusted—an assumption that, it should be reemphasized, he did not make about other sources—and by relying on them for such vital information, Agoncillo was adopting an interpretive stance that mirrored the point of view of his informants. Clearly, Valenzuela, Dizon, and Masangkay had favorable things to say about the early Bonifacio—the sort of things that one might expect to hear from people who were on close personal terms with the man, particularly when they were discussing him with a historian engaged in writing a biography about him. Like many friends and close acquaintances, they might have been inclined to, and probably did, exaggerate Bonifacio's virtues and understate his shortcomings. Their testimony on those matters was, therefore, far from conclusive evidence, but Agoncillo treated it as such.

Agoncillo's picture of the early Bonifacio is almost certainly too flattering. One source that tells us much about the supremo—and one that Agoncillo did not use in preparing his book—is the lengthy memoir by the katipunero Santiago Alvarez, published in the 1920s. Although Alvarez was a strong supporter of Bonifacio in the internecine struggles of 1896–97, one finds in his account a subtly shaded and by no means uniformly complimentary sketch of the early Bonifacio. Among other things, we learn that, even before his arrival in Cavite, Bonifacio manifested many of the same traits of personality that later led to his downfall: hypersensitivity, extreme irritability, and volatility.[13] Such evidence suggests, in other words, that Bonifacio's behavior in Cavite may not have been especially out of character.

Yet, even if we judge Agoncillo on the basis of the documents he actually consulted, his depiction of the early Bonifacio can be faulted. Consider, for one, the testimony of Valenzuela to the Spanish authorities—the source upon which Agoncillo relied in discussing Bonifacio's intelligence. Although Valenzuela did indeed say complimentary things about Bonifacio's intellectual powers, he was extremely critical of his personality, picturing him as easily offended and hotheaded. According to Valenzuela, when some of Bonifacio's fellow katipuneros refused to accept posts to which he had appointed them, the supremo became irate and threatened to "cut off the head" ("cortar la cabeza") of anyone who disobeyed him. When Bonifacio learned that Rizal was opposed to launching an armed revolt against Spain, he again became angry and poured insults on Rizal. At one meeting of the Katipunan's leadership, Bonifacio became enraged with the current head of the secret society, Deodato Arellano, calling him a coward. At another, he traded insults with Arellano's successor, Roman Basa.[14]

Of course, given the fact that Valenzuela was probably providing all this information under duress, we might reasonably wonder whether his unflattering picture of Bonifacio can be believed. Throughout his testimony, Valenzuela adamantly asserted that he was a most unenthusiastic member of the Katipunan; many of the things he did, he told the Spaniards, were done only because he was frightened of Bonifacio. It is possible, then, that the many details about Bonifacio's temper were included to support the notion that Valenzuela's fears were justified and to bolster his case for clemency. But, it is likewise possible that, for the same reasons, Valenzuela would have been inclined to exaggerate Bonifacio's intellectual powers as well. A clever man would have been a much more formidable opponent. In any event, what is striking about Agoncillo's use of Valenzuela's testimony is that, as was elsewhere the case, he treated evidence inconsistently. Parts of it were deemed valid and were mobilized to flesh out the story; parts were considered unreliable and were ignored. Significantly, the ignored data were those that called into question the author's central thesis.

Furthermore, even without the information furnished by Valenzuela, Agoncillo did have at his disposal an extensive body of evidence suggesting that Bonifacio was anything but calm, humble, tolerant, and patient—to wit, the sources he cited in the second half of his book relating to the *later* Bonifacio, the prima donna and subversive. Agoncillo might reasonably have been expected to wonder whether, in light of all that evidence, the early Bonifacio could really have been the model individual that Valenzuela, Dizon, and Masangkay claimed him to be. Rather than questioning the reliability of his informants, however, Agoncillo merely tried to reconcile the apparent contradictions by arguing that a change in surroundings had produced a personality transformation.

If Agoncillo was inclined to be sympathetic to the early Bonifacio, it was not at all evident in his treatment of the later man. In his view, the supremo became a divisive influence soon after his arrival in Cavite. He adopted an imperious air, showed favoritism toward one provincial "faction" (the Magdiwang) at the expense of the other (the Magdalo), attempted to annul the elections at Tejeros that resulted in Aguinaldo's elevation to the presidency of the revolutionary government, and subsequently refused to acknowledge Aguinaldo's authority.[15] As it happens, there is good reason to believe that Bonifacio contributed mightily to the divisions in the revolutionary ranks: various sources—including several not used by Agoncillo—tell us of the supremo's seemingly bizarre behavior during the last six months of his life.[16] That does not mean, however, that Agoncillo presented a fair picture of the later Bonifacio. For, if we again scrutinize the notes at the end of his book, it seems clear that, in telling the story of Bonifacio's downfall, Agoncillo continued to use his sources in questionable ways.

As before, Agoncillo placed inordinate faith in interviews—in this case, his interviews with Emilio Aguinaldo. In the 104 notes for the final six chapters of his book (which cover events from the outbreak of the revolution in Cavite through Bonifacio's execution), Agoncillo cited the interviews with Aguinaldo twenty-two times. The only source he cited more often (thirty-three times) was the memoirs of Ricarte. But, whereas Agoncillo found that Ricarte's version of events was "not always accurate and reliable" (ix; see also 356–57, 358–59, and 360–61), he voiced no concerns about Aguinaldo's.

> With the help of General Emilio Aguinaldo, who was very cooperative with me, I was able to throw light on hitherto obscure and highly controversial episodes, thereby correcting serious mistakes and misconceptions about some phases of the Revolution. (x)

Just as Agoncillo's discussion of the early Bonifacio mirrored the point of view of Valenzuela, Dizon, and Masangkay, his discussion of the later Bonifacio was decisively shaped by Aguinaldo, the supremo's principal antagonist.

Hence, Agoncillo's account of Bonifacio's arrival in Cavite in late 1896 was based entirely on an interview with Aguinaldo (203,

355). According to Agoncillo, when Aguinaldo and two other important revolutionaries from Cavite greeted Bonifacio at Zapote, "a misunderstanding arose between the *Magdalo* leaders and Bonifacio, for the former, rightly or wrongly, saw from Bonifacio's gestures and behavior that he regarded himself as superior and 'acted as if he were a king'" (203). He leaned on Aguinaldo again in his account of the opening of the Imus assembly, a meeting of revolutionary leaders that took place shortly thereafter, and again he presented Bonifacio in an unfavorable light.

> In the assembly hall, the two factions met and exchanged the usual greetings. Bonifacio entered, proceeded to the head of the table and unceremoniously occupied the chair. He beckoned to the *Magdiwang* Ministers to sit at his right side. This obvious partiality to the *Magdiwang* was resented by the *Magdalo*, for as Supreme Head of the *Katipunan* who was called upon to mediate between the two factions, Bonifacio was expected to show impartiality. (205, 356)

Even more instructive was Agoncillo's treatment of the aftermath of the Imus assembly. One source that touched on the subject was Ricarte's memoirs, and in his notes Agoncillo provided a loose translation of Ricarte's account: "Days later, when Bonifacio demanded the copy of all the minutes of the Assembly, the *Magdalo* men promised to send him a copy as soon as all the members present during the meeting had signed the minutes" (357). But Bonifacio never received the minutes, and Ricarte's obvious implication was that those Magdalo men were at fault.

Agoncillo was unwilling to believe Ricarte. He pointed out that Bonifacio and his supporters were in charge of the meeting, and that Bonifacio showed partiality toward the Magdiwang organization throughout the proceedings. "How, under the circumstances, could the *Magdalo* men have been responsible for the minutes when they were in fact ignored by the *Magdiwang* men, particularly by Bonifacio, who, as Supreme Head of the *Katipunan*, should have shown prudence in dealing with the members of both factions?" (357). It was at this juncture that Agoncillo made the highly critical comments about Ricarte's memoir quoted in chapter 4:

In studying Ricarte's memoirs of the Revolution I found several obviously unreliable statements that documents, discovered later on, belied. His strong personal prejudices, so apparent in his delineation of characters, are too pronounced to escape the attention of even a casual reader.

Agoncillo was obviously correct that there were major deficiencies in Ricarte's memoirs, but that did not mean that Ricarte was mistaken about the Imus assembly. The evidence on which Agoncillo based his critical assessment of Ricarte's account—the purported fact that Bonifacio and the Magdiwang controlled the meeting—was derived solely from his interview with Aguinaldo. Was it sensible to believe that Aguinaldo's statements were less tainted by prejudice than Ricarte's? Aguinaldo, too, had reasons to dissemble, and, besides, it seems likely that in discussing matters in the 1940s he would have been at least as shaky about details of the revolutionary period as was Ricarte, who wrote his memoirs in 1908 or 1909.

So, once again, Agoncillo had dismissed a written source on the basis of contradictory information provided by his own informant. Again, his narrative reflected the interpretive stance of that informant: he made no mention in the text of the incident relating to the minutes. By omitting it, he was conveying the impression that the Magdalo, Aguinaldo's organization, was less responsible than Bonifacio and the Magdiwang for the escalating tensions in the revolutionary ranks.

A close reading of the final chapters of Agoncillo's book reveals that the examples discussed above were typical. Time and again, he placed his faith in sources (usually, but not always, his interviews with Aguinaldo) that conveyed a favorable impression of the actions of Aguinaldo and his followers, and he discounted others indicating that the Magdalo men exacerbated the conflict. Time and again, he failed to do justice to the actions of Bonifacio and the Magdiwang.[17] This is not to say that Bonifacio and his followers were not partly responsible for the disunity in the ranks; it is merely to point out that Agoncillo's account consistently understated the contributions of Aguinaldo and the Magdalo. The second half of *The Revolt of the Masses* amounts to nothing more nor less than an apologia for Emilio Aguinaldo.

IV

If Agoncillo's book has such striking weaknesses, we need, I think, to examine why that is so. The preceding critique may seem to suggest that Agoncillo was simply a bad historian—or, at least, a much less able one than he was generally credited with being. But there are other possible explanations for the deficiencies of his study—one that points to extenuating circumstances and three that hint that Agoncillo may have had his own reasons for doing what he did.

One obvious explanation for the book's flaws is hasty composition. It should be recalled that *The Revolt of the Masses* was submitted as an entry to a biography competition and that Agoncillo was working under considerable time pressure. In an interview with Ambeth Ocampo, Agoncillo revealed that he wrote the book "at the spur of the moment" and that he had "no time to edit" the manuscript.[18] His endnotes indicate that he was still conducting interviews as late as October 1947, and we know from the book's introduction that the manuscript was completed by April 1948. No doubt some of the inconsistencies and lapses in logic would have been eliminated if Agoncillo had been able to work at a more leisurely pace. But time pressure cannot account for everything. It cannot, for example, explain Agoncillo's most distinctive methodological quirk—his seemingly unqualified faith in interviews.

Three other lines of explanation are wholly conjectural, but perhaps they merit a hearing. The first—let us call it the functionalist explanation—is that the book's deficiencies may have been due largely to the author's predisposition to reach certain conclusions. That is, Agoncillo may have had practical—in this case familial—reasons for writing the sort of book he did.

Recall that *The Revolt of the Masses* was written for a contest honoring Bonifacio's memory. Agoncillo may already have been inclined to pen good things about Bonifacio, but the contest doubtless gave him an added incentive to do so. At the same time, though, he had reasons to be sympathetic toward Aguinaldo—not only because Aguinaldo had granted him interviews but because he was related to Aguinaldo by marriage. In July 1930, Maria Agoncillo of Taal, one of Teodoro Agoncillo's relatives, had become Emilio Aguinaldo's second wife. Agoncillo would hardly have been disposed to write critical things about a famous member of the family, especially one who was still very much alive when the book appeared.[19] Seen in this light, then, Agoncillo's curious portrait of Bonifacio may have been less the product of flawed methodology than of a predisposition to praise Bonifacio without criticizing Aguinaldo.

The second—let us call it the cultural explanation—is that the book's deficiencies (in particular, Agoncillo's overriding faith in his interviewees) may have been, in a certain sense, culturally based. Although I do not claim that all or even many Filipino historians share the tendency, it seems possible that certain distinctively Filipino concepts about indebtedness and reciprocity—concepts such as *utang na loob* ("debt of gratitude") and *hiya* ("shame" or "embarrassment"), which have been discussed extensively in the social science literature—may predispose some of them to deal differently with the interviews they conduct than with other sources they consult. To call into question a written source or the conclusions of another historian is to engage in an intellectual exercise. To call into question the words of an interviewee, however, is to slight an individual who has done the scholar a favor. Agoncillo may have given more credence to his interviewees, therefore, because from his perspective it would have been unthinkable to do otherwise.

Having raised this possibility, let me emphasize that, like many conjectures, it may be wide of the mark. A few decades ago, there was a tendency on the part of historians of the Philippines to see many past actions by Filipino actors as being influenced by indigenous notions of indebtedness, reciprocity, and shame, and I must admit that I have not always found the line of analysis convincing. Hence, while I am *suggesting* that Filipino historians may be influenced by such notions as well, I make the suggestion somewhat gingerly. The explanation may fit the facts—that is, it may account for the major flaws in Agoncillo's book—but it may also be wrongheaded. Beyond that, it should be acknowledged that non-Filipino historians often seem to place inordinate faith in oral sources as well. Rather than being a manifestation of a cultural predisposition to avoid giving offense, Agoncillo's apparent trust in his interviewees may have been an example of a nearly universal human tendency to treat less skeptically information conveyed face to face.

One final possibility might be dubbed the nationalist explanation—and it is, I should point out, merely a modified version of the explanation offered earlier to account for the scholarly deficiencies of Artigas, de los Santos, and Santos.[20] We should remember that Agoncillo produced his book shortly after the Philippines had finally achieved independence from the United States and that a number of leading Filipino thinkers of the day were intent on declaring intellectual independence from their former colonial overlords. In that historical context, Philippine historians were particularly inclined to rethink and rewrite their country's past, and one event that would have been a likely candidate for rethinking was the revolution of 1896, a struggle that, while it had been honored by home-grown nationalists like Artigas, de los Santos, and Santos, had not always received favorable treatment from earlier clerical, reactionary, and American writers. Agoncillo's book might be seen, then, as an effort to valorize the revolution, rescue it as well as its heroes from the critics, and reiterate—and, to a certain extent, update—the celebratory message of earlier generations of Philippine nationalists. Perhaps, for that reason, it was important for Agoncillo to present the revolution of 1896 as a popular, mass movement, even though his evidence was not especially compelling. And perhaps, for that reason, Agoncillo attempted to valorize *all* of the heroes of the revolutionary struggle, even though his effort to do so resulted in hopeless contradictions. If, for the sake of argument, we assume that Agoncillo had such an agenda—to portray both Bonifacio and Aguinaldo as heroes—his seemingly incomprehensible use of sources suddenly appears to make a good deal of sense: Agoncillo may have settled on his methodology in order to achieve his nationalist objectives.

Yet, whatever the explanation, it is clear that Agoncillo's book is a very odd piece of scholarship. At some points it is a sympathetic portrait of Bonifacio and at others an apologia for his principal opponent. At all points, it is characterized by a problematic use of problematic sources. To be fair to Agoncillo, we should not discount the enormous difficulties posed by the latter. No historian writing about Bonifacio in 1947–48 was even vaguely aware of the untrustworthiness of so many key documents of the revolutionary period, and Agoncillo should not be faulted for being fooled by the inventions of previous writers. If fault there was, it was in privileging a particular genre of sources—his interviews—to fit his framework.

But, even though Agoncillo was not a mythmaker in the way that de los Santos and Santos appear to have been, nor a dissembler like Ricarte, and even though there is much difference between possibly fabricating information on the one hand and privileging certain sources on the other, the fact remains that Agoncillo played as important a role as the others did in creating the distorted image of Bonifacio we have before us today. However much credit we may give to Agoncillo for his lively prose, his narrative skills, and his combative comments about other scholars, we must recognize that at bottom *The Revolt of the Masses* is a misleading account of Andres Bonifacio. The Bonifacio depicted in that book is Teodoro Agoncillo's invention.

Having subjected Agoncillo's invented Bonifacio to scrutiny, I feel compelled, in conclusion, to address a question raised by my analysis: whether, given the problematic nature of the available sources, an uninvented Bonifacio is knowable. Although there is good reason to doubt that we will ever learn a great deal more about the early Bonifacio, that is not necessarily the case for the later man. True, the extant body of source material relating to Bonifacio's role in the Philippine Revolution is far from extensive; but, even so, we have at our disposal today considerably more documentation than Agoncillo used in preparing *The Revolt of the Masses*. For example, only a handful of historians have looked closely at the Philippine Insurgent Records or the holdings of the religious orders for information about the revolution.[21] Few have used the memoirs of Carlos Ronquillo. Moreover, better-known, frequently used sources (like Valenzuela's testimony and Alvarez's memoir) can, and should, be examined with fresh eyes.

    The difficulties confronting scholars who attempt to reconstruct the later Bonifacio should not be underestimated. They must come to terms with the manifest biases of memoirists. When the sources are in conflict, they must, like Agoncillo before them, determine which, if any, of the conflicting accounts to trust. But it is possible, by examining the full documentary record and using those sources judiciously, to present a fuller, more believable picture of Bonifacio the revolutionary than the one Agoncillo was able to produce. There is much more to be said about the manner in which he led the Katipunan, his approach to warfare, and the reasons for his conflict with the Magdalo men.

    I cannot say for sure what that reconstructed Andres Bonifacio will look like. I do not know if he will still qualify for inclusion in the ranks of national heroes. But there is one thing about which I am reasonably certain: when all the evidence is examined and weighed, there will be no reason to believe that Andres Bonifacio underwent a psychological transformation when he crossed the Cavite border. The Bonifacio who came into conflict with Aguinaldo in Cavite was the same man who earlier squabbled with fellow katipuneros in Manila.

Children playing at Bonifacio monument, Liwasang Bonifacio, Manila

(Credit: Jose Duran)

CHAPTER FIVE

Ileto's Bonifacio

While it is true that Manuel Artigas, Epifanio de los Santos, Jose P. Santos, and Teodoro Agoncillo were largely responsible for constructing the popular image of Andres Bonifacio, scholarly views of the national hero have been fundamentally *reshaped* in recent years by the work of another historian—a Philippine-born, Cornell-educated, Australia-based academic named Reynaldo Ileto, the author of a brilliant, provocative book entitled *Pasyon and Revolution: Popular Movements in the Philippines, 1840–1910*.[1] As the title of Ileto's monograph suggests, the principal subject of his inquiry is not Andres Bonifacio or the revolution of 1896. Out of 319 pages of text, only 47 of them are devoted to a discussion of Bonifacio and the Katipunan.[2] The rest deal with a range of millenarian movements in the Tagalog-speaking provinces of central Luzon, beginning with Apolinario de la Cruz's Cofradia de San Jose in the mid–nineteenth century and ending with the uprising of Felipe Salvador's Santa Iglesia in 1910. Even so, as any reader of the book eventually discovers, Ileto's most arresting findings relate to the revolution of 1896, and his treatment of both Bonifacio and the Katipunan is decidedly revisionist.[3]

It would be difficult to overestimate the impact that *Pasyon and Revolution* has had in academic circles, both inside and outside the Philippines. The book was the subject of perhaps the most heated debate in Philippine historical circles since World War II; it has gone through multiple reprintings; due in large measure to its influence on

U.S.-based Southeast Asianists, Ileto was awarded the prestigious Harry Benda Prize of the Association for Asian Studies, an honor conferred on young scholars who have made significant contributions to the field of Southeast Asian studies; and in recent years, despite the fact that he continues to teach in Australia, Ileto has been lionized by many Philippine historians.[4] But, while there can be no doubt that *Pasyon and Revolution* has many merits, it presents a view of Bonifacio that cannot be supported by reliable documentation.

I

Reynaldo Ileto (1946–) is a scholar of rare talent. Acutely perceptive, thoughtful, and highly imaginative, he is capable of finding something new and exciting to say about virtually any historical subject. Ileto's academic career began auspiciously. After compiling a strong record at the Jesuit-run Ateneo de Manila University, he went on to graduate study at Cornell University, long considered the leading center of Southeast Asian studies in the United States. Ileto entered Cornell's M.A. program in Southeast Asian studies in the late 1960s, at a time when the United States was deeply mired in the Vietnam conflict and prominent Cornell academics (George Kahin being perhaps the best known) were highly critical of U.S. involvement. Intellectually, those were exciting times at Cornell. The quality of graduate students in the program was extraordinarily high, and the competition was intense. But Ileto excelled, producing in 1970 (and soon thereafter publishing as a monograph) a valuable M.A. thesis on the late-nineteenth-century Muslim leader Datu Uto of Buayan.[5]

Ileto moved on to the Ph.D. program in Cornell's History Department. Throughout his doctoral work, his supervisor was Oliver W. Wolters, an accomplished scholar of early Southeast Asian history who had a knack for getting the most out of his students. But, as Wolters himself would freely admit, he was only one of several Southeast Asianists at Cornell who affected the way Ileto approached the study of the Philippine past. Just as influential were two specialists on Indonesia, James Siegel and Benedict Anderson. Although neither is a historian by training—Siegel is an anthropologist and Anderson a political scientist—both have written a good deal about the past, Siegel about Achenese religion and Anderson about the Indonesian revolution.[6] Even more important, both are talented explicators of Southeast Asian culture, producing books and articles that provide an informed understanding of Southeast Asian social, religious, and political phenomena. At the heart of their approach is a nuanced reading of a range of "texts," some literary and many not.[7] The operating assumption of both, an assumption they share with Siegel's mentor, Clifford Geertz, is that the key to understanding the Southeast Asian past and present is to recognize the fundamental importance of "culture"—that is, to be attuned to the cultural distinctiveness of the many societies found in the region, and, beyond that, to understand that in a myriad of important ways Southeast Asian perceptions, rituals, and practices are very different from those of the West. Both Anderson and Siegel had a profound impact on Ileto's scholarship. According to Ileto, still another influence was Cornell's Chinese historian Knight Biggerstaff, although it is difficult to see any connection between Biggerstaff's published work and Ileto's. Biggerstaff, reputed to be a great teacher and adviser of graduate students, most probably worked his magic on Ileto in the classroom and in interpersonal contacts. Ileto completed his doctoral dissertation—which he entitled *"Pasión* and the Interpretation of Change in Tagalog Society (ca. 1840–1912)"—in 1975; four years later, after making substantial revisions to the text, he published *Pasyon and Revolution*.

Ileto generously thanked all four of his Cornell mentors in the acknowledgments to *Pasyon and Revolution*, and his words are worth repeating.

> Benedict Anderson, Knight Biggerstaff, James Siegel, and Oliver Wolters made me realize that in order for one to fully understand his society, he must step out of it at some point in order to view it from a distance, before returning to its fold. Somehow, the study of such diverse topics as anthropology, modern Chinese history, Indonesian politics and Southeast Asian history always resulted in some new insights about *Inang Bayan*, some connections which would not have surfaced had I studied under less experienced and provocative professors.[8]

By his own account, then, Reynaldo Ileto is to some degree a product of a foreign intellectual environment, and in that regard he is a very different historian from Teodoro Agoncillo, Jose P. Santos, Epifanio de los Santos, and Manuel Artigas, none of whom had such an intense exposure to outside intellectual influences. Yet Ileto is also very different from the dozens of Philippine historians of his own era who received doctoral training in the United States, principally because he is so committed to the cultural approach championed by Siegel and Anderson. Unlike the others, he also has a strong grounding in Southeast Asian anthropology and political science. Furthermore, because his academic field of vision is not limited to the Philippine past, and also because he is so bright, Ileto was destined to have an impact beyond the field of Philippine history. *Pasyon and Revolution* is not merely an important contribution to an ongoing debate among Filipinists about the nature of Philippine popular movements; it is also a landmark work in the larger field of peasant studies.

What makes *Pasyon and Revolution* a great book is what it tells us about what might be called the "Tagalog peasant *weltanschauung*." Like many Southeast Asianists (and other academics interested in the so-called Third World) of the 1960s and 1970s, Ileto probed the mentality of the rural masses, the common men and women who had been relatively neglected by academic historians and who, to the extent that they had been studied, had typically been portrayed as irrational, ignorant, and otherwise "backward." He focused on the participants in millenarian movements, explicating their rituals, the writings of their leaders, and their actions. But in a sense his unstated, larger subject was the entirety of the rural Philippines. The "texts" generated by popular uprisings and popular movements—the rituals, writings, and actions he explicated—were the lenses he used to gain glimpses into the worldviews of the rural masses. Although his book is filled with details about a succession of rebellions, its real subject is the culture that generated them.

In the pages that follow, I will write some critical things about Ileto's treatment of both the Katipunan and Andres Bonifacio. He was demonstrably wrong about both and contributed significantly to the Bonifacio myth. But I want to make it clear that, those criticisms notwithstanding, I still believe that Ileto's book is superb. That is so precisely because its contributions to scholarship go far beyond what it tells us about the era of the Philippine Revolution. *Pasyon and*

Revolution may be the best book ever written about the mentality of common people in Southeast Asia.

II

The thesis of *Pasyon and Revolution* is that a wide variety of nineteenth- and early-twentieth-century popular movements in the Tagalog region, *including* the revolution of 1896, can only be understood by recognizing that they were deeply influenced by the common people's experience of Holy Week (the week before Easter). In particular, the *pasyon*—the epic of Christ's life that is chanted during Holy Week—provided Filipinos with a language for articulating their expectations, hopes, and values. Ileto maintained that, in thinking about their lives and the world around them, and even in thinking about revolution, common people used the language, images, and metaphors found in the pasyon. According to Ileto, the pasyon shaped the folk mind, and, "because of their familiarity with such images, the peasant masses were culturally prepared to enact analogous scenarios in real life in response to economic pressure and the appearance of charismatic leaders" (24).

Five important points need to be made at this juncture about Ileto's approach. The first is that Ileto was less interested in the events that transpired during the popular uprisings he studied than in the perceptions of those events by the common men and women who took part in them. That is to say, he wanted to know how those people conceptualized and understood what was happening around them. To do so, he looked at a wide range of sources, some of which might be classified as traditional (memoirs, bureaucratic records, newspaper accounts) and others of which would not (folk songs, poems, prayers), paying particular attention to evidence that was either composed by or directed at lower-class Filipinos, since those presumably would provide him with insights into how and what the masses thought. Historical actors like Bonifacio, Jacinto, and Ricarte were of interest to him not so much for what they did or thought but for what their writings conveyed about the perceptions and worldviews of the lower classes.

Second, Ileto made a strong case in his book that those lower classes thought very differently from Westernized, upper-class Filipinos. Whereas the latter were inclined to see the struggles against Spain and the United States as straightforward efforts to gain political autonomy, lower-class Filipinos, in Ileto's view, understood them in very different ways. His study explored at some length popular understandings of the Tagalog word *kalayaan,* which in our own day is usually translated into English as "freedom." But, according to Ileto, nineteenth-century peasants would have understood it to mean a condition of bliss, brotherhood, contentment, abundance, and equality. Hence, when charismatic and/or revolutionary leaders called on the masses to join their ranks and fight for kalayaan, those people would have interpreted the appeal as a call for a fundamental change in society, a leveling of a kind.

Third—and for our immediate purposes even more importantly—Ileto explicitly raised troubling questions about much that had earlier been written about the origins of the revolution of 1896. Before the appearance of *Pasyon and Revolution*, most historians of the revolutionary period, including Teodoro Agoncillo, had depicted the Katipunan as a kind of mutant offshoot of the Propaganda Movement. According to the then-standard account, the Propagandists, heavily influenced by European liberal ideas, agitated for reform. But, when the Spaniards proved reluctant to concede them, the torch was passed from the Propagandists to Bonifacio and the Katipunan. Now convinced that Spain would not undertake meaningful reforms, the members of that secret society aimed to win independence from Spain.

Even though this view of the revolutionary period was widely held, it left at least one important question unanswered. How did a presumably lower-class secret society issue from an upper-class reform movement? It will be recalled that Agoncillo described Bonifacio as plebeian and claimed that "none of [the Katipunan's] charter members were of the middle or aristocratic class." Renato Constantino, writing in the mid-1970s, situated Bonifacio and the other early katipuneros slightly higher on the socioeconomic ladder: "The original leadership of the Katipunan may be classified as lower-middle to middle-middle class." But he went on to assert, without supporting evidence, that their sympathies lay with the lower classes.

> Coming as they did from the lower echelons of the middle class, Bonifacio and his companions instinctively identified with the masses. Although the early leadership of the Katipunan was essentially middle class, many members of this class could be considered almost plebeian in social status, for in the evolving society of that time, class differentiation was not very marked in the lower levels. Thus it was possible for a bodeguero like Bonifacio or a book binder like Aguedo del Rosario or court clerks and other small employees like the others to feel an instinctive affinity for the workingmen in the cities and for the peasants in the countryside. It was therefore possible for this middle-class organization to become the triggering force that would galvanize the masses into action because it expressed the masses' own demands for freedom from Spanish colonialism and friar despotism.[9]

But none of this really accounts for the emergence of the Katipunan. Even if Agoncillo was right about the social composition of the Katipunan—and several scholars doubt that he was[10]—why would these people have been galvanized into action by the writings of the Propagandists? And, even if they were, why would their program—which, according to both Agoncillo and Constantino, differed from that of the Propagandists principally in its call for political independence—have appealed to the lower classes? Why was the establishment of an autonomous government of any compelling interest to them?

Ileto savaged the standard account. He essentially eliminated the Propaganda Movement from the history of the Philippine Revolution, linking Bonifacio and the Katipunan not to a reform program shaped by European liberal ideology but to a tradition of homegrown popular uprisings. In his view, the key to understanding the Philippine Revolution was to recognize that the Katipunan appealed to the preexisting, deeply rooted, distinctively Filipino, millenarian beliefs of the peasantry.

> In order to mobilize large numbers of Filipinos, the revolutionary Katipunan had to speak the common language of katipunans, tap the undercurrent of popular expectations and hopes, and channel the people's energies toward achieving independence from Spain. (101)

The fourth point follows directly from the third. If Ileto was correct that Bonifacio's revolution was not a mutant offshoot of a liberal reform campaign and that it should more properly be situated in the context of a Philippine millenarian tradition, then it follows that the uprising was a much less "Western" phenomenon than it had thus far been seen to be. In fact, before the appearance of *Pasyon and Revolution*, the Philippine Revolution had always been considered something of an anomaly in the history of Southeast Asia. At a time when the rest of the region was experiencing small-scale rural protest movements, often millenarian in character, the Philippines had seemingly witnessed a somewhat "modern" and "secular" revolution—one in which, if the standard version was to be believed, the masses fought for national independence. Ileto called all of this into question. By emphasizing the revolution's traditional character and deemphasizing the links to the Propaganda Movement, he placed it squarely in the mainstream of nineteenth-century Southeast Asian popular rebellions. Almost overnight, Andres Bonifacio was transformed from a revolutionary "plebeian" to the leader of a millenarian movement, a figure comparable not only with charismatic Filipino leaders like Apolinario de la Cruz and Felipe Salvador but with a Javanese like Prince Dipanagara and a Burmese like Hsaya San.[11]

Fifth, like Artigas, de los Santos, Santos, and Agoncillo before him—and like most other historians on the planet—Ileto appeared to have a political agenda. He briefly hinted at it in the second paragraph of the book.

> My choice of subject matter was determined by much the same conditions that led the Filipino youth to question the nature of their society during the late sixties and early seventies. Being home in 1971 doing research was most rewarding, not only because the libraries and archives offered interesting material, but also because people around me were asking similar questions about the relationship of the past to the present. (iii)

In other words, Ileto conceptualized his research project at a time of great ferment in the Philippines, when intellectuals on college campuses were protesting vehemently against the deficiencies of the country's leadership, the close relations between the Philippines and the

United States, and the exploitation of the nation's working classes, and were actively forging alliances with the urban and rural poor. In those times, a heated debate was also going on in leftist circles in the Philippines about the relevance of history. Presumably, Ileto believed that the study of the past could shed light on the issues of the present.

He explicitly made that point in the book's first chapter. Addressing himself to "modern Filipinos," he explained that his book attempted to provide them with a "set of conceptual tools, a grammar, that would help [them] to understand the world" of the indigenous lower classes. And then he discussed why such a grammar was needed.

> In the interest of social reform we can either further accelerate the demise of "backward" ways of thinking . . . in order to pave the way for the new, or we can graft modern ideas onto traditional modes of thought. Whatever our strategy may be, it is necessary that we first understand how the traditional mind operates, particularly in relation to questions of social change. (3)

Ileto's underlying objective was, therefore, the improvement of the lot of the downtrodden, and his chosen means of achieving that goal was to provide elite "modern" Filipinos who were interested in social change with some insight into the worldviews of the lower classes.[12]

Clearly, Ileto's agenda was very different from that of the nationalist historians I have discussed in earlier chapters. Artigas, de los Santos, and Santos, writing during the era of U.S. colonial rule, wanted to keep alive the ideal of national independence. Agoncillo, whose book on Bonifacio was composed when the Philippine Republic was in its infancy, aimed to instill a sense of national pride in its citizenry. Ileto, writing as the Marcos dictatorship was consolidating itself, was interested both in the promotion of nationalism and the rectification of social ills. His chief target was not the former colonial powers but the existing social structure. Like the others, he celebrated the struggles of the lower classes, but unlike them he sought social change in the present.

III

But is Ileto's analysis—in particular, his treatment of the Katipunan and Bonifacio—correct? Does he make a convincing case that the secret society and its supremo should be situated in the context of the Philippine millenarian tradition? In my view, he does not. To understand the deficiencies of his analysis, we must pay particular attention to two aspects of the book: Ileto's construction of his argument and the evidence he used.

Like anthropology and various other disciplines, history is at its core a discursive enterprise, one in which authorial strategies typically determine the conclusions reached. As Clifford Geertz has shown in *Works and Lives*, his thoughtful analysis of the literary products of four leading figures in the field of anthropology, all scholars, including great ones, adopt certain "text-building strategies," which are designed not only to establish (and to convince readers of) their "authority" but to make their substantive case.[13] In *Pasyon and Revolution*, Ileto adopted a text-building strategy that might best be described as discursive blurring—by which I mean that he constructed his text in such a way as to blur important distinctions and link things that should not necessarily be linked. The first major casualty of that strategy was the Katipunan, the secret society Bonifacio led.

The blurring begins in the first paragraph of the book's third chapter, which is devoted to an examination of the revolution of 1896. In that paragraph, Ileto made it clear to the reader that in discussing the revolution he was not inclined to restrict his focus to the battlefield encounters between the Spaniards and the military units commanded by Bonifacio, Aguinaldo, and other leaders of the Katipunan. In fact, he looked initially at the activities of a religious brotherhood known as the Colorum Society, an organization that had never been seen as playing a significant role in the Philippine Revolution or having any intimate connection with the Katipunan.[14]

According to Ileto, who derived most of his information about the Colorum Society from the memoirs of Santiago Alvarez, the brotherhood was drawn into the rebellion, sometime after the fighting spread from Manila to the countryside, by its pastor-prophet Sebastian Caneo. Caneo, who attracted a large following and was said to have miraculous powers, believed that "the Katipunan revolt against Spain was a sign of an approaching cataclysm that would bring about the fulfillment of the faithful's hopes" (94). One day, Caneo informed his assistants that he had communicated with the *Santong Boces* ("Holy Voice"), who told him that he should assemble his followers and march with them to the Spanish garrison at the town of Tayabas (in Tayabas Province). All of them were to wear a piece of rope around their waists. When Caneo's followers came close to the garrison, they would throw their ropes at the Spaniards who "would be miraculously tied up." The power of their prayers would be sufficient to overcome the enemy (94–95).[15]

Caneo's assistant, Juan Magdalo, dutifully carried out Caneo's orders, and eventually about five thousand people gathered at the foot of Mt. Banahaw, a sacred mountain and a center of Colorum activity. Magdalo told them that the Santong Boces had commanded them "to fight for the country's *kalayaan*, and that their strongest weapon would be prayer." He also explained how their ropes were to be used. Then, on the morning of June 24, 1897, "a huge procession of men, women, and children, all praying in unison and carrying lighted candles, entered the town of Tayabas." Some of the older people wore long white robes. In the middle of the procession was a platform "on which stood Juan Magdalo dressed in the attire of John the Baptist." As the people approached the garrison and reached for the ropes around their waists, the Guardia Civil began firing at them. All at once, "scores of men and women of all ages fell dead or wounded" (95). The remaining followers of Caneo fled in panic.[16]

Later, Caneo spoke to the Santong Boces about the fiasco, and he heard the following explanation: "They did not have enough faith and during the time of battle those who died or sustained wounds had failed to utter my name." When Caneo passed on the Santong Boces's words to the brothers, they appeared to be satisfied and returned to their devotions. According to Alvarez's account, they did not even feel "sadness and loss at the death of their brothers, spouses, children or parents" (95–96).[17]

That is a marvelously evocative story, one that appears to provide more than a little insight into the activities and worldviews of the members of the millenarian movements that are the focus of Ileto's book. But we would be naive if we failed to recognize that Ileto placed it at this crucial juncture—at the beginning of his chapter on the Philippine Revolution—not simply because of its evocativeness and the light it presumably sheds on the general phenomenon of

Philippine millenarianism, but because he also wanted to provide a radically new context in which to view that revolution and the people who participated in it. That is to say, the placement of the anecdote at this particular point in his book was dictated by the author's text-building strategy. Ileto's intent was to present the revolution of 1896 as something issuing from an indigenous millenarian tradition, not from the Propaganda Movement, European liberal thought, or a moderate reform agenda.

Furthermore, at the same time that (through his text-building strategy) Ileto was distancing Bonifacio's uprising from the Propagandists, he was also attempting to distance himself from several generations of historians who had written about the Philippine Revolution. He provided his harshest criticism of those earlier historians in a lengthy footnote.

> That the events of the revolution have not been interpreted in terms of traditional ideas can perhaps be traced to the social and cultural background of Filipino scholars. Bred in the intellectual milieu of Philippine universities, they have unconsciously inherited the nationalist and revolutionary language of the ilustrados who not only dominated the post-Bonifacio stages of the revolution but left behind the bulk of written documents upon which histories have been based. The perspective, therefore, has been that of the educated nationalist glancing with puzzled or condescending approval at the "poor and ignorant" who prayed and waved amulets as much as they fought. (99)

Hence, unlike Agoncillo, who dismissed the Colorum attack on the Spanish garrison as nothing more than "an interesting sidelight," Ileto saw it as central.

> Actually, the incident of 1897 is a manifestation of how the revolution, in its Katipunan phase, was perceived from below. Santiago Alvarez, in his account, hardly regards the Colorum as a curiosity. In fact, he notes that, with the exception of the brotherhood's unique rituals and devotions, it was "just like the Katipunan of the Sons of the People at the time brotherly love had not

been dissolved." This is a key statement. . . . By seeing the Katipunan as only one of many types of brotherhoods that Filipinos from all walks of life were attracted to join, and by asking ourselves what part these brotherhoods played in the interpretation of everyday experience, we may begin to assess the real impact of the revolution upon the masses. (96–97)

Here, then, is Ileto's key point: the Colorum, far from being a mere sideshow, irrelevant to the revolutionary experience, was illustrative of its true character because that brotherhood was, according to the testimony of one of the revolution's undisputed leaders, similar to the Katipunan. But were the two organizations really so similar? My own suspicion is that they were not. True, in discussing the Colorum Society, Alvarez did make a statement similar to the one Ileto attributed to him, but Ileto's interpretation of it is misleading. At that point in his account, Alvarez was discussing not the Colorum's attack on the Spanish garrison at Tayabas but the first days of the society's existence, when its members were living together in a forest in southern Cavite. After describing their cooperative endeavors and the hardships they faced, Alvarez commented:

> The society of prayer and mutual aid [that began] in the forest spread over a wide area and gave much comfort, to the satisfaction of all. Therefore, except for the prayers, the way people treated one another was very similar to [the way people were treated by] the Society of the Sons of the People, at the time before the spirit of brotherly love had been destroyed.
>
> (Ang samahan ng dasalan at abuluyan na nasa gubat na iyon ay lubusang lumaganap at nakapagbibigay ng kaluwagan sa pagtutulungan na, kinasisiyang-loob ng isa at isa, kaya, maliban lamang sa dansalan, ang mga pagpapalagayan at pagsasamahan ay tulad na tulad sa katipunan ng mga Anak ng Bayan noong kasalukuyang di pa nangasisira ang mga pag-iibigang-kapatid.)[18]

Alvarez's point was not that the Colorum Society and the Katipunan were similar organizations, nor was he claiming that the worldviews of the people who marched on the Spanish garrison at Tayabas resembled those of the members of the Katipunan. Rather, he was pointing out that in the early stages of both organizations the personal relationships among the members were similar.

Furthermore, it is noteworthy that, while Ileto quoted extensively from Alvarez's discussion of the Colorum Society, he largely ignored the account of the organization that appeared in Artemio Ricarte's memoirs.[19] One important difference between the two is that Ricarte, unlike Alvarez, actually described the beliefs and rituals of the Colorum at some length. A second is that Ricarte saw no similarities of *any* kind between the Colorum and the Katipunan and manifested only disdain for the former. He opined, for example, that Juan Magdalo, by dressing up as a saint, had shown "intentional audacity" ("sadyang kapangahasan") and also intimated that the members of the society were guilty of "superstition or arrogance" ("lubhang pagkapaniwalain o kapalaluan").[20] All in all, Ricarte—who, like Alvarez, was a prominent katipunero—seemed intent on distancing himself and his own society from the Colorum just about as much as Ileto tried to distance himself from the elitist historians he criticized.

In any event, having raised the possibility that the Katipunan was somehow linked to the Philippine millenarian tradition, Ileto then introduced additional evidence on that same head—a book written after the revolution by the Filipino radical Isabelo de los Reyes, which, according to Ileto, hinted that "the 'poor and ignorant' masses who swelled the ranks of the Katipunan had certain ideas about the world and their places in it, ideas quite different from those of the 'better classes' of society" (99). Again, Ileto's point was that the common people who joined the secret society perceived things in very different ways from the elite Filipinos who were attracted by the liberal ideas of the Propaganda Movement.

But de los Reyes's text is, as Ileto seemed to sense, a troublesome source. De los Reyes had never been a member of the Katipunan. His knowledge of the organization, initiation rites, and objectives of the secret society was based, according to his own account, on information provided to him after the fact by people with whom he had been incarcerated in Bilibid Prison. Furthermore, de los Reyes's comments about the ideas held by the katipuneros were curious. Among other things, he stated that "the highest aspiration of the Katipunan was a communist republic" ("el *summum* de las aspiraciones del

Katipunan era una República comunista") and that the members of the secret society had faith in its triumph and "the sought-after community of property" ("la pretendida comunidad de bienes").[21] Ileto himself acknowledged that de los Reyes might have been projecting "socialist ideas" onto his informants and that his "radical sympathies" might have "colored his interpretation of the Katipunan" (100). In light of this, it would be difficult to argue that de los Reyes provided especially useful insights into the worldviews of the katipuneros.

So, here, in the introductory matter of this chapter on the revolution of 1896, an authorial text-building strategy was already unfolding and a discursive groundwork was being laid. Caneo's Colorum, Ileto told his readers, was similar in nature to Bonifacio's Katipunan. The rank-and-file katipuneros, he intimated, had radical objectives. The first claim was based to some extent on Ileto's debatable translation of a key source, the second on the statements of a man whose powers of observation were, in Ileto's own view, compromised by his political agenda. Having set the stage, Ileto now was in a position to analyze the core texts of the revolution—a number of documents supposedly generated by the leading revolutionaries themselves, which, he believed, supplied clues to the masses' "perception of the Katipunan and their role in it" (100). At this point, Andres Bonifacio enters Ileto's story.

IV

The first texts Ileto turned to were certain articles in *Kalayaan*, the newspaper published by the Katipunan. Like many other historians of the revolutionary period, he attributed a great deal of importance to that newspaper, and, like those other historians, his belief in its importance apparently had its origins in a passage in the memoirs of Pio Valenzuela. According to Valenzuela, the Katipunan experienced a stupendous increase in membership in the months immediately preceding the outbreak of the revolution: as of January 1, 1896, the organization had only three hundred members, but eight months later the number had grown to thirty thousand. "Hundreds of people nightly joined the Katipunan in the municipalities of San Juan del Monte, San Felipe Neri, Pasig, Pateros, Marikina, Caloocan, Malabon, and other places," Valenzuela wrote. His explanation for the expansion was elegantly simple: it was "due the effect of the periodical [*Kalayaan*] on the people."[22]

As I have written elsewhere, Valenzuela's account—which claims that a newspaper with a print run of no more than two thousand (and one that could not have circulated easily because of the subversive nature of its contents) alone had such an impact on the populace—should not automatically be accepted.[23] But Ileto did accept it. What is more, he believed that, if *Kalayaan* had actually won as many converts as Valenzuela maintained it had, one could perhaps learn something about the mind-set of the converts by looking closely at its contents. By explicating the articles in *Kalayaan*, he hoped to gain insights into the ways in which the Katipunan tapped "the undercurrent of popular expectations and hopes."

The first article that he examined—"the most important item in the *Kalayaan* issue"—was "Ang Dapat Mabatid ng mga Tagalog" ("What the Tagalogs Should Be Aware Of"), which he attributed to Andres Bonifacio. Of course, as we know, it is by no means certain that Bonifacio authored that piece. Like other historians of his generation, Ileto believed that Bonifacio had written it because earlier scholars told him so. In particular, he placed his faith in Teodoro Agoncillo, since his footnotes reveal that he used the Tagalog text of "Ang Dapat Mabatid ng mga Tagalog" published in Agoncillo's edition of Bonifacio's writings (102). Agoncillo represented that Bonifacio was the author. But, in fact, Agoncillo's representations were based on the findings of other historians—de los Santos and Santos above all—and those historians were not necessarily trustworthy.

For a number of reasons, then, we should be more than a little skeptical of what Ileto was attempting to do in his analysis of the newspaper *Kalayaan*. Granted, the newspaper might conceivably have had the impact on the masses that Valenzuela asserted it had. Granted, too, the articles found therein might even have contained clues to the aspirations of the common people. But one thing Ileto could not demonstrate was that there was a clear link between the articles and Andres Bonifacio. For the moment, though, let us cast such doubts aside and allow Ileto to make his case. It is a fascinating case. Much of Ileto's analysis is astute, and its impact has been enormous. When Ileto has had his say—and readers have had an opportunity to see how effectively he has managed to embed Andres Bonifacio in the Philippine millenarian tradition—it will be time to examine whether that embedding is supported by the evidence.

According to Ileto, the most significant thing about "Ang Dapat Mabatid ng mga Tagalog" is that it placed the anti-Spanish struggle in a "framework of meaning which is 'traditional'" (102). By that, Ileto meant that, even though some of the ideas found in the article were probably influenced by the writings of Rizal and other Propagandists, the metaphors, allusions, and vocabulary employed by the writer echoed those found in the core texts of earlier popular movements, many of which were themselves derived from the pasyon. Referring to Bonifacio, Ileto wrote at one point: "To communicate what he regarded as a matter of sublime importance to each Filipino, he used the form that traditionally conveyed such matters—the pasyon form" (103).

Ileto's conclusions rest squarely on his analysis of the language of the article. To make his case, he quoted extensively from the Tagalog text, including four complete paragraphs of the version found in Agoncillo's edition of Bonifacio's writings. He also provided an English translation of those four paragraphs, but it was his own, not the one in the Agoncillo volume. "I have made a new translation," he explained in a footnote, "not because Agoncillo's is inadequate but because certain nuances of Tagalog terms relevant to this study are not brought out in his translation" (102).

"Ang Dapat Mabatid ng mga Tagalog" begins with a discussion of conditions in the Tagalog region (Katagalugan) before the arrival of the Spaniards. The first sentence of Ileto's translation runs as follows: "In the early days, before the Spaniards set foot on our soil which was governed by our compatriots, Katagalugan enjoyed a life of great abundance (*kasaganaan*) and prosperity (*kaginhawaan*)" (103). In his reading of that passage, Ileto called attention to the specific words Bonifacio used to describe the pre-Spanish era—*kasaganaan* (root word *sagana*) and *kaginhawaan* (root word *ginhawa*). Those words were significant, he felt, because Bonifacio was invoking images from the pasyon: *kasaganaan* and *kaginhawaan* were "common attributes of paradise." He went on: "The word *ginhawa* connotes, besides 'prosperity,' a general ease of life, relief from pain, sickness, or difficulties" (103). Ileto returned to the paradise theme, a central element in the pasyon, in his discussion of another passage in the article's first paragraph. His translation read: "Young and old, women included, could read and write using their own alphabet." In discussing that passage, Ileto pointed out that, since the Tagalogs were able to read and write, they "thus had knowledge, just as Adam and Eve could name all the plants and animals in paradise" (103).

He emphasized the paradise theme, as well, in his analysis of the last few sentences of the first paragraph, which dealt with the initial contacts between the Spaniards and the Tagalogs. As before, he focused on the author's use of language, and in this regard it is significant that his translation of those sentences varies markedly from that found in the Agoncillo edition. Consider the following short passage in Agoncillo's version:

> The Spaniards came and offered us friendship. The self-governing people, because they were ably convinced that we shall be guided toward a better condition and led to a path of knowledge, were crumpled by the honeyed words of deceit.[24]

Ileto, however, translated it as:

> Then the Spaniards came and appeared to offer to guide us toward increased betterment and awakening of our minds; our leaders became seduced by the sweetness of such enticing words. (103)

One particularly striking difference between the two versions is that Ileto's, unlike Agoncillo's, features the metaphor of seduction. That metaphor is, in Ileto's opinion, the key element in the passage.

> Any reader of the manifesto would immediately think in terms of the pasyon story, particularly when Bonifacio says that the leaders of Katagalugan "became seduced by the sweetness of such enticing words." For in the pasyon the delightful existence of Adam and Eve begins to fall apart precisely when Eve, because of her "weak mind," succumbs to the words of the serpent. . . . The serpent's description matches that of the Spanish friars in Katipunan documents. (104)

One question worth asking at this point is whether Ileto's translation (as well as his interpretation) of that passage in Bonifacio's article can be trusted. As Ileto pointed out, he went to the trouble of retranslating the text of the article precisely because "certain nuances . . . relevant to [his] study" were not "brought out" in Agoncillo's translation. Is it possible that, in attempting to make his case, Ileto did not do justice to the meaning of the Tagalog text?

Actually, Ileto did do justice to the Tagalog text, and his translation of the passage under consideration is, in my view, considerably better than Agoncillo's. In particular, his use of the word *seduced* is apt, since two words in the final clause—*nalamuyot* (root word *lamuyot*, meaning "seduction" or "persuasion") and *paghibo* (root word *hibo*, meaning "adulation," "flattery," or "seduction by flattering")—convey the idea that a verbal seduction of a sort has taken place. Ileto was definitely not reading into the Tagalog text meanings that were not intrinsic to it; if anything, his retranslations simply restored to the text meanings that Agoncillo's version had taken from it.

This example of Ileto's skill as a translator is by no means atypical. One of the strengths of *Pasyon and Revolution* is the high quality of Ileto's translations. His feel for English is superior to Agoncillo's, and often he revealed a better understanding of the nuances of Tagalog. On some occasions, it is true, he omitted possibly significant details found in the Tagalog texts, and on others he added words that changed the meaning of those texts ever so slightly.[25] One might quibble, too, with his rendering of certain phrases. But those are the sort of criticisms one can make about every translation ever undertaken. To Ileto's great credit, in this book of more than three hundred pages with several hundred lines of translation, he rarely misrepresented or obscured the sense of the Tagalog texts.

Having thus situated Bonifacio firmly in the pasyon tradition, Ileto went on to analyze the second, third, and fourth paragraphs of the article, which detailed the suffering experienced by the Tagalogs in the three hundred years since the Spaniards' arrival. As before, he highlighted those portions of the text that recalled metaphors and themes in the pasyon. So, for example, Ileto called attention to the fact that Bonifacio described the "fall" of the Tagalogs since the Spanish takeover in terms of "increasing blindness or absence of *liwanag*" (105). According to Ileto, *liwanag*, or light—a key element in many rituals and texts of Philippine millenarian movements—was associated with both knowledge and love. A bit later, after discussing the sad state of the Tagalogs under Spanish rule, Ileto commented: "Bonifacio's description of the pain and hardship of the people is reminiscent of the lengthy pasyon passages describing not only the suffering of Christ but also of those like his mother, Mary, who participated in Christ's experience" (105).

In the final half of the article's fourth paragraph, the author turned from a depiction of Spain's mistreatment of the Tagalogs to a discussion of what needed to be done to change that state of affairs. The gist of his message was that in the future the Tagalogs had to rely on themselves. In the Tagalog text, the word *katwiran* (*katuiran*) appeared in each of the last five sentences of that fourth paragraph, and Ileto made an effort to explain its meaning in the context of the article.

> The word "reason" does not quite bring out the root meaning of *katwiran*, which is "straightness." This connotation is important because in the context of blindness or darkness what is lost is the ability to keep to the "straight path." Katwiran is also associated with the liwanag of the sun which shows the "way" (landas). . . . The "sun of reason," then, is a beacon that enables the Tagalogs to "see," but does not by itself restore wholeness; it merely points to the path toward death that must be taken. It is characteristic of both the Katipunan and Colorum appeals that the mere awaiting of ginhawa is discouraged, that man must participate by "taking the straight path." (106–7)

V

As I have indicated, Ileto's analysis has a certain persuasive power, and that power stems from two of its characteristics. On the one hand, there is the weight of the accumulated body of evidence he presented. Ileto was able to show that in a wide array of seemingly disparate social movements a number of distinctive images and a particular type of discourse recurred. As different as those movements might have seemed on the surface, one cannot deny the many rhetorical linkages. On the other hand, there is Ileto's skillful, subtle translations and explications of the texts.

This is not to say, however, that Ileto's analysis is correct. For, even if Ileto's translations do justice to the language of the texts, they do not necessarily do justice to Andres Bonifacio. That is so for two simple reasons: because there is no solid proof that Bonifacio authored "Ang Dapat Mabatid ng mga Tagalog" and because Ileto incorrectly assumed that the Tagalog-language version in the Agoncillo collection corresponded to the original text of the newspaper article. I have touched on both points already. Permit me to elaborate on the second.

It will be recalled that Jose P. Santos published the Tagalog text of "Ang Dapat Mabatid ng mga Tagalog" in his 1935 biography of Bonifacio, the first time a Tagalog version of that famous article had appeared in print since its original publication in the newspaper *Kalayaan*. But Santos never explained where he had located a copy of the text. A Tagalog version of the article subsequently appeared in Agoncillo's collection of Bonifacio's writings, but Agoncillo merely reproduced the one found in Santos's book. So where did Santos find the original?

My search for an answer to that question sent me back to the writings of Santos to see if perhaps there were some additional clues therein. I discovered only one, and it was, all things considered, not much of a clue. In Santos's unpublished manuscript "Si Andres Bonifacio at ang Katipunan," in the same chapter in which he described the history of the Bonifacio letters, he mentioned that, among the items purchased by his father from the man in Tondo who possessed Bonifacio's correspondence, in addition to the letters themselves and the Acta de Tejeros, there were "some other papers, the originals of which have not been published until now" ("iba pang mga kasulatan na pawang hindi nalalathala ang mga orihinal hanga[ng] ngayon").[26] Conceivably, one of those "papers" was a copy of Bonifacio's supposed newspaper article. But, just as conceivably, it was not, and even more conceivably, given what I have revealed about Santos, the entire story about the man in Tondo was an invention.

There is, however, a much better answer to our question about the origins of the Tagalog text, and curiously it was Ileto himself who steered me in its direction. In his chapter on the revolution of 1896, immediately following his analysis of "Ang Dapat Mabatid ng mga Tagalog," Ileto provided a discussion of another contribution to the newspaper *Kalayaan*, this one allegedly written by Bonifacio's close associate Emilio Jacinto. But, as he revealed in a footnote, Ileto had been unable to locate "the original," by which he meant a Tagalog-language version of the contribution attributed to Jacinto. The text he used, and upon which he based the English translations found in his book, was the Spanish-language one that appeared in Wenceslao Retana's collection of documents on the Philippine Revolution (the same source in which the testimony of Pio Valenzuela and other captured katipuneros was reproduced). Ileto went on in that footnote:

> Agoncillo himself [in *The Revolt of the Masses*] had to rely on the Spanish translation in Retana and on a translation, presumably by Epifanio de los Santos, in *The Philippine Review* ([June]1918). This [article by Jacinto] is not found in the published collection of Jacinto's writings, *Buhay at mga Sinulat ni Emilio Jacinto* (Manila: Jose P. [Bantug], 1935), edited by Jose P. Santos. In other words, it appears that an extant copy of the influential first (and only distributed) issue of *Kalayaan* has not been found. Even the translation by de los Santos, Agoncillo concludes, is from the Spanish version in Retana. (109)[27]

Ileto's observations actually raised more questions than they answered. For, if no issues of *Kalayaan* were available (and to the best of my knowledge, they were not),[28] and if Santos did not include a Tagalog version of Jacinto's piece in his collection of Jacinto's writings (which he did not),[29] how was it possible for Santos (and hence Agoncillo) to publish a Tagalog text of the article attributed to Bonifacio—an article that appeared in the same issue of *Kalayaan* as did Jacinto's contribution? If we assume for the sake of argument that it was not among the Bonifacio papers passed on to his father by the man from Tondo, and if we take Santos's track record into account, an answer seems clear enough: Santos—a man who, it has been demonstrated, failed to reveal the sources he relied on, failed to indicate where important documents were located, covered up the possible wrongdoing of his father, and produced faulty transcriptions of documents he probably thought to be forgeries—may have created the Tagalog text himself. After all, if Santos did such bizarre things with the Bonifacio letters, is there any reason to believe that he would have seen anything wrong with translating into Tagalog either the Spanish or English version of Bonifacio's supposed article and then passing it off as an original? There is none. In my view, the Tagalog text of "Ang Dapat Mabatid ng mga Tagalog" that Ileto used in his research was most probably the literary production not of Andres Bonifacio but of Jose P. Santos.

And, because of that, virtually everything Ileto wrote about it—about the author's choice of words and the presence in it of certain images and themes found in texts generated by other millenarian movements—cannot be accepted. If the chief virtue of Ileto's approach is his nuanced reading of Tagalog-language sources, the chief deficiency is his failure to make certain that the sources he analyzed merited the attention he gave them. True, sometime in 1896, an article entitled "Ang Dapat Mabatid ng mga Tagalog" was published in a newspaper called *Kalayaan*. True, in light of the fact that the newspaper was the official organ of the Katipunan, it seems likely that the article was written by a katipunero and expressed ideas that were held by other katipuneros. But it was not necessarily written by Andres Bonifacio. No copy of the original Tagalog text has survived, and the only Tagalog text we have is one that was in all likelihood fashioned out of an English or Spanish translation sometime in the 1930s by Jose P. Santos.

This is not to say that the Tagalog text used by Ileto bore no resemblance to the real "original"—the article that appeared in *Kalayaan*. The basic ideas found in the text were surely preserved, even after multiple retranslations. But it is not at all likely that the vocabulary, images, symbols, metaphors and the like—the linguistic elements that are at the core of Ileto's analysis—survived in anything like their original form. Some of them may even have undergone a radical transformation.

To see how unreliable the Tagalog text used by Ileto may have been, let us look at a few previously discussed passages in "Ang Dapat Mabatid ng mga Tagalog." Recall the first sentence of the article in which, in describing conditions before the arrival of the Spaniards, the author used the nouns *kasaganaan* ("abundance") and *kaginhawaan* ("prosperity"). As we have seen, Ileto made much of the word choices (102–4). But, if we turn from the dubious Tagalog text to the Spanish translation in Retana, which evidently was based on the real original in the newspaper, the nouns used were *abundancia* ("abundance") and *bienestar* ("well-being").[30] Whereas the first has approximately the same meaning as the Tagalog word *kasaganaan*, the latter is not especially close to *kaginhawaan*. As Ileto himself pointed out, *kaginhawaan* connotes, in addition to prosperity, "a general ease of life, relief from pain, sickness, or difficulties." Had that Tagalog word appeared in the original, however, it is far from certain that the translator would have chosen *bienestar* as a Spanish equivalent, since *bienestar* connotes not only physical comfort but peace of mind and tranquility. Instead of *kaginhawaan*, the word in the original could have been *kapanatagan* ("tranquility," "peacefulness," "calmness of mind"), *katiwasayan* ("tranquility," "freedom from agitation"), or several other possibilities.

Or consider the opening sentence of the article's third paragraph: "Ngayon sa lahat ng ito'y ano ang sa mga guinhawa nating paggugugol nakikitang kaguinhawahang ibinigay sa ating Bayan?" Ileto's translation, which calls attention to the repetition of the key root word *ginhawa* (*guinhawa*), reads: "Now, after all this, what prosperity [*ginhawa*] have they given to our land?" (104–5). But, when we consult the Spanish translation in Retana's collection, we find no reference to "prosperity" at all.

> Ahora, después de todo esto, qué es lo que hemos recibido de ella por tanto gasto que sea digno de mencionarse?
>
> (Now, after all that, what have we received from [Spain] in exchange for such expense that merits being mentioned?)[31]

In light of that Spanish version of the text, how likely is it that the real original would have included the root word *ginhawa*?

Consider, finally, the paragraph in the Tagalog text in which the word *katwiran* (or *katuiran*—"reason," "straightness") appears five times. Ileto placed a great deal of emphasis on the word choice. The second sentence of the paragraph begins with the phrase "ang araw ng katuiran," which Ileto translated as "the sun of reason." The first words in every subsequent sentence in the paragraph are "ytinuturo ng katuiran," which Ileto rendered in English as "reason shows" (106). But, when we turn once more to the Spanish text, we find words that do not come close to the meaning of the Tagalog ones. Instead of "ang araw ng katuiran" ("the sun of reason"), there is "el día de justicia" ("the day of justice"), and instead of "ytinuturo ng katuiran" ("reason tells us"), there is "enseña la justicia" ("justice teaches us").[32] It seems unlikely, in my view, that the word *katwiran* (*katuiran*) was actually in the Tagalog original, for, had it been, the most logical translation would have been *razón*.[33]

Of course, I cannot be certain that some of the words analyzed by Ileto did not appear in the article in *Kalayaan*. But it is doubtful that there is a great deal of correspondence between the text he used and the true original; the possibility of slippage from one translation to the next is simply too great. In the end, therefore, the person who made the crucial linguistic choices in the Tagalog version of "Ang Dapat Mabatid ng mga Tagalog" was probably a historian writing in the 1930s, not the revolutionary of the 1890s. We will never know for sure why Santos made those choices, and in truth it doesn't matter. The only thing that *does* matter is that, since Bonifacio apparently didn't make them, and may not have even written the article in the first place, they tell us nothing of importance about Andres Bonifacio's relationship with the Philippine millenarian tradition.

Nor, unfortunately, does anything else Ileto wrote about Bonifacio in *Pasyon and Revolution*. Later in his chapter on the revolution of 1896, Ileto analyzed in depth the poem "Katapusang Hibik ng Pilipinas" (126–28), which he attributed to the supremo. Yet, as we have seen, it is highly unlikely that Bonifacio composed the poem. Beyond that, given the fact that it first came to light in a book written by Jose P. Santos, there is some reason to suspect that the real author may have been Santos himself. Still later in the chapter, Ileto attempted to place Bonifacio's conflict with Aguinaldo within the context of his thesis about the millenarian character of the revolution of 1896. One of the sources he used, alas, was the tainted Bonifacio-Jacinto correspondence (138).

VI

Thus, there are major flaws in Ileto's discussion of the Katipunan and Bonifacio. No reliable evidence links the Katipunan to the Colorum and Juan Magdalo, and none links Bonifacio to the pasyon and the Philippine millenarian tradition. Having demonstrated all that, however, I need to add some important qualifications. I am not suggesting that we should discount everything Ileto has told us about the

Philippine Revolution. Nor do I believe that we should return to the traditional view of the revolution, which regarded it as a derivative offshoot of the Propaganda Movement. In fact, other evidence mobilized by Ileto (which I have not analyzed here) demonstrates that strong connections existed between the Philippine Revolution and earlier as well as later millenarian movements. I find that evidence convincing. My point is that, as far as I can see, Ileto has failed to prove Bonifacio's link to those movements.

Furthermore, a number of things can be said in Ileto's defense. For one, there is no evidence that he consciously violated accepted canons of historical scholarship or aimed to mislead. For another, he has been to some extent a victim of the mythmakers. He read their books, used the documents they represented to be genuine, and constructed part of his elaborate historical edifice on them. Ileto was, moreover, far from alone in making the assumptions he made about the scholarship he relied on. Every historian who has written about the Philippine Revolution in the past fifty years has made such assumptions.

Yet, if Ileto can be characterized as a victim of Santos, he was also, in a certain sense, a victim of his own unique approach. No other historian of the Philippines has given as much attention to the linguistic elements of the texts of the revolutionary period or placed so much weight on them. But because of the very uniqueness of his approach—because his interpretation of Bonifacio, the Katipunan, and the revolution of 1896 was based almost exclusively on his close reading of a number of core texts—the value of his scholarship ultimately depends on the reliability of those texts. Because those texts are tainted, his view of Bonifacio must be rejected. Thus, however insightful Ileto may have been about some of the popular movements he studied in *Pasyon and Revolution,* and however much those insights may have contributed to social change in the present, his book does nothing to advance our understanding of the Philippine national hero. Andres Bonifacio remains more hidden than ever.

AFTERTHOUGHTS

Nationalism and Myth

What remains of the Philippine national hero, Andres Bonifacio? The data we have about his early years turn out to be undocumented, and hence unproven. Some of them may be true, but we have no way of determining which are and which are not. His famous writings—the newspaper article "Ang Dapat Mabatid ng mga Tagalog," the poems that schoolchildren have committed to memory, the translation of Rizal's poem, and the others—cannot be shown to be his compositions. He may have written some of them; then, again, he may not have. Bonifacio's letters to Jacinto—the core of his personal correspondence and, up to now, a major source on Bonifacio's role in the Philippine Revolution—also may not have been his literary products. Indeed, my examination of their provenance, physical appearance, and linguistic properties suggests that they are probable forgeries. The standard account of the most important event in his life, the Tejeros assembly, has been exposed as a deception designed to hide the true role played at Tejeros by the author of the narrative, the former revolutionary Artemio Ricarte. Bonifacio's personality turns out to be a historian's imaginative construction. The claim that he was intimately connected with the Philippine millenarian tradition cannot be supported. In the end, the Bonifacio we have before us is mostly an illusion, the product of undocumented statements, unreliable, doctored, or otherwise spurious sources, and the collective imagination of several historians and a memoirist.

On one level, the story I have told here can be read as merely a cautionary tale about the perils of doing historical research—a case study, as it were, of the problems of document authentication, the deficiencies of some secondary literature, the dangers of relying on published sources, and the like. On another level, however, it is a tale about nationalism and the function of history in emerging nation-states. In my view, to understand the invention of Andres Bonifacio, we must recognize that the process of posthumous re-creation was as much concerned with the promotion of Philippine nationalism as it was with historical reconstruction. Let me return briefly to the question of nationalism.

In his important book on the subject, Hugh Seton-Watson pointed out that nationalist movements generally have three objectives: independence ("the creation of a sovereign state in which the nation is dominant"), national unity ("the incorporation within the frontiers of this state of all groups which are considered, by themselves, or by those who claim to speak for them, to belong to the nation"), and nation building ("to build a nation within an independent state, by extending down to the population as a whole the belief in the existence of the nation, which, before independence was won, was held by only a minority").[1] The first objective is pursued before the nation is created, the second either before or after, and the third only after.

Three of the Philippine biographers of Bonifacio—Artigas, de los Santos, and Santos—all of whom lived in a colonial state ruled by the United States, focused on the first two objectives: independence and national unity. Their writings, which honored the memory of an earlier, anticolonial struggle and transformed the life of the leader of that struggle into a classic hero story, were intended to build pride in things Filipino and keep alive the notion of an independent Philippines. By attempting to promote nationalist feeling in a colonial environment, they directly attacked the traditional order. Still, there were limits to their commitment to the nationalist cause—none of them suggested manning the barricades, and two, Artigas and de los Santos, depended on the colonial regime for their livelihoods.

Although Agoncillo was only five years younger than Santos, he should properly be classified as a historian of a different era. Whereas Santos wrote virtually all his books in the 1930s, all of Agoncillo's historical writings were produced after 1946, the year in which the

Philippines received its independence from the United States. Not surprisingly, then, his objectives were different from those of the prewar historians: with independence no longer at issue, he focused on national unity and nation building. The demands of both evidently affected his construction of Bonifacio. To bind the new nation together and heal the festering old wounds, he found it necessary to expand the pantheon of heroes and make room for the once discredited Emilio Aguinaldo. Thus was born the two Bonifacios, the hero of Manila and the demon of Cavite.

Ileto, too, was a participant in this nationalist discourse, and he also significantly altered our view of Bonifacio. But he was very different kind of nationalist. When he wrote *Pasyon and Revolution*, the Philippine state had been independent for more than thirty years. But in the eyes of Ileto and other college-educated people of his generation many citizens were not being well served by it: true nation building had not taken place because a majority of the people were excluded or exploited. With Ileto, the Bonifacio story, somewhat transformed, became a vehicle for both social change and a new type of nation building. Ileto moved the locus of nationalism from the dominant elites to the common people.

Throughout this book, I have repeatedly used the word *myth* to describe the stories that have been told about Andres Bonifacio and *mythmakers* to describe the nationalist storytellers. No doubt, some readers will object to such usage, believing that it betrays an unduly critical stance toward both. But, in fact, I have chosen those words because they accurately describe the phenomena I have examined.

Michael Kammen, who has written much on the subjects of myth, tradition, and memory, tells us that myths have at least three key characteristics: they are likely to be fabulous, they typically involve a story, and the story is likely to concern "deities, demigods, or heroes in order to explain a society's cosmology or sense of identity."[2] Most myths are of indeterminate origin, but that is not essential. The best-known mythical stories of the American past—the tales about George Washington invented by Weems—can be dated fairly precisely, as can some of those about Jackson and Lincoln.

The works of Artigas, de los Santos, Santos, Agoncillo, and even to some extent Ileto, in addition to being historical studies and contributions to an ongoing nationalist discourse, are, at their core, modern-day Philippine varieties of "hero myths"—stories in the tradition of Greek tales about Theseus and Herakles and Indian ones about Krishna and Karna.³ But, within that genre, they fall within a distinct, somewhat underexplored, contemporary category—the national hero myth, the national hero being a relatively modern mythical figure since the nation-state is itself of recent vintage. Not surprisingly, then, both in form as well as content, many of the stories told by the Philippine mythmakers bear a striking resemblance to those found in Weems's biography of Washington and other early books about the heroes of the American Revolution. The hero's humble origins and intellectual powers are emphasized, even when, as in the case of Washington, the evidence does not necessarily support the claims. Also emphasized are the hero's virtues and strength of character.⁴ For American and Filipino mythmakers alike, the hero served as a model to be emulated.

But national heroes differ from truly legendary heroes in one important respect. As modern historical figures, their lives can be studied by historians. Furthermore, historians being what they are, the lives of the great and presumably great are much more likely to be studied and restudied, and then restudied again, than are the lives of anyone else. If modern-day hero stories are based on weak or nonexistent evidential foundations, it seems inevitable that they will eventually be exposed.

The exposure of hero myths invariably causes pain, since all of us, regardless of our nationality, have a deeply felt need for heroes. Doubtless, admirers of the mythical Bonifacio will find it difficult to accept the notion that he was probably not the humble plebeian, the literary master, and the superpatriot he has long been thought to be. Admirers of the mythmakers may find it just as difficult to credit my assertions that their writings are deficient. But I can only hope that any distress experienced will soon subside and that the loss of the mythical Bonifacio will not be mourned too long, because much important work remains to be done. Almost a century after his death, the time has come to devote our undivided attention to uncovering the real Andres Bonifacio.

Notes

Introduction

1. Glenn Anthony May, "Agoncillo's Bonifacio: *The Revolt of the Masses* Reconsidered," *Pilipinas* 17 (fall 1991): 51–67.

2. As I demonstrate in chapter 2, most scholars have assumed that Teodoro Agoncillo executed the transcriptions. In fact, the person responsible for transcribing the letters was Jose P. Santos.

3. On the questions of objectivity and political agendas, see, for example, Peter Novick, *That Noble Dream: The "Objectivity Question" and the American Historical Profession* (Cambridge: Cambridge University Press, 1988); Joyce Appleby, Lynn Hunt, and Margaret Jacobs, *Telling the Truth about History* (New York: W. W. Norton, 1994); and Stanley Mellon, *The Political Uses of History* (Stanford: Stanford University Press, 1958). In communist states, however, Marxist scholars typically adopt "conservative" agendas, defending the reigning political system.

4. For useful discussions of this subject, see Appleby, Jacobs, and Hunt, *Telling the Truth*, 90–125; Donald Denoon and Adam Kuper, "Nationalist Historians in Search of a Nation: The 'New Historiography' in Dar Es Salaam," in *African Nationalism and Revolution*, ed. Gregory Maddox (New York: Garland Publishing, 1993), 1–21; J. D. Fage, ed., *Africa Discovers Her Past* (London: Oxford University Press, 1970); Arnold Temu and Bonaventure Swai, *Historians and Africanist History: A Critique* (London: Zed Press, 1981); Caroline Neale, *Writing "Independent" History: African Historiography, 1960–1980* (Westport: Greenwood Press, 1985), 103–26; Jan Vansina, *Living with Africa* (Madison: University of Wisconsin Press, 1994), 56–57, 197–99; Jack Ray Thomas, *Biographical Dictionary of Latin American Historians and Historiography* (Westport: Greenwood Press, 1984), 3–77; Arthur P. Whitaker, "Developments in the Past Decade in the Writing of Latin American History," in *Latin American History: Essays on Its Study and Teaching, 1898–1965*, ed. Howard Francis Cline, 2 vols. (Austin: University of Texas Press, 1967), 2:397–412; and Anthony Reid and David Marr, eds., *Perceptions of the Past in Southeast Asia* (Singapore: Heinemann Educational Books [Asia], 1979), 263–98.

5. On Carlyle, see Fritz Stern, ed., *The Varieties of History* (Cleveland: World Publishing, 1956), 90–107; G. P. Gooch, *History and Historians in the Nineteenth Century*, rev. ed. (Boston: Beacon Press, 1959), 301–9; and Pieter Geyl, *Debates with Historians* (Cleveland: World Publishing, 1958), 48–69.

6. On American heroes, see Marshall W. Fishwick, *American Heroes: Myth and Reality* (Washington, D.C.: Public Affairs Press, 1954); Marshall Fishwick, *The Hero, American Style* (New York: David McKay, 1969); Dixon Wecter, *The Hero in America* (New York: Charles Scribner's Sons, 1941); and Michael Kammen, *Mystic Chords of Memory: The Transformation of Tradition in American Culture* (New York: Alfred A. Knopf, 1991).

7. See , for example, Jerome R. Adams, *Liberators and Patriots of Latin America* (Jefferson, N.C.: McFarland, 1991); John Womack, Jr., *Zapata and the Mexican Revolution* (New York: Random House, 1968), 418–20; and Anna Makolkin, *Name, Hero, Icon: Semiotics of Nationalism through Heroic Biography* (Berlin: Mouton de Gruyter, 1992), 13–23.

8. Hugh Trevor-Roper, *Hermit of Peking: The Hidden Life of Sir Edmund Backhouse*, rev. ed. (New York: Penguin Books, 1978); John Clendenning, "Thomas Beer's *Stephen Crane*: The Eye of His Imagination," *Prose Studies* 14 (May 1991): 68–80; Milton W. Hamilton, "Augustus C. Buell, Fraudulent Historian," *Pennsylvania Magazine of History and Biography* 80 (October 1956): 478–92; John Y. Simon, "In Search of Margaret Johnson Erwin: A Research Note," *Journal of American History* 69 (March 1983): 932–41; Charles Hamilton, *The Hitler Diaries: Fakes That Fooled the World* (Lexington: University of Kentucky Press, 1991); Robert Harris, *Selling Hitler* (New York: Pantheon, 1986); Lawrence W. Lynch, *The Marquis de Sade* (Boston: Twayne Publishers, 1984); William Spence Robertson, "The So-called Apocryphal Letters of Colombres Mármol on the Interview of Guayaquil," *Hispanic American Historical Review* 23 (February 1943): 154–58. Also see Robin Myers and Michael Harris, eds., *Fakes and Frauds: Varieties of Deception in Print and Manuscript* (Winchester: St. Paul's Bibliographies, 1989); Richard Landes, *Relics, Apocalypse, and the Deceits of History: Ademar of Chabannes, 989–1034* (Cambridge: Harvard University Press, 1995); and W. Thomas Taylor, *Texfake: An Account of the Theft and Forgery of Early Texas Printed Documents* (Austin: W. T. Taylor, 1991).

9. William Henry Scott, *Prehispanic Source Materials for the Study of Philippine History*, rev. ed. (Quezon City: New Day Publishers, 1984), 91–140, 149–54; William Henry Scott, *Looking for the Prehispanic Filipino* (Quezon City: New Day Publishers, 1992), 159–70. The first edition of *Prehispanic Source Materials* was published in 1968.

10. John N. Schumacher, "The Authenticity of the Writings Attributed to Father Jose Burgos," in John N. Schumacher, *The Making of a Nation: Essays on Nineteenth-Century Filipino Nationalism* (Quezon City: Ateneo de Manila University Press, 1991), 44–70, 216–24. Schumacher's essay on the Burgos documents first appeared in *Philippine Studies* in 1970.

11. Scott, *Prehispanic Source Materials*, 129.

12. Mason L. Weems, *The Life of Washington*, ed. Marcus Cunliffe (Cambridge: Harvard University Press, 1962), xv–xx (the quotation is on p. xv); Harvey Wish, *The American Historian: A Socio-Intellectual History of*

the Writing of the American Past (New York: Oxford University Press, 1960), 46–50; Garry Wills, *Cincinnatus: George Washington and the Enlightenment* (Garden City: Doubleday, 1984), 27–53.

13. Bertram D. Wolfe, *Three Who Made a Revolution*, rev. ed. (New York: Dell Publishing, 1964), 405–26 (the quotation is on p. 426); Robert C. Tucker, *Stalin as Revolutionary, 1879–1929* (New York: W. W. Norton, 1973), 115–43.

14. The classic account of this economic transformation—never published—is Benito Legarda, "Foreign Trade, Economic Change, and Entrepreneurship in the Nineteenth Century Philippines," Ph.D. diss., Harvard University, 1955. See also John A. Larkin, *The Pampangans* (Berkeley: University of California Press, 1972); John A. Larkin, *Sugar and the Origins of Modern Philippine Society* (Berkeley: University of California Press, 1993); Alfred W. McCoy and Ed. C. de Jesus, eds., *Philippine Social History: Global Trade and Local Transformations* (Quezon City: Ateneo de Manila University Press, 1982); and Norman G. Owen, *Prosperity without Progress: Manila Hemp and Material Life in the Colonial Philippines* (Berkeley: University of California Press, 1984).

15. Edgar Wickberg, *The Chinese in Philippine Life, 1850–1898* (New Haven: Yale University Press, 1965), 128–30; U.S. Bureau of the Census, *Census of the Philippine Islands: 1903*, 4 vols. (Washington, D.C.: U.S. Bureau of the Census, 1905), 3:633–34; Glenn Anthony May, *A Past Recovered: Essays on Philippine History and Historiography* (Quezon City: New Day Publishers, 1987), 53–65; John N. Schumacher, *The Propaganda Movement: 1880–1895* (Manila: Solidaridad Publishing House, 1973), 17–35.

16. Schumacher, *Propaganda Movement*, 36–220.

17. My characterizations of Rizal and the Liga Filipina are heavily influenced by John N. Schumacher, "The *Noli Me Tangere* as Catalyst of Revolution," in Schumacher, *Making of a Nation*, 91–101. Also see Schumacher, *Propaganda Movement*, 221–53; and Leon Ma. Guerrero, *The First Filipino: A Biography of Jose Rizal*, rpt. (Manila: National Historical Institute, 1979), 384–432.

18. *Minutes of the Katipunan* (Manila: National Historical Institute, 1978), iii–ix, 1–86; Isabelo de los Reyes, *La Religión del "Katipunan"* (Madrid: Tipolit. de J. Corrales, 1900). On the point that historical accounts have relied on both, see, for example, Teodoro A. Agoncillo, *The Revolt of the Masses: The Story of Bonifacio and the Katipunan* (Quezon City: University of the Philippines, 1956), 49–54, 76–77, 322–24.

19. The following brief overview of the revolutionary period is based primarily on my reading of the extant, admittedly problematic, primary sources. In particular, I have relied on Santiago Alvarez, *The Katipunan and the Revolution: Memoirs of a General* (Quezon City: Ateneo de Manila University Press, 1992); Carlos Ronquillo, "Ilang Talata Tungkol sa Paghihimagsik nang 1896–97," manuscript, Filipiniana and Asia Division, University of the Philippines (Diliman) Library; Emilio Aguinaldo, *Mga*

Gunita ng Himagsikan (Manila: n.p., 1964); Artemio Ricarte, *Himagsikan nang manga Pilipino Laban sa Kastila* (Yokohama: "Karihan Cafe," 1927); Pedro S. Achútegui and Miguel A. Bernad, *Aguinaldo and the Revolution of 1896: A Documentary History* (Quezon City: Ateneo de Manila, 1972); and Manuel Sastrón, *La insurrección en Filipinas y Guerra Hispano-Americana en el archipiélago* (Madrid: Imp. de la Sucesora de M. Minuesa de los Ríos, 1901).

20. It is unlikely, though, that the membership numbered thirty thousand, as Pio Valenzuela asserted in his memoir. For Valenzuela's assertion, see *Minutes of the Katipunan*, 106. On Valenzuela's reliability, see John N. Schumacher, "The Religious Character of the Revolution in Cavite, 1896–1897," *Philippine Studies* 24 (fourth quarter, 1976): 401; and Glenn Anthony May, *Battle for Batangas: A Philippine Province at War* (New Haven: Yale University Press, 1991), 38.

21. May, *Battle for Batangas*, 48–51.

22. My discussion of the sangguniang bayan is based on Ricarte, *Himagsikan*, 2–19, 35, 52; Aguinaldo, *Mga Gunita*, 32, 42, 57, 103, 138, 142, 177; Alvarez, *Katipunan and the Revolution*, 281–82, 306, 326; Ronquillo, "Ilang Talata," pt. 1, 84–85, 95, and pt. 2, 2, 12; and Achútegui and Bernad, *Aguinaldo and the Revolution*. In the text of this book, I refer to the two organizations as the Sangguniang Magdiwang and the Sangguniang Magdalo. Some of the sources refer to them in that way; others refer to them as the Sangguniang Bayang Magdiwang and the Sangguniang Bayang Magdalo.

In fact, the organization known as the sangguniang bayan first came into existence well before the outbreak of the revolution. As the secret society expanded, the Katipunan established administrative units with that name in provinces and larger towns; in smaller towns, Katipunan chapters were known as *sangguniang balangay*. The exact functions of both are unclear, but it is doubtful that they were invested with much authority. The term *sangguniang bayan*, which I translate in the text as "municipal consultative body," has typically been translated by other historians as "popular council," a rendering conveying the impression—an incorrect one in my view—that the organization had some governing authority.

After the outbreak of the revolution, the sangguniang bayan of Kawit and Noveleta definitely acquired a measure of authority. They served as the foundations upon which the local military units were built and took on certain governmental tasks. Ricarte, Aguinaldo, Alvarez, and Ronquillo all agreed that the province of Cavite was by that time essentially administered by the two sangguniang bayan (Ricarte, *Himagsikan*, 2–8; Aguinaldo, *Mga Gunita*, 142; Alvarez, *Katipunan and the Revolution*, 281–82; Ronquillo, "Ilang Talata," pt. 2, 2), and Ricarte even called them *sangguniang lalawigan* ("provincial consultative bodies"). Clearly, though, there were limits to the perceived authority of both organizations, since they were subordinate to the secret society itself. Indeed, it was precisely because the powers of the sangguniang bayan were understood to be circumscribed that many Caviteños ultimately decided to change the organizational structure of the revolutionary movement.

NOTES

Much of the literature on the revolution claims that there was considerable tension between the Magdalo and the Magdiwang, and the sources support that claim to a certain extent. But they also indicate that two other types of conflict were just as apparent in the revolutionary ranks—conflict within each individual sangguniang bayan and conflict between Caviteños and non-Caviteños (one of whom was Andres Bonifacio). Beyond that, it is worth noting that the dividing line between Magdiwang and Magdalo was by no means as clear at the time as it has appeared to historians writing long after the events. Noveleta and Kawit, the two supposedly rival power centers, were no more than three miles apart, and the men associated with one sangguniang bayan were, by and large, well known to those associated with the other. They went to the same secondary schools, socialized together, and were even related to each other. To provide one example, Emilio Aguinaldo, the eventual Magdalo leader, was recruited to the Katipunan by Santiago Alvarez, a key figure in the Magdiwang.

23. The Tejeros meeting is discussed at length in chapter 3.

Chapter 1

1. Gregorio F. Zaide, *Philippine Political and Cultural History*, 2 vols., rev. ed. (Manila: Philippine Education Company, 1957), 2:147–58; Teodoro A. Agoncillo and Milagros C. Guerrero, *History of the Filipino People*, 5th ed. (Quezon City: R. P. Garcia Publishing, 1977), 156–57, 169–85; Renato C. Constantino, with the assistance of Letizia R. Constantino, *The Philippines: A Past Revisited*, 5th printing (Quezon City: Renato C. Constantino, 1979), 157–70; Jose S. Arcilla, *An Introduction to Philippine History*, 2d ed. (Quezon City: Ateneo de Manila University Press, 1973), 99–102; O. D. Corpuz, *The Roots of the Filipino Nation*, 2 vols. (Quezon City: AKLAHI Foundation, 1989), 2:209–24. While I have used the fifth edition of Agoncillo and Guerrero's text, two subsequent editions have been published—the sixth in 1984 and the seventh in 1986. The publisher remained R. P. Garcia. Also see the brief sketch of Bonifacio and the Katipunan in David J. Steinberg, ed., *In Search of Southeast Asia: A Modern History*, rev. ed. (Honolulu: University of Hawaii Press, 1987), 270–71.

A few other historical surveys should be mentioned: Antonio M. Molina, *The Philippines through the Centuries*, 2 vols. (Quezon City: U.S.T. Textbook Series, 1960–61); Antonio M. Molina, *Historia de Filipinas*, 2 vols. (Madrid: Instituto de Cooperación Iberoamericana, 1984); Eufronio M. Alip, *Philippine History: Political, Social, and Economic*, 8th rev. ed. (Manila: Alip, 1969); and Eufronio M. Alip, *Political and Cultural History of the Philippines*, 2 vols., 5th rev. ed. (Manila: Alip, 1968). It should also be noted that, during the administration of Ferdinand Marcos, a group of scholars (principally from the History Department of the University of the Philippines and the National Historical Institute) undertook to write a comprehensive history of the Philippines, which was entitled *Tadhana*. Several volumes were produced, all of them crediting Marcos as the author. But the project was never completed and the published volumes did not reach the era of the Philippine Revolution.

2. The spelling of the name of the second company varies in the literature. Some authors (Agoncillo, Santos, and Artigas) spelled it Fressell; others (Zaide, Fast, and Richardson) spelled it Fressel.

3. Agoncillo and Guerrero, *Filipino People*, 177.

4. Zaide, *Political and Cultural History*, 2:151. See also Agoncillo and Guerrero, *Filipino People*, 169 (they repeatedly used the word *radical* in describing the Katipunan); and Constantino, *Past Revisited*, 159.

5. Agoncillo and Guerrero (*Filipino People*, 171) indicated that the year was 1895, as did Zaide (*Political and Cultural History*, 2:154) and Corpuz (*Roots of the Nation*, 2:213). Constantino (*Past Revisited*, 173) seemed to imply that Bonifacio was in charge by 1894. Teodoro Kalaw, who wrote one of the earliest scholarly accounts of the revolution and whose book was (as we shall see) cited by Constantino, also wrote that the year was 1894. See Teodoro M. Kalaw, *The Philippine Revolution* (Manila: Manila Book Company, 1925), 9.

6. Gregorio F. Zaide, *History of the Katipunan* (Manila: Loyal Press, 1939); Gregorio F. Zaide, *The Philippine Revolution* (Manila: Modern Book Company, 1954); Gregorio F. Zaide, *The Philippine Revolution*, rev. ed. (Manila: Modern Book Company, 1968). On Zaide's career, see *Filipinos in History*, vol. 3 (Manila: National Historical Institute, 1992), 299–300.

7. Zaide, *Political and Cultural History*, 2:152.

8. Agoncillo and Guerrero, *Filipino People*, 668.

9. Agoncillo, *Revolt of the Masses*, 327–29. Although Agoncillo and Zaide both mentioned Jose P. Santos, they referred to different books authored by him. Zaide cited *Si Andres Bonifacio at ang Himagsikan* (Manila: n.p., 1935), while Agoncillo cited *Ang Mahiwagang Pagkapatay kay Andres Bonifacio* (Manila: n.p., 1935).

10. Aguedo Cagingin, *The Life of Andres Bonifacio* (Manila[?]: n.p., 1922). I am grateful to Ambeth Ocampo for providing me with a xeroxed copy of Cagingin's hard to find book.

11. See, in particular, Constantino, *Past Revisited*, 184–85.

12. Ibid., 425.

13. Leopoldo R. Serrano, "Mga Pangyayari sa Buhay ni Andres Bonifacio," *Historical Bulletin* 4 (September 1960): 90–99; Esteban A. de Ocampo, "The Life and Achievements of Bonifacio," *Historical Bulletin* 10 (December 1966): 23–39.

14. Kalaw, *Philippine Revolution*, 21–22.

15. Ibid., 318–19.

16. Constantino cited the book incorrectly on two occasions (*Past Revisited*, 423, 425). The first citation included publishing details. The correct citation should be Epifanio de los Santos, *Marcelo H. del Pilar, Andres Bonifacio, Emilio Jacinto* (Quezon City: Kapisanang Pangkasaysayan ng Pilipinas, 1957).

NOTES

17. Jose L. Magbanua and Rolando R. Mijares, eds., *The Philippine Officials Review* (Pasay City: M & M Publications, 1967), 348; O. D. Corpuz, *The Bureaucracy in the Philippines* (Manila: Institute of Public Administration, University of the Philippines, 1957); O. D. Corpuz, *The Philippines* (Englewood Cliffs, N.J.: Prentice-Hall, 1965). Some biographical information is also drawn from the cover of Corpuz, *Roots of the Nation*.

18. Manuel Artigas y Cuerva, *Andres Bonifacio y el "Katipunan"* (Manila: Imp. de "La Vanguardia," 1911).

19. The Spanish version of the article is Epifanio de los Santos, "Andres Bonifacio," *Philippine Review* 2 (November 1917): 59–82. For the English version, see Epifanio de los Santos, "Andres Bonifacio," *Philippine Review* 3 (January-February 1918): 34–58. The monthly in which the two versions of de los Santos's article appeared is generally referred to as the *Philippine Review*, and I have done so here, but a point of clarification is in order. That periodical, published in Manila, contained contributions in both English and Spanish. The *Philippine Review* was the title of the English section; the Spanish section was called *Revista Filipina*. On the point that Nieva, then editor of the monthly, executed the translations, see Epifanio de los Santos, *The Revolutionists: Aguinaldo, Bonifacio, Jacinto*, ed. Teodoro Agoncillo (Manila: National Historical Commission, 1973), xii, 83.

20. The work I will focus on in this chapter is Santos, *Si Andres Bonifacio*.

21. On Artigas, see E. Arsenio Manuel, *Dictionary of Philippine Biography*, 3 vols. (Quezon City: Filipiniana Publications, 1955–86), 1:68–79; and Zoilo M. Galang, ed., *Encyclopedia of the Philippines*, 3d ed., 20 vols. (Manila: Exequiel Floro, 1950–58), 3:326–28.

22. Manuel Artigas y Cuerva, "El Fundador del Katipunan," *Renacimiento Filipino*, December 7, 1910, 3–7.

23. On the date of completion, see Artigas, *Bonifacio*, 5, 101.

24. Ibid., 7–8.

25. Francis St. Clair [William Brecknock Watson], *The Katipunan; or the Rise and Fall of the Filipino Commune* (Manila: Tip. "Amigos del País," 1902), 44; John Foreman, *The Philippine Islands: A Political, Geographical, Ethnographical, Social, and Commercial History of the Philippine Archipelago*, 3d ed. (New York: Charles Scribner's Sons, 1906), 370–71. Neither Brecknock Watson nor Foreman was especially reliable.

26. Theodore Friend, *Between Two Empires: The Ordeal of the Philippines, 1929–1946* (New Haven: Yale University Press, 1965), 15; Renato Constantino, *Dissent and Counter-Consciousness* (Quezon City: Malaya Books, 1970), 125–45; Glenn Anthony May, *Social Engineering in the Philippines: The Aims, Execution, and Impact of American Colonial Policy, 1900–1913* (Westport: Greenwood Press, 1980), 88; David P. Barrows, *A History of the Philippines* (New York: American Book Company, 1905), 280–85.

27. De los Santos, "Andres Bonifacio," *Philippine Review* 2 (November 1917): 59–82; 3 (January-February 1918): 34–58.

28. See Foreman, *Philippine Islands*, 370–71, for evidence of Aguinaldo's efforts to influence the historical record. Aguinaldo also spoke to Artigas, and Artigas reported Aguinaldo's comments in his biography (see Artigas, *Bonifacio*, 85–90).

29. Hence, the only source mentioned by Artigas concerning Bonifacio's early years is the baptismal entry in Tondo's parish records, which he discussed in the text. He failed to specify, either in the text or the footnotes, the sources he relied on for all other data (*Bonifacio*, 8–9).

30. On the "professionalization" of historical scholarship in Europe and the United States, see Novick, *Noble Dream*, 21–278; Appleby, Hunt, and Jacobs, *Telling the Truth*, 15–125; Gooch, *History and Historians*, 72–150, 317–96; Arthur Marwick, *The Nature of History* (New York: Dell Publishing, 1970), 24–122. On the changes in the Philippine historical community in the twentieth century, see the contributions by N. J. Casambre and Bonifacio Salamanca in *Philippine Encyclopedia of the Social Sciences* (Quezon City: Philippine Social Science Council, 1993), 19–52. The first Filipino scholar writing about Philippine history to receive a Ph.D. in the United States was Leandro Fernandez in 1926, but there were only a handful of others prior to 1960. See *Dissertations in History: An Index to Dissertations Completed in History Departments of United States and Canadian Universities*, 2 vols. (Lexington: University of Kentucky Press, 1965–72).

31. In the Philippines today, for example, Nick Joaquin and Ambeth Ocampo, both of whom write "popular history," have made major contributions to scholarship.

32. John N. Schumacher, "Sources on the Cavite Mutiny," in Schumacher, *Making of a Nation*, 83–88, 228.

33. Manuel, *Dictionary*, 1:76–77.

34. Schumacher, "Sources," 85.

35. This sketch of de los Santos is based on Gregorio F. Zaide, *Great Filipinos in History: An Epic of Filipino Greatness in War and Peace* (Manila: Verde Book Store, 1970), 575–81; Galang, *Encyclopedia of the Philippines*, 3:420–21; de los Santos, *Revolutionists*, ed. Agoncillo, viii–xii; Teodoro A. Agoncillo, "Philippine Historiography in the Age of Kalaw," *Solidarity* 5, no. 99 (1984): 3–16.

36. May, *Battle for Batangas*, 311, 317.

37. I have taken the quotation from the English-language version of the de los Santos article, which conveys the sense of the Spanish version. For the English version, see *Philippine Review* 3 (January-February 1918): 34; for the Spanish version, see *Philippine Review* 2 (November 1917): 59.

38. See Epifanio de los Santos, "Andres Bonifacio," *Philippine Review* 3 (January-February 1918): 51, 53, 54, 58.

NOTES

39. Wenceslao Retana, *Archivo del Bibliófilo Filipino*, 5 vols. (Madrid: Vda. de M. M. de los Ríos, 1895–1905), 3:387; Epifanio de los Santos, "Andres Bonifacio," *Philippine Review* 2 (November 1917): 61; 3 (January-February 1918): 36.

40. Epifanio de los Santos, "Andres Bonifacio," *Philippine Review* 2 (November 1917): 61; 3 (January-February 1918): 36.

41. See Zaide, *Katipunan*, 52–53, on the date of composition of the memoir.

42. A number of Valenzuela's interviews and accounts of the revolutionary era can be found in Jose P. Santos, "Si Andres Bonifacio at Ang Katipunan," 380–95 (unpublished manuscript, written in 1948), Filipiniana and Asia Division, University of the Philippines Library, Diliman, Quezon City.

43. Agoncillo, *Revolt of the Masses*, 321, 324, 329; Schumacher, "Religious Character," 401; May, *Battle for Batangas*, 38; N. Zafra, G. Fores-Ganzon, J. M. Saniel, D. Taylo, and J. A. Saltiva, "A Critique of Agoncillo's 'The Revolt of the Masses,'" *Arellano Standard*, November 1956, 2, 4–8.

44. Artigas, *Bonifacio*, 85–90; Epifanio de los Santos, "Andres Bonifacio," *Philippine Review* 2 (November 1917): 59, 73–82.

45. For biographical information on Ronquillo, see *Filipinos in History*, 3:254–56. For examples of Carlos Ronquillo's nationalistic writings, see his articles in *Renacimiento Filipino*, July 14, 1910, 26–28; September 7, 1910, 7–8; June 7, 1911, 34; September 14, 1911, 343–45; September 7, 1912, 299–300; and November 12, 1911, 675–76.

46. On Santos, see Agoncillo, "Philippine Historiography," 13. Santos listed his writings at the end of several of his books, but he included on those lists a few items that were never published. For one such list, see Santos, *Si Andres Bonifacio*, 45–47. To determine which books actually were published, see, among other sources, American Library Association, *The National Union Catalog of Pre-1956 Imprints*, 754 vols. (London: Mansell Publishing, 1968–81), 520:213–14; Maxima Magsanoc Ferrer, ed., *Union Catalog of Philippine Materials*, 2 vols. (Quezon City: University of the Philippines Press, 1970–76), 2:1425–26; Abraham C. de Guzman and Ursula C. Villarino, comp., *Bibliography of Materials in Philippine Vernacular Languages* (Manila: Bibliography Division, National Library, 1973), 622–25; *Filipiniana 1968: A Classified List of Filipiniana Books and Pamphlets in the University of the Philippines Library as of January 1, 1968*, 2 vols. (Diliman: University of the Philippines Library, 1969), 2:1299; and *Catalogue of Filipiniana Materials in the Lopez Memorial Museum*, 5 vols. (Pasay City: Lopez Memorial Museum, 1962–71). On Santos's continuing influence, see, for example, Reynaldo C. Ileto, *Pasyon and Revolution: Popular Movements in the Philippines, 1840–1910* (Quezon City: Ateneo de Manila University Press, 1979), 109, 123, 129, 138.

47. Santos, *Si Andres Bonifacio*, 1–5. On Bantug, see *Filipinos in History*, 3:42.

48. I touch on this issue in chapters 4 and 5. One important question that needs to be addressed is whether the Katipunan was from the outset a revolutionary organization. The evidence suggesting that it was strikes me as both thin and unreliable.

49. Readers familiar with both Tagalog and Spanish will perhaps observe that the title of one of the poems—"Ang mga Cazadores"—is somewhat irregular. Since the Tagalog word *mga* signifies that any noun it precedes is plural, one should not use the Spanish plural noun *cazadores* in the title. Thus, the poem should be entitled "Ang mga Cazador." But I have encountered the combination of *mga* and Spanish plural words in other Tagalog texts.

50. Virgilio S. Almario, *Panitikan ng Rebolusyon (g 1896): Isang Paglingon at Katipunan ng mga Akda nina Bonifacio at Jacinto* (Manila: Sentrong Pangkultura ng Pilipinas, 1993), 137–55; Bienvenido L. Lumbera, *Tagalog Poetry, 1570–1898: Tradition and Influences in Its Development* (Quezon City: Ateneo de Manila University Press, 1986), 147–49, 234–39; Bienvenido Lumbera and Cynthia Nograles Lumbera, eds., *Philippine Literature: A History and Anthology* (Manila: National Book Store, 1982), 93–95.

51. Agoncillo, *Revolt of the Masses*, 96–97; Zaide, *Philippine Revolution*, rev. ed., 92.

52. As before, I compiled this list of key sources by looking first at the historical surveys written by Zaide, Agoncillo and Guerrero, Constantino, and Corpuz and then following their references back to secondary literature and published primary sources. As before, my list is somewhat selective; that is, I have focused on the items that, in my judgment, have most influenced historians' views of Bonifacio's literary output. One other secondary account might conceivably have been added to the list: Teodoro Kalaw's book, *The Philippine Revolution*, which appears to have had some influence on later studies. Kalaw claimed that Bonifacio penned the decalogue and provided a translation of that text. But, even if I had included a discussion of that book (which, by the way, did not indicate where the information provided by Kalaw about Bonifacio's writings was derived), my conclusion about Bonifacio's writings would be the same—the evidence concerning Bonifacio's authorship of those texts is unconvincing.

53. Retana, *Archivo*, 3:132–48. At one point in the collection, however, that title was also rendered as "Lo que conviene que sepan los tagalos."

54. Artigas, *Bonifacio*, 38–39.

55. Valenzuela's memoir is published in *Minutes of the Katipunan*, 89–108. See pages 105–6 for Bonifacio's involvement with *Kalayaan*. A typescript version of the memoir can be examined on microform at the Rizal Library, Ateneo de Manila University. There are only minor differences between it and the one found in *Minutes of the Katipunan*.

56. It seems unlikely that he saw a copy of *Kalayaan*. I personally don't know anyone who has seen a copy of the paper. None exists in any

Philippine library, and to my knowledge no photographs of the newspaper have ever appeared in Philippine periodicals.

57. Epifanio de los Santos, "Andres Bonifacio," *Philippine Review* 2 (November 1917): 63–66; 3 (January-February 1918): 38–41. One can find a copy of the English translations of the decalogue and "Ang Dapat Mabatid ng mga Tagalog" in Gregorio F. Zaide (with the assistance of Sonia M. Zaide), ed., *Documentary Sources of Philippine History*, 12 vols. (Manila: National Book Store, 1990), 8:200–203. As I have indicated, de los Santos did not do the English translations himself; they were executed by Gregorio Nieva, then editor of the *Philippine Review*.

58. This quotation is taken from the English-language version of de los Santos's article (*Philippine Review* 3 [January-February 1918]: 39). The translated passage preserves the sense of the Spanish text. For the latter, see *Philippine Review* 2 (November 1917): 64. In rendering the quotation, I capitalized several words that were not capitalized in article itself, eliminated the italicization of the Tagalog titles, placed those titles in quotation marks, and changed a few words.

59. Santos, *Si Andres Bonifacio*, 5–13, 15–16, 19–22, 34. In these totals, I am excluding from consideration the correspondence attributed to Bonifacio, which is the subject of chapter 2.

60. On the last point, see chapter 5.

61. Santos, *Si Andres Bonifacio*, 5.

62. Ibid., 10.

63. Ibid., 10–13.

64. Cagingin, *Life of Bonifacio*, 31–34; Ricarte, *Himagsikan*, appendix, x–xiii.

65. Santos, *Si Andres Bonifacio*, 19–21, 31.

66. Ibid., 21–22. Earlier the proclamation was published in Kalaw, *Philippine Revolution*, 46–47. Also see Zaide, *Katipunan*, 121.

67. Teodoro A. Agoncillo (with the collaboration of S. V. Epistola), ed., *The Writings and Trial of Andres Bonifacio* (Manila: Manila Bonifacio Centennial Commission, 1963), 1–12, 67–80. Among the scholars who relied on the collection were Ileto and Corpuz. See Ileto, *Pasyon and Revolution*, 102, 126, 172; and Corpuz, *Roots of the Nation*, 2:219–20, 607.

68. The proclamation can be found in Agoncillo, *Writings*, 4, 70. On its authorship, see Santos, *Si Andres Bonifacio*, 21.

69. See, for example, Almario, *Panitikan ng Rebolusyon*, 29–75, 97–129; Lumbera, *Tagalog Poetry*, 147–49; B. S. Medina, *The Primal Passion: Tagalog Literature in the Nineteenth Century* (Manila: Centro Escolar University Research and Development Center, 1976), 153–76; and Ileto, *Pasyon and Revolution*, 93–139.

70. My discussion of Bonifacio's writings is based on the Tagalog texts in Agoncillo, *Writings*, 67–80. As I will eventually show, those texts—or rather Santos's versions of them, on which Agoncillo's were based—are even more unreliable than I have indicated, but they suffice for the purpose of trying to identify the themes to which readers of the texts were exposed. The English translations are in most cases my own, but I have consulted existing translations for guidance, especially the ones found in the Agoncillo volume, Ileto's *Pasyon and Revolution*, Zaide's *Documentary Sources*, and Lumbera's *Tagalog Poetry*.

71. The Tagalog text can be found in Agoncillo, *Writings*, 75–77.

72. Ibid., 70.

73. The Tagalog text is in ibid., 67. The Tagalog is somewhat difficult to render in English, and in making my translation I borrowed a bit from translations in Kalaw, *Philippine Revolution*, 22; Agoncillo, *Writings*, 1; and Epifanio de los Santos, "Andres Bonifacio," *Philippine Review* 3 (January-February 1918): 38.

74. For the Tagalog text, see Agoncillo, *Writings*, 76.

75. I am aware, of course, of Reynaldo C. Ileto's argument that the word *kalayaan* has multiple layers of meaning. I discuss that issue in chapter 5. Among other things, Ileto's argument calls attention to the fact that translations (such as the ones provided here) often fail to convey important distinctions. If he is right about *kalayaan*, my use of the English word *liberty* here might be misleading.

76. The Tagalog text is in Agoncillo, *Writings*, 71.

77. For the Tagalog texts of these poems, see ibid., 72–75.

78. Nick Joaquin, *A Question of Heroes: Essays in Criticism on Ten Key Figures of Philippine History* (Makati: Ayala Museum, 1977), 90–94, 98–102.

79. Jonathan Fast and Jim Richardson, *Roots of Dependency: Political and Economic Revolution in 19th Century Philippines* (Quezon City: Foundation for Nationalist Studies, 1979), 67–70. The proletarian nature of the revolution was also called into question by John Schumacher (see "Religious Character," 400).

80. In fact, Corpuz, whose lengthy synthesis appeared in 1989, did not even list Fast and Richardson's book, published a decade earlier, in his bibliography.

Chapter 2

1. Zaide, *Political and Cultural History*, 2:162–71; Agoncillo and Guerrero, *Filipino People*, 192–206; Constantino, *Past Revisited*, 175–91; Corpuz, *Roots of the Nation*, 2:224–55.

2. Agoncillo, *Writings*, 82–91.

NOTES

3. The Agoncillo collection contains Tagalog texts that, according to the editors, were "published . . . exactly as they appear in the original" (ibid., v)—a statement that is patently incorrect. It also includes English translations, but these were not done by Agoncillo; rather, they are the ones that had appeared in 1918 in the *Philippine Review*. Furthermore, for reasons that will become clear in due course, those translations do not do justice to the Tagalog texts. In the pages that immediately follow, the Tagalog words are those found in the Agoncillo collection; the English translations are mine (that is, they are my efforts to translate the texts published by Agoncillo). They are not the ones found in the *Philippine Review*.

4. Agoncillo, *Revolt of the Masses*, 370.

5. In my discussion of the letters, I refer to the author (or authors) as Bonifacio, despite the fact that he was probably not the author. I do this to avoid having to subject readers to a succession of sentences containing such hedging phrases as "Bonifacio, or rather the person who authored the letters attributed to Bonifacio."

6. Epifanio de los Santos, "Andres Bonifacio," *Philippine Review* 2 (November 1917): 67–73; 3 (January-February 1918): 42–49. Curiously, Manuel Artigas referred briefly to that correspondence in his short 1911 biography of Bonifacio, and he even provided details found in two of those letters. Typically, Artigas did not indicate where the letters were located (or whether he had seen them). Several possibilities exist. He may have seen the letters, which were then in Epifanio de los Santos's hands; he may have received information about them from de los Santos; or he may have read something about them written by de los Santos. (I am unaware, however, of any pre-1917 publication by de los Santos that referred to the Bonifacio-Jacinto correspondence.) See Artigas, *Bonifacio,* 92–98.

7. De los Santos, *Revolutionists*, ed. Agoncillo, xii.

8. Epifanio de los Santos, "Andres Bonifacio," *Philippine Review* 2 (November 1917): 66; 3 (January-February 1918): 41–42. I have used the English-language version from the *Philippine Review* since it clearly conveys the meaning of the Spanish text.

9. De los Santos, *Revolutionists*, ed. Agoncillo, ix–x.

10. Jose P. Santos, *Mga Kasulatang Lumiliwanag sa Pagkakapatay kay Andres Bonifacio* (Manila: n.p., 1935), 46; Santos, *Si Andres Bonifacio*, vii.

11. Jose P. Santos, "Si Andres Bonifacio at Ang Katipunan," 234–43, unpublished manuscript, Filipiniana and Asia Division, University of the Philippines Library, Diliman.

12. Telephone conversation with Teresita Pangan, September 8, 1994.

13. In his introduction to the collection of de los Santos's writings, Agoncillo claimed that "the best parts of [de los Santos's] wonderful

collection of rare Filipiniana were kept by his eldest son, the late Jose P. Santos who, before the last world war, placed them in the Filipiniana Section of the University of the Philippines Library for safekeeping—and lost all of them when the Japanese soldiers used the books of the University Library as fuel to cook their food on the old campus on P. Faura Street in Manila" (de los Santos, *Revolutionists*, ed. Agoncillo, xi). Santos himself stated that part of his father's collection had been deposited in the library and destroyed during the war, but he claimed that the Bonifacio papers had not been included in the deposited material ("Si Andres Bonifacio," 240).

14. Santos, *Pagkakapatay*, 46.

15. For a partial list of the finding aids consulted, see chapter 1, note 46.

16. Santos, "Si Andres Bonifacio," 126–33.

17. One difference that is particularly noteworthy relates to the two versions of the letter of April, 24, 1897. The Tagalog text is actually somewhat unclear about whether Emilio Aguinaldo was forced to resign his presidency, but the Spanish version suggests that strongly.

18. In these examples, there is no appreciable difference in meaning between the two variations of the texts.

19. Agoncillo, *Revolt of the Masses*, 408–19.

20. On the point that it was somewhat revised, see Jose M. Hernandez and Simeon G. del Rosario, *"The Revolt of the Masses": The Story behind Agoncillo's Story of Andres Bonifacio* (Manila: Hernandez and del Rosario, 1956), 2–8. Agoncillo discussed Aguinaldo's objections to the book in an interview with Ambeth Ocampo. See Ambeth R. Ocampo, *Talking History: Conversations with Teodoro A. Agoncillo* (Manila: De La Salle University Press, 1995), 45.

21. Agoncillo, *Revolt of the Masses*, 370–71.

22. Ambeth Ocampo, who knows the sources of the revolutionary period better than anyone, believes that the copy reproduced by Agoncillo in his book was not actually provided by Santos. According to Ocampo, photographic copies of the Acta could be found in the Philippine National Library in the 1930s, and they also appeared in Philippine magazines. He thinks that Agoncillo probably used one of them (personal communication, August 1, 1995).

23. Ambeth Ocampo, "Andres Bonifacio: Mito o Realidad?" paper delivered as the first annual Andres Bonifacio/Parian Lecture, Manila, November 1989, 5. Ocampo learned about the Agoncillo-Santos rivalry from E. Arsenio Manuel, who knew both men well (personal communication, August 1, 1995).

24. Telephone conversation with Teresita Pangan, September 8, 1994.

25. Ocampo, "Mito o Realidad?" 5–6. According to Ocampo, photocopies of the "original" Bonifacio letters were provided to him by the

documents' owner, Emmanuel Encarnacion. Ocampo indicates further that he had an opportunity to see the "originals" before he was supplied with the photocopies (personal communication, August 1, 1995).

26. Agoncillo, *Writings*, v.

27. Ibid., 13.

28. Carlos Quirino, *The Young Aguinaldo: From Kawit to Biyak-na-Bato* (Manila: Regal Printing, 1969), 127; Alfredo B. Saulo, *Emilio Aguinaldo: Generalissimo and President of the First Philippine Republic—First Republic in Asia* (Quezon City: Phoenix Publishing House, 1983), 128, 145; Schumacher, "Religious Character," 412; Constantino, *Past Revisited*, 185, 427; Corpuz, *Roots of the Nation*, 2:203–4, 247–52, 604–5, 613; Zaide, *Documentary Sources*, 8:400–401; May, *Battle for Batangas*, 57–58, 317–18.

29. To be more precise, Quirino cited a 1957 reprint of Epifanio de los Santos's sketch of Bonifacio; Corpuz used the version found in the volume of de los Santos's writings edited by Agoncillo; and Saulo credited Agoncillo's *Revolt of the Masses* in one footnote, though in another he indicated only that his source was one of Bonifacio's letters and did not specify which published source he had consulted.

30. This account of the sale of the Bonifacio letters is based on my conversation with Teresita Pangan, September 8, 1994. Details about Pangan's efforts to sell the documents to the government and their purchase by de Asis and Encarnacion were confirmed by Encarnacion (interview with the author, November 1993).

31. Ocampo, "Mito o Realidad?" 5. In attempting to render the coded passages in Tagalog, Ocampo discovered that the code keys supplied by Agoncillo in *Revolt of the Masses* (52–54) did not work. To decipher the text, he devised his own code key based on the coded words on the Bonifacio monument in Caloocan designed by Guillermo Tolentino (Ocampo, personal communication, August 1, 1995). As it happens, the code worked out by Ocampo (see "Mito o Realidad?" 21–22) is virtually identical to the one reproduced in Artigas, *Bonifacio*, 34.

32. Santos, "Si Andres Bonifacio," 126.

33. Ocampo, "Mito o Realidad?" 25.

34. Copies of what seems to be Bonifacio's signature have been published over the years. A photographic copy of a form letter bearing his signature appeared in the *Philippines Free Press*, November 30, 1929, 8. The reproduced letter came from the collection of Jose P. Santos and accompanied an article by Santos. Bonifacio's signature also appeared in a facsimile of the records of his trial, which was published in *The Trial of Andres Bonifacio: The Original Documents in Tagalog Text with English Translation* (Manila: Ateneo de Manila, 1963).

35. Handwriting experts disagree considerably about how best to determine the authenticity of texts. Some adopt a method that approximates the letter-by-letter scrutiny described here; others insist that the examiner

must focus not on the formation of letters but on the "feel" of the handwriting based on his or her knowledge of the writer's script. In this case, given the fact that there are few if any certifiably authentic examples of Bonifacio's script, a letter-by-letter scrutiny was the only available option. On "feel," see Hamilton, *Hitler Diaries*, 83–96.

    36. I have discussed this episode in Glenn Anthony May, "Vanishing Archives," *Far Eastern Economic Review*, January 27, 1994, 34–35.

    37. A number of other possibilities exist, though some are so farfetched that I have not discussed them in the text. For example, it is possible that de los Santos at one time possessed original Bonifacio letters and that someone made copies of them at a later date, perhaps intending to sell them. In this scenario, the letters now owned by Encarnacion would be the copies not the originals; the author of the words would nonetheless have been Bonifacio.

    38. I do not want to leave the impression that scientific testing and "expert" handwriting analysis are infallible. On the problems of detecting forgeries and the reliability of handwriting and ink analysis, see two useful, often amusing, and ultimately sobering books: Hamilton, *Hitler Diaries*; and Harold Rhoden, *High Stakes: The Gamble for the Howard Hughes Will* (New York: Crown Publishers, 1980).

    39. Another reason for limiting access to the correspondence was, of course, to prevent it from being seen by someone, such as Gregoria de Jesus, who was familiar with Bonifacio's handwriting.

    40. Goal-focus verbs might be divided into two subtypes: object-focus and directional-focus. On these linguistic issues, see Paul Schachter and Fe T. Otanes, *Tagalog Reference Grammar* (Berkeley: University of California Press, 1972), 60–62, 69–71, 283–409; Paul Kroger, *Phrase Structure and Grammatical Relations in Tagalog* (Stanford: CSLI Publications, 1993), 13–15, 57–69; Teresita V. Ramos and Resty M. Cena, *Modern Tagalog: Grammatical Explanations and Exercises for Non-native Speakers* (Honolulu: University of Hawaii Press, 1990), 53–59; and Teresita V. Ramos and Maria Lourdes S. Bautista, *Handbook of Tagalog Verbs: Inflections, Modes, and Aspects* (Honolulu: University of Hawaii Press, 1986), v–xvi, 1–3.

    41. In Santos's version, the double *g* (as in *tumanggap*) was used exclusively, as the examples provided in this paragraph suggest. In Ocampo's transcription, the letter writer tended to use a single *g*.

    42. Tagalog readers/speakers can see my point about verb forms in "older" Tagalog by examining the writings of Bonifacio's fellow revolutionaries—for instance, the memoirs of Carlos Ronquillo, Santiago Alvarez, and Emilio Aguinaldo. Consider, for example, the first paragraph of the second chapter of Ronquillo's unpublished memoir, "Ilang Talata Tungkol sa Paghihimagsik nang 1896–97," which is housed in the Filipiniana and Asia Division, University of the Philippines Library (the chapter is entitled "Si Bonifacio sa Kabite"):

> Natapus nañga ang pagtatangol ñg Paghihimagsik sa lalawigan ñg Cavite. Ang kaniyang fuersa ay wala na kaniyang kalaparan; na sa mga bundok na at doon na lamang nagaantay ñg ano mang kararatnan. Naghihiñgalo nañga sa matuid sa sabe, ang mabayani't nakapañgiñgilabot isipin na revolucion. Bakit? Ano ang dahil?
>
> (The defense of the Revolution in the province of Cavite has ended. Its force no longer extends over the same area as before. It now resides upon the hills and there awaits its fate. In other words, it is dying, the heroic and terrifying revolution. Why? What is the reason?)

Or consider the first paragraph of the introduction to Santiago Alvarez's memoir (*Katipunan and the Revolution*, 239):

> Samantalang sumusulong sa pagbabago ang Bayan, ay bumubukas sa Kabataan ang matalinong isipan ng pagsusuri sa karapatan at kakayahan ng isang nagsasalita o gumagawa, at kinikilala kung dapat o hindi dapat paniwalaan, lalo't sa mga bagay na maselang, gaya ng pagsulat ng isang buong "Kasaysayan ng Bayan," o kahi't ng bahagi man lamang; kung bakit nagawa o nasulat, at ano ang mga pinagkunan o pinagbatayan.
>
> (While the Country moves forward toward renewal, the Youth are coming to have powerful faculties of analysis concerning the worth of any word or deed, and they are discerning about what they should or should not believe, and they are especially hard to please about a "History of the People," or even a part of one; they want to know why it was written, and what are the sources or the bases [on which the writers have relied].)

Both Ronquillo and Alvarez tended to use actor-focus verbs, and the same was true of Aguinaldo (see Aguinaldo, *Mga Gunita*).

But it is worth noting that there are exceptions. Whereas Rizal tended to use actor-focus verbs when he wrote in Tagalog, Marcelo H. del Pilar typically used goal-focus verbs. See Jose Rizal, *Escritos de Jose Rizal*, 13 vols. (Manila: Jose Rizal National Centennial Commission, 1961), vol. 2, book 3, pts. 1 and 2 (*Cartas entre Rizal y su Colegas de la Propaganda*).

43. It is also worth pointing out that John Schumacher has raised questions about sources found in another of Santos's books. While Schumacher has found no evidence of wrongdoing on Santos's part, he seems suspicious. See John N. Schumacher, "The Civil and Religious Ethic of Emilio Jacinto," *Landas* 9 (January 1995): 37–52 (in particular, notes 12 and 20).

Chapter 3

1. On Agoncillo's reliance on Ricarte, see chapter 4. Also see Zaide, *Philippine Revolution*, rev. ed., 123, 143–46, 152; Quirino, *Young Aguinaldo*, 58–62, 118–28, 144, 145; and Saulo, *Emilio Aguinaldo*, 116–57.

2. As this chapter will show, the sources do not agree about many of the details of the Tejeros assembly. Even establishing the date of the meeting is no simple task. Agoncillo and others have asserted that it took place on March 22, 1897, and that the Tanza meeting occurred on March 23 (Agoncillo, *Revolt of the Masses*, 208, 220). That may be so, and in this book I accept that dating, but it should be noted that the evidence on the matter is contradictory. In his memoir, Emilio Aguinaldo indicated that the Tejeros meeting occurred on March 22. But, according to Santiago Alvarez, it began on March 25, and Carlos Ronquillo and Telesforo Canseco placed it on March 21. Ricarte's memoirs are silent about the date. Three supposedly contemporary sources indicate that the date was March 22, but all three of them—one of Bonifacio's letters to Jacinto, a declaration by Ricarte, and the so-called Acta de Tejeros—are of dubious reliability. The authenticity of the Bonifacio letter was discussed in the previous chapter; questions about the other two will be raised in this one.

3. Constantino, for one, has written: "Tejeros was the defeat of the revolution of the masses; it was the victory of a clique intent on taking advantage of the historic initiative of the people and the momentum the Revolution had already acquired" (*Past Revisited*, 186).

4. Readers should be advised that my analysis of the Tejeros meeting largely ignores—or, to be more precise, avoids—any discussion of two related questions: why there was so much overt conflict at Tejeros and why the delegates chose to replace Bonifacio as head of the revolutionary movement. Both are important, since it is clear that the tensions and divisions within the revolutionary ranks had a major impact on the course of the Philippine struggle. My silence should not be interpreted as a tacit acknowledgment that existing accounts of the divisions in the revolutionary camp—which explain them as caused by either regional differences, class conflict, or dissatisfaction with Bonifacio's personality—are satisfactory. On the contrary, I believe that our understanding of the revolution—like our understanding of Bonifacio—has been clouded by problematic sources and, on occasion, the ideological predispositions of the historians who have interpreted them. I avoid those questions here, first, because it is impossible to answer them adequately in short compass and, second, because a full discussion would not be appropriate in this book.

But, for what it's worth, let me touch briefly on those matters now, stating an argument I have made in an unpublished paper (Glenn Anthony May, "The Philippine *Levée* of 1899: Conscription, Nationalism, and National Amnesia," paper prepared for the Seminar on Force in History, Institute for Advanced Study, Princeton, N.J., November 1995). One important substantive reason for dissatisfaction with Bonifacio was his style of military leadership. Often accused of being autocratic, Bonifacio tended to be hyperdemocratic as a military commander: he consulted subordinates and even common soldiers constantly, even in the heat of battle. This style contrasted with Aguinaldo's more strictly hierarchical approach. At a time when the Filipinos were doing so poorly in the war against Spain, the latter approach evidently had greater appeal to other revolutionary leaders. This difference in approach, I believe, led directly to Bonifacio's fall from power.

5. Artemio Ricarte, *Memoirs of General Artemio Ricarte*, ed. Armando J. Malay (Manila: National Heroes Commission, 1963), xvi.

6. Ricarte, *Himagsikan*, vii.

7. On the points that the original version of the memoirs was once in the Watson Collection and that it was written in Tagalog, see Ricarte, *Memoirs*, xxi–xxii. On the location of the Watson Collection, see *Minutes of the Katipunan*, v. I discuss the disappearance of the collection in May, "Vanishing Archives," 34–35.

8. Artemio Ricarte, *The Hispano-Philippine Revolution* (Yokohama: n.p., 1926); Ricarte, *Himagsikan*; Artemio Ricarte, *Gubat dagiti Pilipino ken Kakastila* (Yokohama: The Ohm-Sha, 1929); Ricarte, *Memoirs*.

9. In doing this, I am operating on the assumption that the Tagalog text preceded the English one, a point suggested by Malay, who evidently saw the originals. In my opinion, both the very incomplete 1926 English version and the 1963 English version seldom convey the sense of the Tagalog text. One would expect the Ilocano edition, *Gubat dagiti Pilipino ken Kakastila*, to be the definitive one, since Ricarte was an Ilocano, but it is the sketchiest of all.

10. Agoncillo, *Revolt of the Masses*, 357.

11. This summary is based on Ricarte, *Himagsikan*, 52–63.

12. Ricarte did not indicate the date of the meeting, although his text implies that it was shortly before March 25. See note 2 for a discussion of the date.

13. Alvarez, *Katipunan and the Revolution*; Aguinaldo, *Mga Gunita*; Ronquillo, "Ilang Talata"; Telesforo Canseco, "Historia de la Insurrección Filipina en Cavite," 1897, unpublished manuscript in the Dominican Archives, Quezon City (a typed copy of the Canseco manuscript is available on microfilm at the Rizal Library, Ateneo de Manila University).

14. For these three documents, see Epifanio de los Santos, "Andres Bonifacio," *Philippine Review* 2 (November 1917): 70–71; 3 (January-February 1918): 46–47; Ocampo, "Mito o Realidad?" 33–36; and Santos, *Si Andres Bonifacio*, 25–26.

15. Santos, "Si Andres Bonifacio," 236.

16. The letter is reproduced in Achútegui and Bernad, *Aguinaldo and the Revolution*, 343. The original document is in the Dominican Archives, Quezon City. For the testimony, see Agoncillo, *Writings*, 91–132.

17. Joanna D. Nicolas, "The National Library: Vaporizing History," *Smart File*, Animal Farm ser., 020 and 021 (1994): 4–21.

18. May, *Past Recovered*, 30–52.

19. For the exception, see Joaquin, *Question of Heroes*, 95.

20. Canseco, "Historia," 77 (page number refers to the microfilm typescript at the Rizal Library, Ateneo de Manila University). To my

embarrassment, I must acknowledge that my own research can be faulted here. As I indicate above, I did not consult the original Canseco manuscript, but rather a typescript; that is, I made no effort to subject this important source to the same scrutiny I have subjected the supposed Bonifacio letters.

21. Alvarez, *Katipunan and the Revolution*, 318. I have provided my own translation of the Tagalog text; another translation is published in that volume (on page 83), but I found it to be somewhat inaccurate.

22. Ibid., 321.

23. I am, of course, merely guessing that there was such a deal, but while I am in the speculative mode allow me to take this line of inquiry a few steps further.

The deal, if there was one, involved a neat political compromise among the Caviteños: Aguinaldo, a leader of the Magdalo organization, was to assume the presidency, but the three other top jobs were to go to Magdiwang leaders. Here was an arrangement that could satisfy the political ambitions of the representatives of both groups. It is difficult to guess exactly who might have been involved in the deal, although three likely Magdiwang candidates were Ricarte, Mariano Trias, and Emiliano Riego de Dios, who were elected to office. One person who clearly was not involved was Bonifacio.

Here is one last guess. The election proceeded according to plan as long as the delegates voted by written ballot. When they switched to open voting, however, the manipulators were unable to produce the result they favored, and consequently Bonifacio was chosen. When Tirona objected to Bonifacio's election, Bonifacio blew up, voiding all the election results.

24. De los Santos indicated that forty-one people signed the Acta, but the copy of the document seen by Ocampo lists forty-five signers. See Epifanio de los Santos, "Andres Bonifacio," *Philippine Review* 2 (November 1917): 71; and Ocampo, "Mito o Realidad?" 33.

25. Baldomero Aguinaldo's letter is the only source indicating unambiguously that the delegates were aware that elections would be held at Tejeros. In addition, the Acta de Tejeros *hints* that the Magdalo leaders engaged in some unspecified mysterious conduct before the Tejeros meeting and singles out Emilio Aguinaldo for blame, but that document is a somewhat dubious source.

26. Quoted in Achútegui and Bernad, *Aguinaldo and the Revolution*, 343.

27. May, *Battle for Batangas*, 56, 317.

28. Ibid., 56–57, 317.

29. Ronquillo, "Ilang Talata," pt. 4 (entitled "Ang Pulong sa Tehero at Tansa").

30. Santiago Alvarez, who wrote his account of the revolution immediately after Ricarte's appeared in print (and who, perhaps as a result, repeated many details found in Ricarte's narrative), also maintained that

Severino de las Alas suggested the idea of reorganizing the government (Alvarez, *Katipunan and the Revolution*, 319).

31. Ronquillo, "Ilang Talata," pt. 4.

32. Aguinaldo, *Mga Gunita*, 178–80.

33. Canseco, "Historia," 77.

34. Ronquillo, "Ilang Talata," pt. 4.

35. Ibid. See also Aguinaldo, *Mga Gunita*, 185. In his declaration of March 24, 1897, Ricarte reported that when he arrived at the parish house of Tanza he discovered, among others, Mariano Trias (the vice president elect), Emiliano Riego de Dios (the director of war elect), Vicente Riego de Dios, and Santiago Rillo—all of them affiliated with the Magdiwang organization—as well as various other Magdalo *and* Magdiwang men. Thus, while the memoir conveys the impression that only a few members of the Magdiwang—Trias, de las Alas, Pulido, and Ricarte himself—were in attendance, this declaration (if it is to be believed) implies that Magdiwang participation was more substantial.

36. Aguinaldo, *Mga Gunita*, 186–87.

37. Alvarez, *Katipunan and the Revolution*, 323.

38. Another source that *does* indicate that the results of the elections were voided by Aguinaldo is Bonifacio's letter to Jacinto of April 24, 1897, but that claim—like the tainted document in which it occurs—cannot be credited.

Chapter 4

1. Constantino, *Past Revisited*, 159–98; Milagros C. Guerrero, "Luzon at War: Contradictions in Philippine Society, 1898–1902," Ph.D. diss., University of Michigan, 1977, 10–15, 20–33; Ileto, *Pasyon and Revolution*, 4–6, 96–101. Ileto's critique is discussed in chapter 5.

2. For biographical details, I relied on Ocampo, *Talking History*, v–vi; *Filipinos in History*, 3:6–7; a sketch of Agoncillo by William Frederick ("Southeast Asia," in *Great Historians of the Modern Age: An International Dictionary*, ed. Lucian Boia [New York: Greenwood Press, 1991], 593–624); and another sketch (author unknown), entitled "Ang May-Akda" ("The Writer") in *Pagbabalik sa Bayan: Mga Lektura sa Kasaysayan ng Historiyograpiya at Pagkabansang Pilipino*, ed. Ferdinand C. Llanes (Manila: Rex Book Store, 1993), 12.

3. Agoncillo's surveys, in addition to the one written with Guerrero (*Filipino People*; see chapter 1), include Teodoro A. Agoncillo and Oscar M. Alfonso, *History of the Filipino People* (Quezon City: Malaya Books, 1967); Teodoro A. Agoncillo, *A Short History of the Philippines* (New York: New American Library, 1969); and Teodoro A. Agoncillo, *Kasaysayan ng Bayan*

Pilipino (Manila: National Book Store, 1975). His other major books (aside from *The Revolt of the Masses*) are *Malolos: The Crisis of the Republic* (Quezon City: University of the Philippines, 1960); *The Fateful Years: Japan's Adventure in the Philippines, 1941–1945*, 2 vols. (Quezon City: R. P. Garcia Publishing, 1965); *The Burden of Proof: The Vargas-Laurel Collaboration Case* (Mandaluyong: University of the Philippines Press, 1984); and *Filipino Nationalism, 1872–1970* (Quezon City: R. P. Garcia Publishing, 1974).

4. Agoncillo's Marxist tinge made him the target of a full-fledged rightist-reactionary attack. See Hernandez and del Rosario, *The Story behind Agoncillo's Story*.

5. It is worth noting that Agoncillo's scholarship alone does not explain the enormous shadow he cast in his lifetime and continues to cast today. Agoncillo was also an imposing, dominating presence, a man who inspired awe and great loyalty in some and intimidated others. One can gain some insight into this side of Agoncillo by reading Ambeth Ocampo's extraordinarily revealing interviews with him in *Talking History* and the assorted recollections of the man by former students and colleagues in Llanes, *Pagbabalik sa Bayan*, 7–15.

6. *Minutes of the Katipunan*, vii–ix.

7. Aguinaldo's memoirs—which other historians have used extensively—were not published until 1964, sixteen years after Agoncillo completed his manuscript. I compared the memoirs with the material attributed to Aguinaldo in Agoncillo's book and found no discrepancies.

8. At the time of the book's composition, the records were housed in the U.S. National Archives in Washington, D.C. They had been used by a few Filipino scholars but not extensively. See *Philippine Insurgent Records, 1896–1906, with Associated Records of the United States War Department, 1900–1906*, pamphlet accompanying microcopy no. 254 (Washington, D.C.: National Archives, 1967), 14–16. It should be noted, though, that Agoncillo did consult these records extensively in preparing his next major book, *Malolos: The Crisis of the Republic*.

9. Santos, *Si Andres Bonifacio*, 14.

10. The *Documentos Políticos* referred to by Agoncillo were part of volume 3 of Retana's five-volume *Archivo del Bibliófilo Filipino*, examined in chapter 1.

11. *Minutes of the Katipunan*, vii–ix; Agoncillo, *Revolt of the Masses*, 323.

12. The letter appeared in Santos, *Si Andres Bonifacio*, 14, but Santos did not indicate the date of composition. In his introduction to *Minutes of the Katipunan* (iv), Carlos Quirino indicated that the letter was written around 1930.

13. Alvarez, *Katipunan and the Revolution*, 242–43, 262–64.

14. Retana, *Archivo*, 3:206, 226, 349, 377, 378.

15. Agoncillo used the word *faction* repeatedly in referring to the Magdiwang and Magdalo organizations (see, e.g., chapter 12 of *Revolt of the Masses*).

16. See, for example, Alvarez, *Katipunan and the Revolution*, 301–56; and Ronquillo, "Ilang Talata," pt. 2 (entitled "Si Bonifacio sa Kabite").

17. See, for example, Agoncillo's treatment of the aftermath of the Tejeros meeting, in which he rejected evidence that the Magdalo leaders had failed to attend a conference with the Magdiwang to work out their differences (222–26, 360–62); the meeting of Bonifacio and Aguinaldo at Naik (233–35, 363); and Aguinaldo's decision to withdraw his pardon of Bonifacio (265–66, 368).

18. Ocampo, *Talking History*, 20.

19. The question of Agoncillo's relationship with Aguinaldo—and the effect of that relationship on his historical interpretations—was the subject of a nasty exchange between Agoncillo and Vivencio R. Jose. See Vivencio R. Jose, "The Bankruptcy of the Subjectivist Conception of History," *Solidarity* 10 (September-December 1976): 101; and Teodoro A. Agoncillo, "Distorting Historical Facts," *Solidarity* 11 (January-February 1977): 35.

It is possible that I am making too much of the Agoncillo-Aguinaldo connection. Agoncillo was, as his interviews with Ocampo in *Talking History* clearly indicate, a brutally frank man, and those who knew him well have told me that they think it unlikely he would have taken a pro-Aguinaldo stance merely because Aguinaldo had wed an Agoncillo. Beyond that, Aguinaldo himself felt that Agoncillo's portrayal of him was unsatisfactory, and because of his objections publication of the book was delayed. If Agoncillo's objective was to avoid offending Aguinaldo, he evidently failed.

20. I want to acknowledge my debt to Ben Anderson for suggesting this general line of analysis when he read an early version of my critique of Agoncillo's scholarship. Anderson should not, however, be held responsible for my formulation of the argument here.

21. One scholar who did use the Philippine Insurgent Records was Milagros Guerrero, formerly Agoncillo's coauthor. Her revisionist doctoral dissertation ("Luzon at War"), based on those records, calls into question Agoncillo's assertions about the popular nature of the Philippine Revolution. Why the dissertation has never been published is a mystery.

Chapter 5

1. Reynaldo C. Ileto, *Pasyon and Revolution: Popular Movements in the Philippines, 1840–1910* (Quezon City: Ateneo de Manila Press, 1979). Some of the points I make in this chapter about Ileto's book—especially the favorable ones—were made in a review essay written shortly after the book's publication. See Glenn A. May, "Understanding the Peasant: Reynaldo Ileto's

History from Below," *Bulletin of the American Historical Collection* 9 (January-March 1981): 69–77. I adopted and acknowledged Ileto's analysis in several publications—most notably in *Battle for Batangas* (see, e.g., pages 51, 116, and 214). But recent research in the sources used by Ileto has made me somewhat more critical of his discussion of the Katipunan and Bonifacio.

2. Pages 93 through 139 deal with the revolution of 1896.

3. Reviewers invariably devoted most of their attention to Ileto's discussion of the revolution of 1896. See, for example, the symposium about the book in the *Bulletin of the American Historical Collection* 9 (January-March 1981): 55–77; and the essays by Guerrero and Schumacher cited in note 4.

4. On the debate, see Milagros C. Guerrero, "Understanding Philippine Revolutionary Mentality," *Philippine Studies* 29 (1981): 240–56; Reynaldo C. Ileto, "Critical Issues in 'Understanding Philippine Revolutionary Mentality,'" *Philippine Studies* 30 (1982): 92–119; and John N. Schumacher, "Recent Perspectives on the Revolution," *Philippine Studies* 30 (1982): 445–92. It is worth noting that, while Ileto is today held in high regard in the Philippines, he was not especially well treated by the University of the Philippines when he taught there shortly after receiving his doctoral degree. Indeed, he was savagely criticized by some colleagues.

5. Reynaldo C. Ileto, *Magindanao, 1860–1888: The Career of Datu Uto of Buayan*, Data Paper no. 82 (Ithaca: Southeast Asia Program, Cornell University, 1971).

6. See, for example, James Siegel, *The Rope of God* (Berkeley: University of California Press, 1969); Benedict R. O'G. Anderson, *Java in a Time of Revolution: Occupation and Resistance, 1944–1946* (Ithaca: Cornell University Press, 1972); and Benedict R. O'G. Anderson, "The Idea of Power in Javanese Culture," in *Culture and Politics in Indonesia*, ed. Claire Holt (Ithaca: Cornell University Press, 1972), 1–69. Ileto was also influenced by his fellow graduate student at Cornell, Robert Love, who wrote an important, still unpublished, doctoral dissertation in anthropology on Tagalog religion.

7. For insight into their approaches to Southeast Asian culture—approaches that have been constantly in flux—see, in addition to the studies cited in note 6: James Siegel, *Shadow and Sound: The Historical Thought of a Sumatran People* (Chicago: University of Chicago Press, 1979); James Siegel, *Solo in the New Order: Language and Hierarchy in an Indonesian City* (Princeton: Princeton University Press, 1986); Benedict R. O'G. Anderson and Ruchira Mendiones, eds., *In the Mirror: Literature and Politics in Siam in the American Era* (Bangkok: Editions Duang Kamoi, 1985); and Benedict R. O'G. Anderson, *Language and Power: Exploring Political Cultures in Indonesia* (Ithaca: Cornell University Press, 1990).

8. Ileto, *Pasyon and Revolution*, iii.

9. Constantino, *Past Revisited*, 165, 167.

10. Readers will recall that with this issue was addressed at the end of chapter 1. Also see May, *Past Recovered*, 12–13; May, *Battle for Batangas*, 36–66; Fast and Richardson, *Roots of Dependency*, 67–71; Schumacher, "Recent Perspectives," 468–92.

11. On Prince Dipanagara and Hsaya San, see Michael Adas, *Prophets of Rebellion: Millenarian Protest Movements against the European Colonial Order* (Chapel Hill: University of North Carolina Press, 1979); and Sartono Kartodirdjo, *Protest Movements in Rural Java: A Study of Agrarian Unrest in the Nineteenth and Early Twentieth Centuries* (Singapore: Oxford University Press, 1973).

12. Ileto returned to that point in the last paragraph of his book: "Only those movements were successful that built upon the masses' conception of the future as well as social and economic conditions. . . . As we move forward on the path to kalayaan, we can hardly ignore the voices from below" (319).

13. Clifford Geertz, *Works and Lives: The Anthropologist as Author* (Stanford: Stanford University Press, 1988), 27–29, 69–71, 73–85, 105–9.

14. See, for example, Agoncillo, *Revolt of the Masses*, 194–96.

15. The quotations are from Ileto's text, not from the sources upon which he relied.

16. The quotations are from Ileto's text.

17. Both of the quotations are Ileto's translations of excerpts from Alvarez's account. The Tagalog text of the first reads "Kulang sa pananampalataya, at nang naroroon na ay di na ako nabanggit ng mga namatay at nasugatan." The second (I include the entire clause in which the translated passage appeared) reads "di man halos dinamdam ang namatay at napinsalang kapatid, asawa, anak, o magulang, . . ." For the Tagalog text, see Alvarez, *Katipunan and the Revolution*, 445. Paula Carolina S. Malay translated those passages as follows: (1) "Lack of faith! Why, the dying and the wounded did not even remember to invoke me!" and (2) "They showed almost no concern anymore for their dead and wounded kin" (see ibid., 210). Both versions have strengths and weaknesses. In the case of Ileto's, it is curious that he included words not found in the Tagalog text (in the first case, apparently for clarification; in the second, for no obvious reason). My own, slightly more literal, rendering of the two would be (1) "Lack of faith. Even the dead and the wounded there did not mention my name" and (2) "They felt almost nothing about the dead and injured brothers, spouses, children, and parents."

18. For the Tagalog text, see Alvarez, *Katipunan and the Revolution*, 442–43. My translation differs somewhat from the one by Malay in the same volume.

19. Ileto's only reference to Ricarte's account appears in a footnote: "Artemio Ricarte, a former colleague of Alvarez in the Magdiwang wing of the Katipunan, also wrote about the Colorum in his *Memoirs* (Manila:

National Heroes Commission, 1963), 82–84." See Ileto, *Pasyon and Revolution*, 94. For the Tagalog text of Ricarte's account of the Colorum Society, see Ricarte, *Himagsikan*, 126–31.

    20. Ricarte, *Himagsikan*, 131.

    21. De los Reyes, *La Religión del "Katipunan,"* 37–38. For some reason, Ileto did not use de los Reyes's book itself but rather an English translation of part of it found in John R. M. Taylor, *The Philippine Insurrection against the United States: A Compilation of Documents with Notes and Introduction*, 5 vols. (Pasay City: Eugenio Lopez Foundation, 1971–73), 1:202–11. That translation was inept, however. In the text of this chapter, I have provided my own translation of a few passages from de los Reyes's book.

    22. For Valenzuela's statements, see *Minutes of the Katipunan*, 106. Ileto included the first quotation in his own text (*Pasyon and Revolution*, 102).

    23. May, *Battle for Batangas*, 38.

    24. Agoncillo, *Writings*, 2. The Tagalog text reads: "Dumating ang mga kastila at dumulog na nakipagkaibigan. Sa mabuti nilang hikayat na di umano, tayo'y aakain sa lalung kagalingan at lalung imumulat ang ating kaisipan, ang nasabing nagsisipamahala ay ng yaring nalamuyot sa tamis ng kanilang dila sa paghibo" (for the text, see ibid., 68).

    25. See, for example, note 17.

    26. Santos, "Si Andres Bonifacio," 236. Careful readers will have noted that, at the time Santos submitted his manuscript to the Bonifacio biography contest (1948), an "original" version of Bonifacio's article had, in fact, already appeared—that is, in Santos's 1935 biography of Bonifacio. But that alone fails to prove that he was *not* referring to the article in *Kalayaan* since the 1948 manuscript was filled with mistakes about exactly this kind of factual point. For example, Santos claimed in the manuscript that various other writings attributed to Bonifacio had not been published, whereas he had earlier published them himself. As it happened, in a number of those cases, Santos (or his assistant) had simply copied, word for word, claims that he had made in previous publications that the writings he reproduced had never been published before.

    27. Ileto made two noteworthy slips in the text of his note. He stated that the Jacinto piece appeared in the July 1918 issue of the *Philippine Review*, whereas, in fact, it was published in the June 1918 number (pp. 412–30). Also, he claimed that Agoncillo relied on both Retana and de los Santos, whereas Agoncillo himself (*Revolt of the Masses*, 334–35) admitted that he used the English translation in the *Philippine Review*.

    28. One issue I have not discussed in the text, but which I should at least allude to in the notes, relates to Retana. The translated selections from *Kalayaan* that appeared in Retana's compilation, *Archivo del Bibliófilo Filipino,* were allegedly based on a copy of the newspaper. Since the

compilation appeared shortly after the outbreak of the revolution, it is not improbable that such a copy could have been located at the time. What we don't know is what happened to it afterward.

29. See Jose P. Santos, *Buhay at mga Sinulat ni Emilio Jacinto* (Manila: Jose P. Bantug, 1935), 24–66. On this matter, also see Schumacher, "Civil and Religious Ethic," 42–43.

30. Retana, *Archivo*, 3:145.

31. Ibid., 146.

32. Ibid., 147–48.

33. My guess is that the word in the Tagalog original was something like *katarungan* ("justice," "equity," "sound reason," "rightfulness").

Afterthoughts

1. Hugh Seton-Watson, *Nations and States: An Enquiry into the Origins of Nations and the Politics of Nationalism* (Boulder: Westview Press, 1977), 3. For other valuable efforts to define (and explain) nationalism, see Benedict Anderson, *Imagined Communities: Reflections on the Origin and Spread of Nationalism*, rev. ed. (London: Verso, 1991), 5–7; and Ernest Gellner, *Nations and Nationalism* (Ithaca: Cornell University Press, 1983), 1–7.

2. Kammen, *Mystic Chords*, 25.

3. The books of Joseph Campbell deal most extensively with hero myths. See Robert A. Segal, *Joseph Campbell: An Introduction* (New York: Garland Publishing, 1987), 1–29; Joseph Campbell, *The Hero with a Thousand Faces*, 2d ed. (Princeton: Princeton University Press, 1968); and David Adams Leeming, *The World of Myth* (New York: Oxford University Press, 1990), 217–311.

4. Weems, *Washington*, xv, xliii–xliv, lii–liii; Michael Kammen, *A Season of Youth: The American Revolution and the Historical Imagination* (New York: Alfred A. Knopf, 1978), 41–43, 51–52.

Index

Acta de Tejeros, 93, 108; and de los Santos, 60-62, 157; and Agoncillo, 61, 67-68, 77; and protest against Tejeros assembly, 98, 104-05, 106, 186; as a dubious source, 99, 184; photographic copies of, 180; signers of, 186
Actor-focus verbs, 78-79, 182-83
Agoncillo, Maria, 131
Agoncillo, Teodoro, 19, 21, 140; and *The Revolt of the Masses*, 2-5, 22, 25, 66-69, 70, 113-35, 158, 184, 189; and Bonifacio's personality, 5, 113-17, 133; as author of *History of the Filipino People*, 20, 22, 75, 171; use of interviews by, 22-23, 113-14, 118-21, 123, 124-26, 128-30, 131-33; and Bonifacio's literary tastes, 36; as editor of collected writings of Bonifacio, 37, 43, 54-59, 69, 70, 153, 157, 179, 192; and nationalism, 50-51, 115, 132-33, 164-65; and Bonifacio letters, 60-62; as editor of collected writings of de los Santos, 60-62, 66-69; and Bonifacio biography contest, 66; and Aguinaldo, 66, 116-17, 124-32, 133, 165, 180, 189; and Santos, 67-68, 77, 115, 124, 172; unreliability of, 67-69, 71-73, 80, 113-14, 134, 152, 179; influence of, 70, 113-14, 116, 137, 152; and Ricarte, 85, 128, 129; and Artigas, 113, 115, 124; career of, 114-15; reliance of, on de los Santos, 115, 124; and use of evidence, 119-30; interviews of, with Ambeth Ocampo, 131; and Philippine Revolution, 142; and Katipunan, 142; translations of, 154-55; personality of, 188; treatment of Magdiwang-Magdalo relations by, 189
Aguinaldo, Baldomero, 56, 86, 89, 91; and Tejeros assembly, 93, 100, 105, 110, 186
Aguinaldo, Crispulo, 90

Aguinaldo, Emilio, 70; military leadership of, 14, 17, 184; and conflict with Bonifacio, 16, 23, 55-59, 116, 161; memoir of, 54, 58, 92-93, 103, 108, 184, 188; and Spanish peace overture, 54-58; and Tejeros elections, 57, 88-91, 100, 103-07, 186; portrayal of, by Agoncillo, 66, 116-17, 124-32, 133, 165, 180, 189; and Tanza meeting, 107; interviews with, 118, 120, 124-30; reliability of, 130; and Santiago Alvarez, 171; and actor-focus verbs, 182-83
Alas, Severino de las, 86, 90, 102, 186-87
Alger, Horatio, 21
Alvarez, Mariano: and revolution against Spain, 14; relationship of, to Bonifacio, 16, 117; Bonifacio's letters to, 54, 81, 93; and Tejeros assembly, 57, 58, 86, 88, 89, 98, 100, 101, 104-07, 110
Alvarez, Pascual, 86, 88, 110
Alvarez, Santiago: and revolution against Spain, 14; memoir of, 54, 58, 92, 96-99, 104, 105, 108-09, 118, 126, 134, 146-50, 184, 186-87; and Tejeros assembly, 86-88, 96-99, 100; value of, as informant, 99; and Tanza meeting, 109-10; portrayal of Bonifacio by, 126; and Colorum Society, 146-50; and Aguinaldo, 171; and use of actor-focus verbs, 182-83
Anderson, Benedict, 138-40
Arcilla, Jose, 19, 21
Arellano, Deodato, 20, 127
Army, Philippine: in revolution against Spain, 14, 16-17; problems of, 55-59, 184
Artigas, Manuel: influence of, 4, 22-25, 31, 47, 113, 115, 124, 137; biography of Bonifacio by, 22-30, 34, 37, 38, 47, 179; life of, 25-26; and footnotes, 28-29, 31, 35; nationalism of, 34, 145, 164; and Bonifacio letters, 179
Asis, Severina ("Viring") de, 71

Backhouse, Sir Edmund, 7
Banahaw, Mount, 147
Bantug, Jose P., 35, 158
Barrows, David Prescott, 27
Basa, Roman, 20, 127
Bataan (province), 30, 61
Batangas (province), 31, 70, 114; sugar in, 12; support for Bonifacio in, 16, 57-58; and Tejeros assembly, 101-04, 106-07
Beer, Thomas, 7
Biggerstaff, Knight, 139
Bikol, 12, 58
Bilibid Prison, 85, 150
Bonifacio, Andres: myth of, 1-2, 43, 80, 163-66; personality of, 5, 23, 24, 27, 113-17, 124-30, 133, 134-35; and Katipunan, 13-14, 20, 28, 48, 116, 120-21, 172; as military leader, 14, 184; and problems in Cavite, 16-17, 23, 83-111; and relations with Magdalo, 16, 54-59, 81, 116, 117, 128, 129, 130, 134, 161, 186; sources concerning, 17-18, 27-28, 47-48, 53-54, 81, 118-30, 134; textbook view of, 19-21, 53; birth of, 19, 28; youth of, 19; education of, 19-20, 24, 31, 49-50; family of, 19, 23-24; loves of, 19-20, 35; reading tastes of, 20, 24, 32-33, 35; and Liga Filipina, 20; writings of, 20, 36-47, 157-61, 163, 176, 178; economic status of, 21, 24, 49-50, 142-43; early writings about, 26-28; and conflicts with fellow revolutionaries, 27, 53, 55-59, 86-92, 116, 161, 171, 184; and Rizal, 36, 40, 41, 49, 127; pseudonyms of, 37-39; trial of, 43, 94, 118, 119; image of, conveyed in writings, 44-47; letters of, 54-81, 93, 118, 163, 179; and Tejeros assembly, 56-59, 86-92, 104-09, 128, 186; handwriting of, 75-79, 121-22, 181; literary style of, 78-80; and Ricarte's memoir, 83-84; and relations with Magdiwang, 117, 128-30; and use of codes, 122; and Daniel Tirona, 135; discussion of, by Ileto, 137, 152-61; and millenarianism, 144, 151, 152-56, 161-62; and fall from power, 184, 186. *See also* Heroes
Bonifacio, Santiago, 19
Buell, Augustus C., 7
Burgos, Father Jose, 8-9

Cagingin, Aguedo, 22, 41
Caneo, Sebastian, 146-48
Canseco, Telesforo: narrative of, 93, 105-06; and Tejeros assembly, 95, 99
Cavite (province): Philippine Revolution in, 14, 16-17. *See also* Aguinaldo, Emilio; Bonifacio, Andres; Magdalo; Magdiwang; Tejeros assembly
"Cazadores, Ang mga" (poem), 36, 42, 176
Code: in Bonifacio letters, 55, 60-61, 72-73, 181; in minutes of the Katipunan, 118, 121-24
Cofradia de San Jose, 137
Colorum Society, 146-51, 156, 161, 191-92
Constantino, Letizia, 23
Constantino, Renato, 5, 19, 21; career of, 23; writings of, 23, 114, 172, 184; and nationalism, 50; and Bonifacio letters, 70; and Katipunan, 142-43
Cornell University, 138-40
Corpuz, O. D., 19, 21, 24-25, 50, 70
Cortes, David, 121
Craig, Austin, 22
Crane, Stephen, 7
Cruz, Apolinario de la, 137, 144
Cuenca, Felix, 93, 100

"Dapat Mabatid ng mga Tagalog, Ang" (newspaper article): authorship of, 20, 36-41, 163; themes of, 44; Ileto's interpretation of, 152-61
Diwa, Ladislao, 120, 123
Dizon, Jose, 118, 120
Dizon, Marina, 118, 124

Education: in Philippines, 12; of Bonifacio, 19-20, 24, 31, 49-50
Elections. *See* Tejeros assembly
Encarnacion, Emmanuel, 71, 75, 181
Epistola, S. V., 37, 43, 69
Erwin, Margaret Johnson, 7

Fast, Jonathan, 49
Fleming and Company, 19
Foreman, John, 27, 173
Forgeries: in Philippines, 4, 8-9, 75-80, 93, 158, 163; and Bonifacio letters, 4, 75-80, 93, 158, 163; in other countries, 7; detection of, 181-82
Franco, Domingo, 118
Fressell and Company, 19, 172

INDEX

Gaceta de Manila, 120
Garcia, Pantaleon, 118
Geertz, Clifford, 139, 146
Ginhawa ("prosperity," etc.), 153, 156, 160
Goal-focus verbs, 78-79, 182, 183
Gonzales, Teodoro, 132
Guardia Civil, 12, 147-48
Guerrero, Milagros, 19, 21, 75, 114, 189

Heroes: and Bonifacio, 1, 6, 34, 47, 163-66; in Latin America, 7; in Africa, 7; in United States, 7, 10, 165-66; in Soviet Union, 10-11; creation of, 47
History: and use of evidence, 3; political uses of, 6-8; nationalism and, 6-11, 50-51, 164; and professionalization, 28-29, 174; and motives of historical actors, 33-34
History of the Filipino People, 20, 22, 75, 171
Hiya, 132
Holy Week, 141
Hong Kong, 17, 56, 60
Hugo, Victor, 20

Ileto, Reynaldo, 4, 5, 114; and millenarian movements, 137, 140, 141-44, 162; discussion of Bonifacio by, 137, 152-56, 162; career of, 138-39; mentors of, 138-40, 190; sources used by, 140, 141; interpretation of Katipunan by, 143-44, 146-51; political agenda of, 144-45; nationalism of, 144-45, 165; text-building strategy of, 146-49; questionable interpretations of, 149-51, 159-61, 162; translations of, 153-56, 159-61, 191; and Jacinto, 157-58; and Bonifacio letters, 161; political agenda of, 191
Imus, 16, 56, 58, 90, 103, 129-30
Imus assembly, 129-30
Indang, 58
Independencia, La, 30
Inocentes, Florencio, 43

Jacinto, Emilio: Bonifacio's letters to, 3, 54-81; role in Katipunan of, 20, 36; and proclamation of 1897, 42; burning of house of, 63; and minutes of the Katipunan, 121-22; use of codes by, 122; personality of, 124; newspaper article by, 157-58, 192

Jesus, Gregoria de: and marriage to Bonifacio, 16, 20, 48, 49; Cavite connections of, 16, 117; and Bonifacio letters, 62, 182; memoir of, 118, 124
Joaquin, Nick, 5, 48-49, 174

Kaginhawaan ("prosperity," etc.), 153, 159-60
Kahin, George, 138
Kalantiaw, Code of, 8
Kalaw, Teodoro, 23, 24, 28, 172, 176
Kalayaan ("freedom," "liberty"), 46, 142, 147, 151-61, 178, 191
Kalayaan (newspaper): contribution/s by Bonifacio in, 20, 37-41, 153-61; impact of, 151-52; article by Jacinto in, 157-58
Kasaganan ("abundance"), 153, 159
Katagalugan, 56, 65, 153-54
"Katapusang Hibik ng Pilipinas" (poem), 36, 42, 44, 161
Katipunan: 16, 26, 27, 28, 108; growth of, 13-14, 151-52, 170; Bonifacio's role in, 13-14, 20, 28, 48, 116, 120-21, 172; minutes of, 13, 118, 119, 121-23; administrative subdivisions in, 14-15, 87, 170; goals of, 20; socioeconomic status of members of, 49, 142-43; founding of, 120-21; connection between, and Propaganda Movement, 142-43; connection of, to millenarian movements, 146-51, 156, 161; and Isabelo de los Reyes, 150-51. *See also* Magdiwang, Magdalo
"Katungkulang Gagawin ng mga Z. Ll. B." ("The Duties of the Sons of the Country"), 20, 39
Katwiran ("reason," etc.), 156, 160-61
Kawit, 55-56, 170-71

Liga Filipina, 13, 20, 48-49, 169
Limbon (barrio of Indang), 58
Lincoln, Abraham, 7, 21, 35
Lipa, 58
Liwanag ("light"), 155-56
Lumbreras, Jacinto, 86, 98

Magdalo (Sangguniang Magdalo), 14, 16, 170, 189; and disputes with Bonifacio, 16, 54-59, 81, 116, 117, 128, 129, 130, 134, 161, 186; and conflict with Magdiwang, 56-59,

171; and Tejeros assembly, 86-92, 96-99, 100-01, 105-07, 187
Magdalo, Juan, 147, 150, 161
Magdiwang (Sangguniang Magdiwang), 14, 56-59, 170-71, 189; Ricarte's role in, 84-85; and Tejeros assembly, 86-92, 96-99, 100-04, 106, 186, 187; and Tanza meeting, 106-07, 187; Bonifacio and, 117, 128-30
Malay, Armando, 85
Malvar, Miguel, 102
Manila: and Liga Filipina, 12-13; and Katipunan, 13-14, 120-21
Maragtas Code, 8
Marco, Jose E., 8-9, 79
Marcos, Ferdinand, 23, 25, 171
Masangkay, Guillermo, 118, 124
May, Glenn Anthony, 31, 70
Millenarian movements, 138, 140, 141-44; and Katipunan, 146-51, 156, 161; and Philippine Revolution, 148, 162
Mojica, Diego, 97
Monteclaro, Pedro Alcantara, 8
Montenegro, Antonio, 86-87
Myth, 1-2, 6-11, 43, 80, 163-66

Naik, 56, 61, 189
National heroes. *See* Bonifacio, Andres; Heroes
Nationalism: and history, 6-11, 50-51, 66, 110, 164; and Bonifacio myth, 34, 163-66; and de los Santos, 34, 66, 145, 164; and Artigas, 34, 145, 164; and Santos, 34, 66, 145, 164; and Philippine Revolution, 34, 133; characteristics of, in Philippines, 50-51; and Agoncillo, 50-51, 115, 132-33, 164-65; and interpretation of Bonifacio, 132-33; and Ileto, 144-45, 165; goals of, 164
Nationalist school: and portrayal of Bonifacio, 49-51, 132-33; and Tejeros assembly, 101, 110
National Library. *See* Philippine National Library
Nieva, Gregorio, 25, 173, 177
Nocon, Santos, 86
Noriel, Mariano, 93, 100
Noveleta, 14, 170-71
Nueva Ecija, 30, 61, 63

Ocampo, Ambeth: and Agoncillo, 68-69, 131, 180, 188; and Bonifacio letters, 71-74, 78-79
Ocampo, Esteban de, 23-24
Osmeña, Guillermo, 19

Pacheco, Cipriano, 32
"Pag-ibig sa Tinubuang Bayan" (poem), 36-41, 45-47
Palma, Rafael, 31, 115
Pangan, Teresita, 62, 68, 71, 181
Pasyon, 141, 153-56
Pasyon and Revolution: Popular Movements in the Philippines, 1840-1910. See Ileto, Reynaldo
Patriotism, 45-46
Pavón, José María, 8
Philippine-American War, 24, 96, 115, 118
Philippine Commission, 27
Philippine Insurgent Records, 118, 134, 188, 189
Philippine National Archives, 48, 118
Philippine National Library (National Library and Museum), 71, 180; Artigas and, 26; de los Santos and, 31; documents missing from, 85, 94; and purchase of minutes of the Katipunan, 121-22
Philippine Review: and de los Santos, 22, 24, 25, 31-34, 39-40, 60-61, 69, 70, 158, 179, 192; and nationalism, 34, 60; description of, 173
Philippine Revolution (of 1896): overview of, 11, 13-14, 16-17, 170; and conflicts in the revolutionary ranks, 16, 27, 55-59, 81, 86-92, 170-71, 184; and nationalism, 34, 133; sources on, 53-54, 83-84, 118, 169-70; and establishment of government, 87-92; attitude of elites toward, 116; Ileto's interpretation of, 142-44; connection of, to Propaganda Movement, 142-44, 148, 150, 162; and millenarian movements, 148, 162. *See also* Bonifacio, Andres; Tejeros assembly
Pilar, Marcelo H. del, 12, 37, 183
Ponce, Mariano, 42
Propaganda Movement, 12, 37, 42, 116; connection of, to the Philippine Revolution, 142-44, 148, 150, 162; influence of, 153
Pulido, Jacinto, 90-91

INDEX

Quiason, Serafin, 71
Quirino, Carlos, 50, 70, 188

Renacimiento Filipino, 26, 34
Retana, Wenceslao: publications of, 26, 32, 37-38, 121, 158, 159, 160, 193; Artigas's attacks on, 28
Revolt of the Masses, The. See Agoncillo, Teodoro
Revolution of 1896. *See* Philippine Revolution
Reyes, Isabelo de los, 150-51
Ricarte, Artemio: memoir of, 5, 41, 54, 58, 83-111, 163, 170, 191-92; and letter of protest after Tejeros assembly, 60, 67, 93, 187; and Tejeros assembly, 83-111; influence of, 83, 118; unreliability of, 83-84, 85, 92, 95-96, 99, 107-08, 110, 128-30; role of, in Bonifacio's fall, 84, 97-99, 100-01, 186; career, 84-85; and opposition to the United States, 85, 95-96; critical of Magdalo, 97; and Acta de Tejeros, 106; and Tanza meeting, 107; and Colorum Society, 150, 191-92
Richardson, Jim, 49
Riego de Dios, Emiliano, 88, 110, 186, 187
Riego de Dios, Vicente, 103, 187
Rillo, Santiago, 101-04, 106-07, 110, 187
Rizal, Jose, 23; ideas of, 12-13; and Liga Filipina, 13, 20; and emergence as a hero, 27; Bonifacio and, 36, 40, 41, 49, 127; and Philippine Revolution, 116; arrest of, 120; influence of, 153; and actor-focus verbs, 183
Ronquillo, Carlos: and literary nationalism, 34, 175; narrative of, 93, 100, 102-03, 105-06, 134, 182-83, 184; and Tejeros elections, 100, 102-03, 105-06, 184; and actor-focus verbs, 182-83
Rosario, Aguedo del, 143
Rosario, Jose del, 88-89

Sade, Marquis de, 7
Salvador, Felipe, 137, 144
Sampagita, 118
San Francisco de Malabon, 84, 95, 109
Sangguniang bayan ("municipal consultative body"), 14-15, 87, 101, 170-71
San Miguel, Luciano, 86
San Pedro, Sinforoso, 43
Santa Cruz de Malabon. *See* Tanza

Santa Iglesia, 137
Santong Boces ("Holy Voice"), 147
Santos, Epifanio de los, 4; article about Bonifacio by, 22-25, 27, 31-34, 37, 39-40, 60-61, 64-66, 68-69, 70, 72-73, 93, 158, 173, 186; influence of, 22-25, 47, 70, 113, 115, 124, 137, 172, 181; and footnotes, 29, 31; career of, 30-31, 61-62; interviews by, 31-33; unreliability of, 31-34, 39-40, 43, 64-66, 77-80; nationalism of, 34, 66, 145, 164; and Bonifacio letters, 60-68, 157, 179; as collector of Filipiniana, 179-81
Santos, Jose P., 4, 140, 179-80; influence of, 22-25, 37, 40, 47, 113, 124, 137; writings of, 22-25, 34-35, 37, 40-41, 62-66, 71, 76-80, 93, 157; and footnotes, 29, 35; career of, 34-35; nationalism of, 34, 66, 145, 164; unreliability of, 40-43, 47, 64-66, 73-80; and Bonifacio letters, 62-80, 167; and Bonifacio biography contest, 62, 64, 66, 192; and father's acquisition of Bonifacio documents, 62-63, 157; relationship of, to Agoncillo, 67-68, 77, 115, 124, 180; and Ladislao Diwa, 120, 123; and "Ang Dapat Mabatid ng mga Tagalog," 157-61; and translation of Jacinto's newspaper article, 157-59, 161
Santos, Teresita. *See* Pangan, Teresita
Santo Tomas, University of, 12, 20, 21, 25, 30
Sastrón, Manuel, 26, 170
Saulo, Alfredo, 5, 70
Schumacher, John, 8-9, 29-30, 70, 178, 183
Scott, William H., 8-9
Serrano, Leopoldo, 23-24
Seton-Watson, Hugh, 164
Siegel, James, 138-40
Soviet Union, 10
Spain: rule of, 11-13, 44-47, 154-55; and Guardia Civil, 12, 147-48; army of, 14, 42, 45, 55-56, 86, 90, 99, 102, 103; as depicted in writings attributed to Bonifacio, 44-47; peace overture of, 56-58; conditions in Philippines before arrival of, 153-54. *See also* Philippine Revolution; Propaganda Movement
Sparks, Jared, 10
Stalin, Joseph, 10
Sue, Eugène, 20, 23

Tagalog (language). *See* Actor-focus verbs; Goal-focus verbs
Tanza, 83-84, 89-91, 103-09
"Tapunan ng Lingap" (poem), 36, 42, 47
Tayabas, 147, 149-50
Tejeros assembly, 2-3, 5, 116, 163; elections at, 16, 53, 57-58, 70, 81, 87-92, 94-105, 116, 128, 184, 186, 187, 189; references to, in Bonifacio's letters, 56-59; date of, 83, 184; and Ricarte's memoir, 83-111, 113, 163; conflict at, 86-92; sources about, 93-94; number of delegates at, 105-07; electoral politics at, 110-11, 116; importance of, 184. *See also* Acta de Tejeros
Tirona, Daniel: and conflict with Bonifacio, 16, 88-89, 91, 125; and Tejeros assembly, 86, 88-91, 96-98
Tolentino, Guillermo, 181
Tondo, 19, 28, 62-63, 93, 157, 158, 174
Topacio, Cayetano, 59, 86
Translation: by Bonifacio, 20, 36, 40-42, 163; and de los Santos, 39, 64-66; by Agoncillo, 43, 69, 71, 129, 154-55, 192; by Ileto, 148-50, 151, 153-56, 159-61, 178, 191; by Santos, 159-60
Trias, Mariano, 86, 88, 90, 91, 107, 110, 186

"Ultimo Adiós" (poem), 20, 36, 40-42
United States: heroic biography in, 7, 10, 165-66; and Constantino, 23; colonial administration/rule of, 26, 27, 30-31, 34, 145, 164; and professionalization of historians, 28-29; and Ricarte, 83, 84, 85, 95-96; and Philippine independence, 133, 145; and Ileto, 138-40
University of the Philippines, 171; and Zaide, 21; and Corpuz, 24; library of 64, 180; and Agoncillo, 114, 180; and Ileto, 190
Utang na loob, 132

Valenzuela, Pio, 36; unreliability of, 32-33, 38, 39, 40, 121, 127, 152, 170; testimony to the Spaniards of, 32, 118, 120-21, 126-27, 134; memoir of, 37, 38-39, 125, 151-52; Agoncillo's reliance on, 118, 120, 121, 123; interviews with, 118, 121, 123, 124; and minutes of the Katipunan, 123; and Bonifacio, 124, 125, 126-27; and Daniel Tirona, 125; influence of, 151-52
Villanueva, Ariston, 88, 96
Villegas, Ramon, 75-76

Washington, George, 7, 10, 35, 165-66
Watson, William Brecknock, 27, 85, 173, 185
Watson Collection, 85, 185
Weems, Mason, 10, 165-66
Wolters, Oliver W., 138, 139
Wood, Leonard, 31

Zaide, Gregorio, 50; writings of, 5, 19, 20, 21-22, 30; career of, 21-22; and Katipunan writers, 36; and Bonifacio letters, 70
Zulueta, Clemente J., 32

Center for Southeast Asian Studies
University of Wisconsin-Madison

Monograph Series

Inventing a Hero: The Posthumous Re-Creation of Andres Bonifacio
by Glenn Anthony May

The Mekong Delta: Ecology, Economy and Revolution, 1860-1960
by Perre Brocheux

Autonomous Histories, Particular Truths: Essays in Honor of John Smail
edited by Laurie J. Sears

An Anarchy of Families: State and Family in the Philippines
edited by Alfred McCoy

Salome: A Filipino Filmscript by Ricardo Lee,
translation by Rofel Brion;
introduction by Soledad S. Reyes

Recalling the Revolution: Memoirs of a Filipino General,
by Santiago V. Alvarez; translation by Paula Carolina S. Malay;
introduction by Ruby R. Paredes

Anthropology Goes to War: Professional Ethics and Counterinsurgency in Thailand,
by Eric Wakin

Voices from the Thai Countryside: The Short Stories of Samruam Singh,
edited and translated by Katherine Bowie

Putu Wijaya in Performance: An Approach to Indonesian Theatre,
edited by Ellen Rafferty

*Gender, Power, and the Construction of the Moral Order:
Studies from the Thai Periphery,*
edited by Nancy Eberhardt

Bomb: Indonesian Short Stories by Putu Wijaya,
edited by Ellen Rafferty and Laurie J. Sears

Aesthetic Tradition and Cultural Transition in Java and Bali,
edited by Stephanie Morgan and Laurie J. Sears

*A Complete Account of the Peasants' Uprising in the Central Region
(of Vietnam in 1908),*
by Phan Chu Trinh; translated by Peter Baugher and Vu Ngo Chieu

Publications Committee
Daniel F. Doeppers
Carol J. Compton
Alfred W. McCoy, Chair
R. Anderson Sutton
John Roosa, Editor